RITUALS OF BIRTH, CIRCUMCISION, MARRIAGE, AND DEATH AMONG MUSLIMS IN THE NETHERLANDS

New Religious Identities in the Western World focuses on the mutual challenge between minority religions and the socio-juridical structure of the societies at large, especially with regard to the main world religions (i.e. Islam, Hinduism and Buddhism) within the Western context. Special attention is paid both to the influence of social, juridical and cultural contexts upon the institutionalization of these new religious identities, and to the ability of their adherents to maintain or transform their specific traditions.

NEW RELIGIOUS IDENTITIES IN THE WESTERN WORLD

2

Rituals of Birth, Circumcision, Marriage, and Death among Muslims in the Netherlands

NATHAL M. DESSING

PEETERS

2001

The investigations were supported by the Foundation for Research in the Field of Philosophy and Theology (SFT), which is subsidized by the Netherlands Organization for Scientific Research (NWO).

ISBN 90-429-1059-3
D. 2001/0602/81

CONTENTS

ACKNOWLEDGEMENTS VII

1. INTRODUCTION 1
1.1. Academic Research into Islam in Western Europe 1
1.2. Lifecycle Rituals under Migration 5
1.3. Sources of Evidence 8
1.4. Fieldwork 9

2. BIRTH 15
2.1. Pregnancy and Delivery 16
Home or Hospital Confinement 19; Presence of Men 20; Ceremonies Relating to the Placenta 20; Postnatal Period 21; Amulets 23
2.2. Whispering in the Child's Ear and the *Taḥnîk* 24
2.3. The *ᶜAqîqa* 26
The Religious Qualification of the *ᶜAqîqa* 27; The Sacrifice 30; The *Ḥukm* of the Meat of the Sacrifice 32; Communal Gatherings 33; The Appropriate Time for the *ᶜAqîqa* 35; Shaving the Child's Hair 36
2.4. Naming 38
The Appropriate Time for Naming a Child 39
2.5. Conclusions 40

3. CIRCUMCISION 43
3.1. The Religious Qualification of Circumcision 44
3.2. Age of Circumcision 51
3.3. The Organization of the Operation 55
New Organizational Developments in the Netherlands 58; Rotterdam 58; Utrecht 61; The Hague 62; The Operation in the Countries of Origin 63
3.4. Circumcision Festivities 64
Celebrations in the Netherlands 65; Festive Dress 66; Celebrations at Home 66; Celebrations in a Public Hall 68; Celebrations on the Premises of a Religious Organization 69; Celebrations in the Countries of Origin 70; Religious Part 71; Social Part 73
3.5. Conclusions 75

4. MARRIAGE 79
4.1. Proposal of Marriage 80
4.2. Contracting of Marriage 85
Guardianship 87; Presence of Witnesses 88; The Bridal Gift in Islamic Law 88; Present-Day Marriage Legislation 90; Moroccan Marriage Legislation and Its Influence on the Marriage Practice of Moroccans 91; Turkish Marriage Legislation and Its Influence on the Marriage Practice of Turks 94; Surinamese Marriage Legislation and Its Influence on the Marriage Practice of Surinamese 101; The Bridal Gift 106
4.3. Marriage Festivities 109
The *Ṣadaqa* or *Kitaab* 111; The Henna Party 113; The Wedding Party 120; Wedding Parties in the Netherlands 121; Wedding Parties in the Countries of Origin 127; The Reception of the Bride at the Groom's Home 133
4.4. Conclusions 137

5. DEATH 141
5.1. Death and Burial Preparations 141
Ritual Purification 145; Shrouding 149; *Ṣalât al-Janâza* 153
5.2. Burial 157
Country of Burial 158; The Institution of Funeral Funds 161; Grave Construction and Interment 162; Use of a Coffin 166; Attendance of Women at the Interment 170; Waiting at the Graveside and the *Talqîn* 172
5.3. Condolences and Mourning 173
5.4. Conclusions 178

6. CONTINUITY AND CHANGE 183
6.1. Competence and Consonance 183
6.2. Ritual Attrition 186
6.3. Historical Contingency 190
6.4. Future Trends 192

BIBLIOGRAPHY 195

INDEX 207

ACKNOWLEDGEMENTS

This work would not have been possible without the support of a large number of individuals and institutions. First, I would like to thank my respondents, who are the source of the most important information in this book. They offered me trust and hospitality, and were willing to allow an outsider to witness rituals at important times of their lives. I am indebted particularly to the foundation Al-Gitaan in Rotterdam, the Stichting Ontmoeting met Buitenlandse Vrouwen, and the Juliana Children's Hospital in The Hague, who were helpful in putting me in contact with many of them.

The Foundation for Research in the Field of Philosophy and Theology (SFT) of the Netherlands Organization for Scientific Research (NWO) and the Faculty of Theology of Leiden University facilitated my research. I enjoyed the convivial atmosphere and the company of my colleagues at the Faculty of Theology and the stimulating discussions with other researchers in the section Religious Studies of the research school NOSTER.

I would like to thank my colleagues at the International Institute for the Study of Islam in the Modern World (ISIM) for their support and understanding, and for granting me leave from my post as Educational Coordinator when I needed it.

I am grateful particularly to Sjoerd van Koningsveld and Wasif Shadid, who as my Ph.D. supervisors commented on many versions of the arguments presented here. I am also grateful to Dick Koopman, who checked the orthography of the Turkish terms in this book at very short notice. I am of course responsible for any remaining mistakes in this book.

Léon Buskens first introduced me to the work of Yves Linant de Bellefonds. As a fieldworker he fully understood the challenges of this project and encouraged me to undertake and complete it. I thank him for this and for his confidence in the project's success.

I first met Marrie Bot while she was working on her book, *Een laatste groet*, on death and burial customs of various denominations in the Netherlands, including Muslims. My conversations with her and her postcards were a constant source of pleasure and inspiration.

I would like to thank my mother Thea Dessing-de Bakker, my sisters Veronique and Madeline, my brother Frank and Joossien, Anselma Bueler, and Sabine du Croo de Jongh, who I knew always stood behind me. I am sorry that my father was not able to witness my academic career.

My greatest debt is to my *compagno*, James W. McAllister, who supported me more than I can say. He read several drafts of this manuscript, gave useful comments, and corrected my English on more than one occasion. I hope that I will be able to return the favour at times when he needs it.

Previous versions of chapters in this book appeared as: "The Circumcision of Muslim Boys in the Netherlands: How Change Occurs in a Diaspora", in *Strangers and Sojourners: Religious Communities in the Diaspora*, ed. Gerrie ter Haar, 133–151 (Leuven: Peeters, 1998); "Continuïteit en verandering in de huwelijkssluiting bij Marokkaanse, Turkse en Surinaamse moslims in Nederland", in *Recht van de Islam* 16 (1999), 59–81; "Uitvaart- en rouwrituelen bij moslims in Nederland", in *Handboek Sterven, Uitvaart en Rouw*, III 1.3, 1–16 (Maarssen: Elsevier, 1999), and in *Handboek Interculturele Zorg*, IV 5.1, 1–16 (Maarssen: Elsevier, 2001).

1
INTRODUCTION

The performance of Muslim lifecycle rituals in the Netherlands produces countless incongruities. As everyone is aware, the Netherlands is a densely populated, highly urbanized country with a wet climate and a heavy Christian influence. Muslims who wish to perform rituals marking birth, circumcision, marriage, and death are confronted by considerable challenges. How are such rituals to be transposed and adapted to the Dutch circumstances so that they retain their significance for the participants while remaining within the bounds of practicality?

The variety of answers given by Muslims in the Netherlands to these challenges is the subject of the present study. The snapshot that I present of Muslim lifecycle rituals in the Netherlands today is taken against a background of Islamic prescriptions pertaining to these rituals and the practice in the countries of origin of the Muslim groups that I treat.

The plan of this study naturally follows the lifecycle: we begin in chapter 2 with "Birth" and end in chapter 5 with "Death". I present my conclusions in chapter 6. In this introduction, I begin by offering a bird's-eye view of academic research conducted into the Islamic presence in Western Europe and recapitulating a number of theories on lifecycle rituals. Later I set out the aims of this study, discuss the sources on which I draw, and conclude by giving a brief account of my fieldwork.

1.1. Academic Research into Islam in Western Europe

The number of Muslims living in Europe today is estimated at 31.2 million, or 4.3% of the population.[1] The Muslim population of France is the largest of any Western European country, numbering between 4 and 5 million in 2000.[2] These include 1,246,706 people of Algerian origin, 709,521 Moroccans, 340,752 Tunisians, and 179,392 Turks.[3] Germany, with 3 million Muslims, for the most part from Turkey,[4] and the United

[1] Statistisches Bundesamt, *Statistisches Jahrbuch 2000 für das Ausland*, 223.

[2] Personal communication, Brigitte Maréchal, Unité d'anthropologie et de sociologie, Université catholique de Louvain, Louvain-la-Neuve, Belgium.

[3] INSEE, Institut national de la statistique et des études économiques, *Tableau références et analyses*, 21. These figures relate to 1999.

[4] REMID, Religionswissenschaftlicher Medien- und Informationsdienst e.V., "Religionsgemeinschaften in Deutschland: Mitgliederzahlen (Stand Dezember 2000)", http://www.uni-leipzig.de/~religion/remid_info.zahlen.htm, consulted on 8 January 2001.

Kingdom, with 1.5 to 2 million, for the most part from Pakistan, Bangladesh, and India, follow.[5] The Netherlands takes fourth place with 736,000 Muslims in 2000, or 4.6% of the population.[6]

Muslims living in the Netherlands have diverse national origins: Turkish (299,700), Moroccan (252,500), and Surinamese (approximately 50,000 of the 297,000 people of Surinamese origin living in the Netherlands are Muslim). These groups constitute the focus of my research. Smaller groups are Moluccan (around 1,200 of the 40,000 people originating from the Moluccan Islands resident in the Netherlands are Muslim), Indonesian, Pakistani (15,600), Egyptian (13,600), and Tunisian (6,400). In recent years, refugees have been admitted from Somalia (27,400), Iran (21,800), Iraq (30,000), and the former Yugoslavia, many of whom are Muslims. Furthermore, about 6,000 people of Dutch origin are converts to Islam.[7]

Academic research into Islam as a social phenomenon in Western Europe has been conducted since the mid-1970s. The academic approach varies from country to country. In Britain, the study of Islam was incorporated into the existing strong tradition of ethnic and race relations research, in which the disciplines of anthropology and sociology play a central role.[8] In France, research in this field has been governed above all by the concepts of citizenship and of separation of religion and state. The *foulards* controversy of the late 1980s and early 1990s is emblematic of the French national political discourse on the

[5] Office for National Statistics, *Britain 2001*, 235 and 242; also available at http://www.statistics.gov.uk, consulted on 12 January 2001. See also The Muslim Council of Britain, "Population Statistics", http://www.mcb.org.uk/popstats.html, consulted on 10 January 2001. The UK national census is held every ten years; the most recent census was conducted in April 2001. For the first time, this census contained a question on religious affiliation.

[6] Centraal Bureau voor de Statistiek, *Kerkelijke gezindte en kerkbezoek aan het einde van de 20e eeuw*, 7.

[7] Centraal Bureau voor de Statistiek, "Allochtonen in Nederland (eerste en tweede generatie) naar geboorteland" (Migrants in the Netherlands (first and second generations) by country of origin), updated on 4 May 2000, http://www.cbs.nl/nl/cijfers/kerncijfers/sbv0610d.htm, consulted on 20 December 2000; for the data on Moluccans and Surinamese Muslims, Shadid & Van Koningsveld, *Moslims in Nederland*, 20–21; on Dutch converts to Islam, Crijnen, *Veertien portretten van nieuwe Nederlandse en Vlaamse moslims*, 8. The figures relate to 1 January 1999, except the numbers of Surinamese Muslims and Moluccans, which are older. Hoefte, *De betovering verbroken*, 37 n. 23, estimates the number of Surinamese Javanese in the Netherlands at 10,000. Nico Landman, *Van mat tot minaret*, 204, estimates the number of Surinamese in the Netherlands at 210,000, of whom 26,000 are Muslim: 6,000 Javanese and 20,000 Hindustanis.

[8] Nielsen & Vertovec, "Great Britain", 67–69.

compatibility of Islam and the ideal of *laïcité*. Research into Islam has thus been conducted mainly within the disciplines of political science, anthropology, and socio-legal studies.[9] In the Netherlands, partly because of public policy priorities, the focus has been directed at the socio-economic position of migrants from Muslim countries as well as at educational issues and juvenile delinquency. Research into Islam as a social and religious phenomenon is more recent and has been conducted mainly from within the disciplines of theology and religious studies.[10]

Research into Islam in the West may be subdivided into five main categories.[11] A first category of research aims at quantifying and describing the Muslim presence in Europe by ascertaining for example the numbers of Muslims living in each country, their countries of origin, and the numbers of mosques and prayer halls. This category includes introductory studies on Muslims in Europe,[12] but also in-depth descriptive research aiming for example at producing an inventory of existing religious associations.[13]

Another category concerns the relationship between Islam and the state in European countries. France provides many examples of this type of research, as do the Netherlands and Belgium. This category includes research into the attempts to create national Islamic councils in European countries and the means that Muslim organizations have for obtaining state financial support for their educational and community activities against the background of national legislation regulating the relationship between religion and state.[14]

A third category of research concerns the institutional and juridical integration of Muslims in Europe. Studies dealing with educational matters, such as religious education in state-funded schools, the

[9] Diop, "France", 21–23.

[10] Sunier & Landman, "Nederland", 126.

[11] See Dassetto, *La Construction de l'islam européen*, esp. 75–81; and also the bibliographies in Dassetto & Conrad, *Musulmans en Europe occidentale*, and Shadid & Van Koningsveld, *Religious Freedom and the Position of Islam in Western Europe*.

[12] Muslims in Europe: Shadid & Van Koningsveld, *Religious Freedom and the Position of Islam in Western Europe*; Vertovec & Peach, ed., *Islam in Europe: The Politics of Religion and Community*; Saint-Blancat, *L'Islam de la diaspora*; Nielsen, *Muslims in Western Europe*; Gerholm & Lithman, ed., *The New Islamic Presence in Western Europe*. The Netherlands: Shadid & Van Koningsveld, *Moslims in Nederland*; Rath et al., *Nederland en zijn islam*. Germany: Spuler-Stegemann, *Muslime in Deutschland*. Great Britain: Lewis, *Islamic Britain*. France: Cesari, *Être musulman en France aujourd'hui*; Leveau & Kepel, ed., *Les Musulmans dans la société française*; Étienne, *La France et l'islam*.

[13] The Netherlands: Landman, *Van mat tot minaret*; Sunier, *Islam in beweging*. Belgium: Dassetto & Bastenier, "Organisations musulmanes de Belgique".

[14] See especially Shadid & Van Koningsveld, *Religious Freedom and the Position of Islam in Western Europe*, 51–59.

establishment of Islamic schools, and supplementary religious education at mosque schools fall within this category. Another research area in this category is the ever-growing corpus of jurisprudence concerning Islam and Muslims in Europe, especially in the field of family law.[15]

Publications dealing with the presence of Muslim so-called fundamentalist groups in Europe and the threat that they are supposed to pose to European society fall within a fourth category of research treating the image of Islam in Europe and the relations between Islam and European society. Many European countries have experienced controversies affecting the relations between Muslims and non-Muslims and contributing to an essentialist conception of Islam. The Rushdie affair evoked strong emotions throughout Europe. Similarly, the practice of some young Muslim girls of wearing headscarves at school provoked heated discussions in France, but also in the Netherlands, Germany, and the United Kingdom. The *Koranschule-Debatte* in Germany is an example of the many controversies in the field of Islamic religious education.

Of a more interpretative character, lastly, are publications dealing with the meaning of Islam in the formation of a religious and ethnic identity for its adherents in Western Europe. These publications aim for instance at analysing the various degrees and forms of religiousness observed among Muslims in Western Europe. This type of research is characteristic particularly of Germany, but has been conducted from a somewhat different perspective also in France, Sweden, and the Netherlands.[16] These publications have helped reveal the diversity of Islam and Muslims in Western Europe.

This bird's-eye view leads to the conclusion that the main focus of research hitherto has been on questions of direct socio-political importance, while Islam "from within" has been largely ignored. Remarkably little attention has so far been paid to the transmission of religious knowledge among Muslims in Western Europe through preaching, religious education, publications, videos, and radio broadcasts. Nor have Islamic religious practices as performed in the European context, such as prayers, fasting during the month of Ramadan, the pilgrimage to Mecca, and practices related to the lifecycle, received much attention. The Feast

[15] For example Rutten, *Moslims in de Nederlandse rechtspraak*, and Vestdijk-van der Hoeven, *Religieus recht en minderheden*.

[16] For example, Schiffauer, *Die Migranten aus Subay*; Leveau, "The Political Culture of the '*Beurs*'"; Sander, "To What Extent is the Swedish Muslim Religious?"; Van der Lans & Rooijackers, "Types of Religious Belief and Unbelief among Second Generation Turkish Migrants", and Rooijackers, "Religious Identity, Integration and Subjective Well-Being among Young Turkish Muslims".

of Sacrifices, halal food, and the use of headscarves are exceptions, because of their socio-political implications.[17]

There have been a few studies dealing with Islamic lifecycle rituals or some aspects of them as performed in Western Europe. Cor Hoffer's *Moslimbesnijdenissen in Nederland* (Muslim circumcisions in the Netherlands, 1990) is a policy document providing an inventory of the possibilities for Muslims in the Netherlands to perform the operation of male circumcision. Two important studies on the ritual of marriage are Edwige Rude-Antoine's *Le Mariage maghrébin en France* (1990) and Ibrahim Yerden's *Trouwen op z'n Turks* (1995), which deals with marriage among Turkish Muslims in the Netherlands. *In fremder Erde: Zur Geschichte und Gegenwart der islamischen Bestattung in Deutschland* (1996) contains eight contributions, of which Yasemin Karakaşoğlu's "Die Bestattung von Muslimen in der Bundesrepublik aus der Sicht türkish-islamischer Organisationen" is particularly interesting. Yassine Chaïb's dissertation *L'Islam et la mort en France* remains as yet unpublished. *Een laatste groet: Uitvaart- en rouwrituelen in multicultureel Nederland* (1998) by the Dutch photographer Marrie Bot contains an informative chapter on death and burial customs among Muslims in the Netherlands consisting of photographs, explanatory comments, and extensive background information.

Notwithstanding these works, we do not yet have a systematic and comparative study of Islamic lifecycle rituals as they are performed in Western European societies. I aim to contribute to such a study here. Unlike the studies mentioned above, which focus on one ritual and mostly also on one nationality or ethnic group, I adopt a comparative perspective by describing four lifecycle rituals as performed by four ethnic groups. I treat rituals of birth, male circumcision, marriage, and death among Moroccan, Turkish, Surinamese Hindustani, and Surinamese Javanese Muslims in the Netherlands.

1.2. Lifecycle Rituals under Migration

Lifecycle rituals are rituals that accompany and assure important transitions in human life. Following Arnold van Gennep, one may distinguish three major phases in rituals that accompany human passages: separation (*séparation*), transition (*marge*), and incorporation (*agrégation*).[18] In the preliminal phase, rites of separation, such as purifications or

[17] Dassetto, *La Construction de l'islam européen*, 79–80.

[18] Van Gennep, *The Rites of Passage*, 3–4, uses the broader term "rites of passage" which according to his definition also includes "those rites occasioned by celestial

shaving of hair, dissociate the person or persons undergoing the rites from their previous surroundings. In the liminal phase, rites of transition symbolically place the ritual subjects outside society, for example for the duration of a mourning period. During this phase the normal rules of the community may be suspended for the people concerned. Finally, in the postliminal phase, rites of incorporation, such as a shared meal, new clothes or naming, mark their transition to their new status and normal life resumes.[19]

Building on Van Gennep's theory and the writings of Max Gluckman,[20] Victor Turner has developed the concepts of liminality and communitas, structure and antistructure.[21] Turner characterizes the second phase in the ritual process, the liminal or transitional phase, as one of ambiguity: the ritual subjects are suspended between their former and future positions. This marginal position nurtures communitas or solidarity among the ritual subjects. Communitas is antistructural in that it is characterized by equality and homogeneity. It forms the basis of and is at the same time contrasted with social structure, defined as "the patterned arrangements of role-sets, status-sets, and status-sequences, consciously recognized and regularly operative in a given society. These are closely bound up with legal and political norms and sanctions."[22]

Van Gennep's theory about the basic structure of lifecycle rituals, Turner's concept of communitas experienced in the liminal phase as well as Emile Durkheim's functionalist interpretation of ritual according to which rituals are "a primary mechanism for expressing and reinforcing the sentiments and solidarity of the group"[23] may yield a deeper understanding of what ritual does.[24] These approaches are useful,

changes, such as the changeover from month to month . . . from season to season . . . and from year to year".

[19] This categorization is certainly not rigid. Van Gennep, *The Rites of Passage*, 11–12, recognizes that (1) the three subcategories "are not always equally important or equally elaborated", (2) the pattern may be duplicated within one phase, (3) birth, circumcision and other ceremonies contain rites of passage—rites that ensure transition—but also rites that have a specific aim of their own, such as fertility rites in marriage ceremonies or protection rites in birth and circumcision ceremonies.

[20] Gluckman, "Rituals of Rebellion in South East Africa"; Morris, *Anthropological Studies of Religion*, 248. According to Durkheim, rituals express the cohesion and solidarity of the group, whereas in Gluckman's view rituals tend to exaggerate conflicts and thereby affirm the unity of the group.

[21] Turner, *The Ritual Process*. Cf. Morris, *Anthropological Studies of Religion*, 248 and 252.

[22] Turner, *Dramas, Field and Metaphors*, 202.

[23] Morris, *Anthropological Studies of Religion*, 120.

[24] Ter Haar, *Halfway to Paradise*, 65–69, has applied Turner's concepts to the process of migration. She points out that African Christians living in the Bijlmer quarter of

particularly for research into well-integrated situations where the social and legal context supports and reflects rituals in various ways.

In migration, however, lifecycle rituals lose their firm basis in a social and religious context. For example, in Muslim countries the ritual of circumcision forms, from an organizational point of view and in people's perceptions, an integral part of daily life. In a context of migration, where those who keep to this practice form a small minority, it loses its matter-of-course character. The support network that was normally available in the countries of origin is lacking in the new countries of residence where, for instance, neighbours are unlikely to assist in organizing a circumcision party. Moreover, an organizational infrastructure for the performance of the operation has to be developed afresh. I aim to concentrate on these processes of change and ascertain how lifecycle rituals react and accommodate to the transplantation from one social context to another that does not support them to the same degree.

The different cultural backgrounds of the four ethnic groups on which I concentrate largely account for the different forms that the lifecycle rituals have assumed in the Dutch context. However, the different reasons for their migration to the Netherlands have also influenced the form of these rituals. The presence of Moroccans and Turks in the Netherlands is a consequence mainly of the Dutch need for labour force in the 1960s and early 1970s. Labour migrants from these countries mostly came to the Netherlands as individuals, leaving their families behind. By contrast, the presence of the Surinamese Muslims results from the Dutch colonial past: shortly before Surinam declared independence in 1975, as well as at the end of the 1970s when the Dutch government made preparations to impose visa requirements on visitors from Surinam, many Surinamese decided to move to the Netherlands. Unlike the Moroccan and Turkish labour migrants, the Surinamese came to the Netherlands mostly in family groups. The circumstances of and reasons for migration influence the form of the lifecycle rituals in the Dutch setting. This becomes visible in, for example, the choice between burial in the Netherlands and in the country of origin. Whereas Moroccans and Turks mostly prefer a burial in their countries of origin because of their continuing strong links with them, the Surinamese Javanese and Hindustani Muslims mostly opt for burial in the Netherlands.

Amsterdam belong neither to the community from which they have come, nor yet to Dutch society. In this situation the African church leaders in the Bijlmer promote and cultivate communitas, which they regard as a prerequisite for successful integration of their communities into Dutch society.

In the following chapters I use the terms "rite" and "ceremony" to designate specific units of lifecycle rituals. I take rites as "the individual building blocks, the isolated actions, that, for the purpose of analysis, can be distinguished in ceremonies and rituals", and a ceremony as "the smallest configuration of rites constituting a meaningful whole".[25] For example, the ritual of marriage consists of several ceremonies, such as henna party, civil marriage, and religious marriage. Rites that occur within the ceremonies include the exchange of rings and the signing of the marriage certificate.

1.3. Sources of Evidence

The aim of this study is to describe the evolution of lifecycle rituals of Moroccan, Turkish, Surinamese Hindustani, and Surinamese Javanese Muslims in the Netherlands by comparison with the countries of origin, and where possible to ascertain the influence of the Dutch social and legal context on the form and meaning of these rituals. To circumscribe my research I have chosen to concentrate on the largest groups of Sunnite Muslims in the Netherlands and leave aside the Shiites and the Ahmadiyyas, even though the latter constitute groups of considerable size among the Turks and Surinamese Hindustanis in the Netherlands. Another reason to concentrate on Moroccans, Turks, and Surinamese is that the lifecycle rituals of these groups have begun to take shape in Dutch society, unlike those of more recent immigrants, such as refugees from Somalia and the former Yugoslavia.

My conclusions are based on three forms of evidence: Islamic legal texts, my fieldwork, and anthropological literature. Islamic legal texts (*fiqh*), which have a normative character, form the common reference point of the four ethnic groups on which I concentrate. I have therefore chosen to give an outline of the Islamic prescriptions relating to the lifecycle rituals in each chapter before presenting my fieldwork findings.

Nadia Abu-Zahra has favoured a similar approach in her study of Islamic rituals. She criticizes Ernest Gellner's dichotomy that associates official Islam with the merchant classes in the city and popular Islam with the tribes and their cult of saints. In Abu-Zahra's view this dichotomy obliterates the interaction between Islam and society. She also criticizes Richard Antoun's notion of orthopraxy—as if Islamic rituals were devoid of beliefs—and Nancy Tapper and Richard Tapper's contention that the *mevlüt* poem commemorating the birth and life of the

[25] Snoek, "Initiations", 58.

Prophet Muhammad has Christian origins. Against this background she emphasizes the importance of consulting Islamic texts and demonstrating how Islamic prescriptions are interwoven with social norms in the performance of rituals. She contends that the mode of integration of the two dimensions varies with the prevailing social conditions and that, consequently, the interaction between Islam and society should be the focus of comparative studies of Muslim societies.[26] She illustrates the importance of Islamic texts by using them as a basis of her comparison of death and rain rituals as they are performed in Egypt and Tunisia. However, the outcome is somewhat disappointing, particularly because she refers only to the Koran and the *ḥadîth* collection of Al-Bukhari to identify the relevant Islamic prescriptions.

I have chosen a broader basis than Abu-Zahra, and also a more systematic presentation of Islamic prescriptions. For each lifecycle ritual I begin by presenting an outline of Islamic prescriptions with special attention to present-day Islamic discussions. This part treats the differences of views between and within the four law schools—Malikites, Hanafites, Shafiᶜites, and Hanbalites. A second part of each section deals with the form and meaning of these rituals as they are performed in practice, both in the Netherlands and in the countries of origin. This second part is based partly on anthropological studies, but mainly on my fieldwork data.

1.4. Fieldwork

Between 1993 and 1997 I conducted fieldwork in Rotterdam, The Hague, and other Dutch cities. This fieldwork consisted of participant observation and interviews.

As a participant observer, I attended two Moroccan birth parties. I attended many circumcision operations and the parties organized on the occasion of the circumcisions of a Moroccan, a Surinamese Javanese, and a Turkish boy. I attended 15 wedding parties, of which 14 were in the Netherlands and one in Morocco. I also attended the funerals of Surinamese Muslims. Once, Surinamese Javanese Muslims offered me the rare privilege of attending the washing and shrouding of a dead person of their community.

The other form of data collection was the semistructured interview. I interviewed 54 Moroccan, 51 Turkish, 24 Surinamese Hindustani, and

[26] Abu-Zahra, "The Comparative Study of Muslim Societies and Islamic Rituals", 7–17. Cf. Gellner, *Muslim Society*; Antoun, "Anthropology", 137–228; Tapper & Tapper, "The Birth of the Prophet".

10 Surinamese Javanese respondents about one or more of the lifecycle rituals. Sometimes one session would suffice; more often, I returned to a respondent several times. I was reluctant to use a tape recorder, because in my view it would not contribute to openness and give too formal a character to the interview. I preferred to make notes during the interview, which I worked up immediately afterwards where possible. In my interviews I referred to a check list of questions. At the beginning of my research this question list was drawn up on the basis of anthropological literature and Islamic legal texts; I made subsequent adjustments in the light of the data that I had obtained from interviews.

The interviews were conducted in Dutch. If a respondent did not have a sufficient command of Dutch, we asked his or her family or neighbours for help. It frequently occurred that the respondents answered my questions only in general terms. This was due mainly to language problems. It also occurred that possible respondents declined on second thoughts to give an interview, even though I emphasized the importance of their contribution and guaranteed that the material would be treated confidentially. The following example illustrates the reserve that I sometimes encountered. Surinamese Hindustani, Surinamese Javanese, and Turkish male respondents had described to me in detail how they proceed while washing and shrouding a dead body. At that time I heard of a Moroccan woman who regularly performed these tasks, and was eager to interview her. At first she let me know through an intermediary that she was prepared to cooperate, but later declined because her husband had not given his permission.

About 75% of my respondents were female. In most cases, female respondents were able to provide more details about the lifecycle rituals, particularly concerning birth and marriage celebrations. Moreover, as a female researcher I joined women in most situations. At Moroccan and Turkish birth, circumcision, and wedding parties, male and female guests were mostly received in separate rooms or in separate areas of the venue. At some other parties, particularly Surinamese Hindustani wedding parties, the guests sat in family groups. In these cases, I joined a family that I knew. Of course, being a female researcher limited me on certain occasions, though as a Dutch woman I had in some ways more space than my respondents to interact with both men and women.

To ascertain which changes have occurred in the Dutch context, I needed information on the form and meaning of the rituals in both the Netherlands and the countries of origin. However, I generally had only very indirect access to the data pertaining to the countries of origin, since my fieldwork there was restricted to a brief stay in Morocco in 1993.

To solve this problem, I asked my respondents not only about the rituals performed in the Netherlands but also whether and how a particular rite in the country of origin differed from its equivalent in the Netherlands. I thus learned about the change of the rituals in the Dutch context according to the subjective experience of my respondents. Of course this procedure yields a somewhat biased picture, for a couple of reasons. If the respondents' knowledge of their country of origin dates from the time before their migration to the Netherlands, their accounts cannot reflect any changes in these rituals in the countries of origin in the intervening years. This introduces the risk of attributing a particular development to the Dutch situation whereas it has occurred in the countries of origin too. Furthermore, even if these accounts refer to recent occurrences, observed for example during holidays in the country of origin, they are likely to be coloured by the respondents' experiences in the Netherlands.

These forms of bias have been countered in various ways. Most important, anthropological literature, though necessarily dated and limited to a particular area, helped me gain an understanding of the form and meaning of the lifecycle rituals as performed in the countries of origin. Also, I gained insight into the original situations from the detailed accounts that some respondents gave me of circumcision and wedding parties that they had held in their country of origin. I studied videos and photographs of these events in the company of respondents who commented on the pictures. A wedding party in Morocco of a couple resident in Morocco, which I attended during my fieldwork there, enabled me also to experience the difference between the performance of this ritual in the Netherlands and Morocco. Moreover, since Moroccan and Turkish migrants in the Netherlands mostly opt for a burial in the countries of origin, I was able to form a reliable picture of the course of events there on the basis of the many accounts that they gave me of this ritual. Finally, I conducted interviews about each ritual with several individuals within the same denomination of the same ethnic group. In this way I attempted to ensure that differences that already existed in the home countries would not be attributed to the migrational context.

In the early stages of my fieldwork, I experienced some difficulties in making contact with Moroccan, Turkish, and Surinamese Muslims. I attended cooking and sewing classes run by community centres and Moroccan and Turkish women's organizations in The Hague, Utrecht, and Rotterdam. This approach proved ineffective, since in these settings women were not disposed to talk about their personal situation. They preferred conversations with one another in their mother tongue to my interviews, and, with holidays at hand, chose to finish their sewing.

I also approached Turkish and Moroccan employees at health information services in Utrecht and Rotterdam, who give health classes to Moroccan and Turkish women. Through these teachers I hoped to make contact with individual Muslim women who had recently participated in one or more lifecycle rituals. This approach produced no results either, since the teachers appeared unable to introduce me to the people attending their classes.

Since the number of my respondents remained limited, I seized every opportunity to obtain more information. I conducted interviews with Muslims from the Moluccan Islands, Indonesia, Algeria, and Egypt, and with Dutch converts to Islam, even though they fall outside the scope of this study. Also, I approached Turkish and Moroccan women in supermarkets. This method proved too direct, and consequently ineffective.

In the same period, I conducted interviews with imams and members of mosque boards in Leiden, The Hague, and Rotterdam. Frequently, the imams focused in their replies on the Islamic prescriptions regulating the lifecycle rituals. In this way, I came to know which Islamic legal texts (*fiqh*) they used for reference. For example, one Turkish imam consulted *Büyük islâm ilmihali* by Ömer Nasuhî Bilmen (1883–1971) and *Nimetülislam*. A Moroccan imam used a widespread commentary on the *Risâla* of the Malikite Ibn Abî Zaid al-Qairawânî (d. 996) as his guide.[27] During the interviews the imams often declined to give a description of birth, circumcision, and wedding parties, for these, they argued, are not regulated by Islamic law. For information on the performance of the lifecycle rituals in practice, I was obliged to turn to respondents who had recently participated in these rituals. However, the imams appeared rather cautious in introducing me to the families that they knew and the number of respondents remained limited.

Throughout my fieldwork, I worked as a volunteer for the Stichting Ontmoeting met Buitenlandse Vrouwen, a foundation that provides one-to-one Dutch-language teaching to Moroccan and Turkish women in The Hague at their homes. Over four years I gave Dutch lessons to two Moroccan women, visiting each of them every week. Both women were pregnant and gave birth during this time. Talking, watching television, and sitting with them for many hours gave me the chance to observe the everyday course of events in the household.

In addition, I approached various Islamic organizations. One of these was the Stichting Platform Islamitische Organisaties Rijnmond, a

[27] Shaikh Ṣâliḥ ᶜAbd al-Samîᶜ al-Abî al-Azharî, *Al-thamaru al-dânî*: *Sharḥ Risâla Ibn Abî Zaid al-Qairawânî.*

platform of Islamic organizations in Rotterdam and surroundings; another was the Surinamese Javanese community centre Centrum Santoso in Rotterdam. In The Hague I contacted the Muslim Information Centre, the Stichting Haags Islamitisch Platform, and the Indonesian organization Al-Ittihaad. One of these organizations invited me to its weekly gatherings on Saturdays. The main business of these gatherings was religious education and a communal meal. I attended several of these meetings, but later decided to discontinue my visits because my conversations at these events remained formal and did not spark open discussion of the lifecycle rituals. Nonetheless, with the help of these organizations I gradually gained insight into the performance of the lifecycle rituals in the Netherlands. Moreover, these organizations introduced me to a few respondents whom I interviewed at their homes. This led to better-quality information. The number of respondents remained limited, but things were improving.

The Juliana Children's Hospital in The Hague and the foundation Al-Gitaan, which organizes circumcisions in Rotterdam, were particularly helpful in introducing me to many parents who had had their sons circumcised there. The large number of parents to whom I was introduced proved decisive. Some parents were able to inform me of other lifecycle rituals in which they had recently participated, to introduce me to another respondent or to invite me to a wedding party. In this way, I came into contact with an ever-expanding group of respondents.

As a result of the many interviews, conversations, parties and meetings, I eventually managed to collect data about all four lifecycle rituals, though not spread equally over the four ethnic groups. For example, I was not able to collect enough information about Surinamese Javanese weddings and Surinamese Hindustani circumcisions. Thus, the information that I present in the chapters to follow necessarily remains incomplete, though I have tried to fill in the omissions by returning to respondents and organizations now and then during the past two years.

My findings of course pertain to some 150 respondents out of a total Muslim population in the Netherlands of 736,000. My findings are thus based on limited data. Nonetheless, I claim that my findings are susceptible to generalization over the entire Moroccan, Turkish, and Surinamese Muslim population in the Netherlands. There are two grounds for this claim. One is the manner in which I selected the respondents, who are drawn from a wide variety of contexts and settings. The second reason is the behaviour of the findings over time. After a time, my findings in different settings converged onto a stable pattern, confirming what I had found earlier and yielding no surprises.

I hope that this research will provide insight into the religious and cultural identities of Muslim communities in the Netherlands and contribute to a better understanding of what it means to live in a migrational situation where many religious facilities that can be taken for granted at home have to be reconstructed. A further aim is to show that numerous changes have occurred in the lifecycle rituals as they are performed in the Netherlands: some rites maintain their original form and meaning, others adapt to or are influenced by the new environment, new rites arise in the new setting, and yet other rites disappear. The changes provide evidence that Muslims in the Netherlands have made adaptations in many areas under the influence and in consequence of the new surroundings. Finally, by using the comparative approach I wish to bring out the pluralistic character of Islam in the Netherlands.

2
BIRTH

> O men, if you are in doubt as to the Uprising, surely We created you of dust then of a sperm-drop, then of a blood clot, then of a lump of flesh, formed and unformed, that We may make clear to you. And We establish in the wombs what We will, till a stated term, than We deliver you as infants, then that you may come of age; and some of you die, and some of you are kept back unto the vilest state of life, that after knowing somewhat, they may know nothing.
>
> —Koran 22:5, trans. Arthur J. Arberry

Birth is marked by several rites and ceremonies. They are regulated to varying degrees by Islamic law: there are no ceremonies prescribed during pregnancy, but Islamic law contains detailed regulations, for instance, pertaining to the sacrifice named *ᶜaqîqa* that is performed for the child on the seventh day after its birth.

The changes that have occurred in the ritual of birth due to transplantation to the Dutch context are relatively small, compared to those that have affected other lifecycle rituals. A new organizational infrastructure has developed in the Netherlands for the performance of circumcisions, but Moroccan, Turkish, and Surinamese women who give birth make use of the existing infrastructures in the Netherlands. Similarly, the ceremonies and rites surrounding marriage and burial have changed under the influence and by consequence of the Dutch legal context and other factors, but the ritual of birth takes place mainly within the small family circle where under normal conditions neither Dutch law nor the law of the countries of origin interferes. The rites and ceremonies that take place in the small family circle are not easily maintained in the Dutch context because, among other things, knowledge and experience of them are easily lost in the migration context, as we shall see below.

This chapter begins with a discussion pertaining to ceremonies and rites of pregnacy and delivery, including the *mitoni* ceremony which is performed in seventh month of a Surinamese Javanese woman's first pregnancy. Section 2.2 treats the whispering of the call to prayer in the child's ear shortly after birth and the placing of the chewed pulp of a date in his or her mouth. In section 2.3, there follows a description of the *ᶜaqîqa*, and section 2.4 treats the naming of the child.

2.1. Pregnancy and Delivery

Islamic law considers pregnancy and delivery mainly under the heading of purity, and prescribes no ceremonies or rites during this period. However, Al-Jazîrî and Ibn Ṭûlûn (1475–1546) briefly mention a meal named *khurs* that is held to protect women against the throes of childbirth in their discussion of the permissibility of organizing and accepting an invitation to meals on such occasions as birth, circumcision, marriage, and death.[1]

None of my Moroccan, Turkish, and Surinamese Hindustani respondents mentioned any ceremony to be performed during a woman's pregnancy. Many respondents stressed the importance that the expectant mother be provided with nourishing food. Anyone whom the mother visits is likely to feel responsible for providing any kind of food for which she may express a desire at that moment, even the most elaborate dishes.[2]

By contrast, several ceremonies may accompany a Surinamese Javanese woman's first pregnancy. A ceremonial meal (*slametan*) may be held at several times and a ceremony called *mitoni* or *tingkeban*, derived from *pitu* (seven), consisting of a *slametan* and a ritual bath, may be performed in the seventh month of pregnancy.[3]

Annemarie de Waal Malefijt describes the *slametan* as a socio-religious event consisting of a "sacred meal", a prayer and Koran recitation by a religious leader (*ka'um*), and a formal address by the host stating the specific purpose of the *slametan*.[4] The meal is regarded as an offering to

[1] Al-Jazîrî, *Al-fiqh ᶜalâ al-madhâhib al-arbaᶜa*, vol. 3, 32, and Ibn Ṭûlûn, *Faṣṣ al-khawâtim fîmâ qîla fî al-walâ'im*, 50.

[2] This corresponds with the findings of Nicolas, *Croyances et pratiques populaires turques concernant les naissances*, 59, pertaining to Turkey: "De l'avis général, en Turquie, la femme enceinte doit satisfaire ses «envies», sous peine de voir son enfant en porter l'empreinte. Car, dit-on, les «envies» rentrées se traduisent en signes sur la peau de l'enfant à venir." This ethnographical study is based mainly on Nicolas's fieldwork in the region of Bergama during the summers of 1966, 1967, and 1968: Nicolas, ibid., 2. For similar findings concerning Morocco and Surinam, see respectively Singels, "Op het raakvlak van twee geboortesystemen", 28, and Van den Berg et al., "Javaans-Surinaamse rituelen", 35–36.

[3] In the following, as far as the Surinamese Javanese Muslims in Surinam are concerned, I will frequently refer to Suparlan, "The Javanese in Surinam", and De Waal Malefijt, *The Javanese of Surinam*. Both authors draw their material mainly from fieldwork and both studies contain detailed information about all four lifecycle rituals. Furthermore, especially as regards the period preceding birth, I will refer to Van den Berg et al., "Javaans-Surinaamse rituelen", which deals with Javanese birth rituals in Surinam.

[4] According to Woodward, "The Slametan: Textual Knowledge and Ritual Performance in Central Javanese Islam", 74–83, a *slametan* in Java consists of three elements: (1) the *ujub*—the welcoming speech by the host in which among other things he explains

the spirits, who share in it by smell. In the late afternoon men from neighbouring households gather at the house where the *slametan* will be held. After the religious part of the ceremony they eat a few morsels, package or wrap the remainder of the food, and take it home for their family.[5]

De Waal Malefijt's description of the *slametan* fits the westward-prayers among the Surinamese Javanese Muslims better than the eastward-prayers. The westward-prayers continued to observe the custom of directing prayers to the west after their migration from Indonesia to Surinam, even though Mecca is more naturally regarded as being located to the east of Surinam. They are to a larger extent influenced by Javanese religion (*Agama Djawa*) or by what is taken to be such. This means for instance that they attach great importance to performing *sadjèn* offerings for the spirits, with which the eastward-prayers disagree on the grounds of Islamic teachings. The eastward-prayers prefer to use the Islamic name *ṣadaqa* to the word *slametan*, and to consume the meal together rather than to take the food home. They also refrain from burning incense on this occasion, for this is associated with the *sadjèn* offerings where incense is used to make contact with the spirits. The *daᶜwa* policy of the eastward-prayers, which consists of tolerating those aspects of Javanese religion that are not contrary to Islamic teachings, seems to bring the two groups closer nowadays.

According to Suparlan, a *slametan* is held in each month of a woman's pregnancy except, in some cases, the ninth,[6] whereas De Waal Malefijt mentions only the third, fifth, and seventh months.[7] The *slametan* held in the seventh month of the woman's pregnancy, the *slametan mitoni*, is more elaborate than the ones in the third and fifth months, which may be held in private.[8] The *mitoni* is a ceremony interpreted as marking the couple's transition to parenthood and is to be performed in the woman's first pregnancy only.[9] Suparlan locates this ceremony within the understanding of human beings according to the

the purpose of the *slametan*; (2) *donga*—Arabic prayer consisting of Koran recitation; (3) the distribution of food. See also Beatty, *Varieties of Javanese Religion*, 30–32.

[5] De Waal Malefijt, *The Javanese of Surinam*, 125.

[6] Suparlan, "The Javanese in Surinam", 243.

[7] De Waal Malefijt, *The Javanese of Surinam*, 125–126.

[8] Van den Berg et al., "Javaans-Surinaamse rituelen", 33–34. De Waal Malefijt, *The Javanese of Surinam*, 125–126, provides more details about the scale of these gatherings. According to her, a small *slametan* is held in the third month. In the fifth month, ten to fifteen neighbouring households are invited, and at the *slametan mitoni* about 50 to 100 people take part.

[9] Van den Berg et al., "Javaans-Surinaamse rituelen", 34.

Javanese religion (*Agama Djawa*). Suparlan accounts for this ceremony from the belief that in the seventh month the body and soul of the foetus have become an integrated whole, but the foetus is not yet viable.[10] Mother and foetus are therefore to be strengthened and protected against evil influences.[11] On the basis of the link with the Javanese religion, one would expect the *mitoni* to be performed more commonly by the west-ward-prayers. In fact, some eastward-prayers also keep to this ceremony, albeit in a different form.

The *mitoni* consists among other things of a *slametan* and a ritual bath, which, in Surinam, takes place in the open air.[12] The ceremony is led by a *dukun bayi* (a midwife who will also assist at the delivery), who, as a kind of master of ceremonies, constantly speaks to the people attending the ceremony. In some cases incense is burned, depending on the religious orientation of those concerned. The water for the ritual bath is taken from seven different taps or wells, is flowered, and poured in either two or seven tubs.[13] The water is poured over the future mother and father first by the *dukun bayi* and then by the participants.[14] Thereafter seven *sarong*s are held in turn before the expectant mother while the participants are asked to choose which suits her best. This will always be the seventh.[15] Then the father chops a coconut into two pieces with a knife or cleaver. It is believed that if the two pieces of the coconut are equal in size, the baby will be a boy, and otherwise a girl. Finally the future mother and father, having changed their clothes, will sell *dawet*

[10] Suparlan, "The Javanese in Surinam", 244.

[11] Van den Berg et al., "Javaans-Surinaamse rituelen", 34.

[12] Ibid., 33–34. The following account of this ritual is based mainly on information kindly supplied by Yvonne Towikromo, who also showed me slides of a *mitoni* in Surinam.

[13] Yvonne Towikromo, personal communication, and Van den Berg et al., "Javaans-Surinaamse rituelen", 34.

[14] De Waal Malefijt, *The Javanese of Surinam*, 126.

[15] Suparlan, "The Javanese in Surinam", 245–246, gives a somewhat different account: "After finishing this ritual the mother is led to the center of the house and must stand up there next to seven *tapih* (sarongs) and seven *kemben* (Javanese long waist bands for a woman), especially for a woman after childbirth; this *kemben* is to be wrapped around her waist and it is believed it will make her slim again. The pregnant woman, then, is to dress herself with each of the seven *tapih* and the seven *kemben*, in front of the all female audience. But as she puts on each set, the audience will say to her: '*Durung patut*' (Not fit yet, [or] not proper yet). After all of these seven sets of dress have been tried on, but none of them is proper to her, she again puts on her old clothing without ear-rings, necklace, ring, bracelet, or any flower, and the audience will say: '*Uwis patut, uwis patut*' (It is proper now, it is proper now). The symbolism behind all this is that the pregnant woman is not prepared yet to give birth, because the seven sets of clothing which symbolize the seven months of pregnancy and the clothing of the woman after giving childbirth do not fit her."

(Javanese syrup) and *rudjak* (fruit cocktail) to the people attending the ceremony. Because of its bitter-sweet taste, this cocktail is considered to symbolize the ups and downs in the couple's future life.[16]

The *mitoni* is still practiced in the Netherlands nowadays, albeit in a rather different form. In Surinam, as we have seen, the *mitoni* is performed in the open air, enabling many people to attend the ceremony. In the Netherlands the scale is necessarily smaller, for the *mitoni* is held either at home in the bathroom or in a rented hall. The majority of the Surinamese Javanese Muslims in the Netherlands have no objections to the *mitoni* as such; provided those aspects that are contrary to Islamic teachings, such as the burning of incense in order to make contact with the spirits, are eliminated from the ceremony, the eastward-prayers also accept the *mitoni*.

Home or Hospital Confinement

Among my respondents in the Netherlands, especially among those of Turkish and Moroccan origin, I found a strong preference for giving birth either during a few days' stay at a hospital or as an outpatient in a maternity clinic, partly because this is considered safer than a home delivery. Another reason people prefer a hospital stay is that it affords the mother a few days' rest: "I stayed in hospital for four days. Then you settle down and visits are confined to visiting hours." This preference for a hospital stay endures despite the policy of health insurance companies in the Netherlands to promote home births; in view of the relatively high costs of hospitalization, health insurers no longer automatically cover a hospital stay in order to give birth.

In recent years, the place and manner of the delivery in the countries of origin has changed too. Whereas in the past Javanese people of Java and of Surinam preferred a home confinement,[17] many Javanese babies are nowadays born in hospital or assisted by a nurse.[18]

Similar developments have taken place in Turkey. However, there is a shortage of doctors and particularly of nurses in rural areas, according to Froukje Santing, notwithstanding the Turkish government's attempts to set up a high-quality health service throughout the country. As a consequence, women living in rural areas or in *gecekondu*, especially those over the age of thirty, may give birth without a doctor or a midwife

[16] The description of the *tingkeban* by Geertz, *The Religion of Java*, 42–44, suggests that in Java this ceremony is more elaborate.

[17] Van den Berg et al., "Javaans-Surinaamse rituelen", 37.

[18] Suparlan, "The Javanese in Surinam", 247.

being present. *Gecekondu* are shantytowns in the periphery of large cities which have arisen due to the large-scale migration in Turkey from rural to urban areas. City dwellers and younger *gecekondu* women are more inclined to consult a doctor during pregnancy and delivery. Those belonging to the middle or upper class will give birth in a hospital or the clinic of the doctor involved.[19] Thus, whether a woman gives birth in hospital is determined by the level of the local health services, the age and educational level of the woman, and above all the family's financial means. Sylvia Wing Önder also found that a home delivery is the norm in Turkey. However, she found that a hospital delivery is fashionable and preferred if the family can afford it: a hospital stay makes a woman feel important, it is a demonstration of her husband's love for her that he takes her to the hospital, and a hospital stay is a rare opportunity for her to be spoiled. Furthermore, the dirt associated with childbirth is not brought into the home.[20]

Presence of Men

Women may show a preference for being treated exclusively by female doctors and nurses, although they will allow themselves to be treated by men if there is no alternative. A Turkish respondent gave the following explanation for this: "I had my baby in a policlinic [that is, as an outpatient]. But it is rather unpleasant that men and women work in a hospital. In Turkey gynaecologists are mostly female. A hospital will promote itself [there] as having female doctors. Therefore it is easier to make a choice." A number of respondents expressed regret at the fact that the only women's clinic in The Hague closed a few years ago.

Asked whether their husbands were present at the delivery, women often answered in the affirmative. However, in some cases this meant that the husband was in an adjoining room at the birth, not actually in the delivery room. Other respondents explicitly expressed a preference that the birth be attended only by women, but added that, if this were not possible, a husband was of course allowed to assist his wife.

Ceremonies Relating to the Placenta

The burial of the placenta or afterbirth seems no longer to be common usage in the Netherlands. This also holds true to a lesser degree for the countries of origin. However, in the respondents' accounts of childbirth

[19] Santing, *Die vrouw, dat ben ik*, 58–61.
[20] Wing Önder, "Your Own Mother or Father State?"

in the countries of origin, the custom of burying the placenta or throwing it into a river is frequently mentioned.

Surinamese Javanese people used to bury a girl's placenta outside the home to the left of the entrance and that of a boy to the right of it. A light, such as a paraffin lamp, burned continuously for 35 days at the spot where the placenta was buried. The amniotic fluid is, according to Surinamese Javanese people, the elder sibling of the newborn, whereas the placenta and the umbilical cord are his or her younger sibling. They are believed to protect the baby against illness for the first 35 days.[21]

According to Nicolas, the belief that the placenta is the child's companion is found also in Bergama (Turkey), where the placenta is called *son* (end) or *eş* (companion): "Parce que c'est un «morceau d'homme», il est d'usage d'enterrer le placenta. Le jeter n'importe où et le laisser traîner est considéré comme étant *günah* «peché». Après l'avoir lavé et enveloppé dans un morceau d'étoffe, on choisit un endroit convenable pour l'enterrer."[22] Prevailing custom varies depending on the level of health care in a particular region. A respondent stated for instance: "In Turkey the placenta is buried, at least in villages [with no hospitals or clinics]. In the case of a hospital delivery it is thrown away."

Whereas some handle the placenta with care because it is considered the child's companion, others store it in a safe place to prevent its constituting a danger to mother and child through magic. As a Moroccan respondent put it: "In Morocco, the placenta is buried. All kind of things can happen to it, through magic (for instance it may bring about that the mother cannot bear any more children). Here, in the Netherlands, Moroccan people think that one has to leave the placenta behind in the hospital because it is used for making cosmetics [thus it is used for industrial purposes rather than being thrown away]."

Postnatal Period

Opinions concerning the advisibility of the husband's presence at the delivery and the burial of the placenta are undergoing change in the Netherlands as well as in the countries of origin. This holds true also for the period of time during which the mother and child stay at home.

In Turkey, in former times, a woman was supposed to remain at home for forty days after having given birth, a period known as *lohusalık*. Whether a woman kept to the *lohusalık* depended on where she lived.

[21] Van den Berg et al., "Javaans-Surinaamse rituelen", 39.

[22] Nicolas, *Croyances et pratiques populaires turques concernant les naissances*, 91–92.

In rural areas, a woman probably could not afford to lose more than about four days' work on the land. In towns, by contrast, women would certainly stay at home for twenty days, if not forty. The completion of the *lohusalık*, whether lasting forty days (*büyük kırk*), twenty days (*küçük kırk*) or some other period, is called *kırklama*. On this occasion, a ritual bath, intended to protect mother and child from evil influences, marked their return to normal life.[23] In Morocco, likewise, there is evidence that a mother observes a period of between a week and forty days after the birth, during which she and her child do not leave the home.[24]

The majority of my respondents in the Netherlands do not keep strictly to this practice. The length of this period varies, as in the countries of origin. Alternatively, people may stress that the mother of the newborn child is ritually unclean during this period, rather than insisting on her actually staying at home. A Surinamese Hindustani respondent argued, for instance, as follows:

> It is not obligatory to stay at home for forty days. For fifteen or sixteen days one is weak and unclean. During this period it is therefore not allowed to sleep with your husband. In former days, in Surinam, a woman used to live with her in-laws. In those days, she often had to work very hard. But after the delivery she was released [from her daily tasks] for forty days; she needn't do anything.

Moroccan women may also leave home during this period:

> After this, I stayed with my mother for forty days. I didn't do anything, except for taking care of . . . [name of the baby]. I went out when I really had to, to go to the health centre. I remained indoors much longer than Dutch women do.

However, Moroccan respondents showed some reservations about the idea of a young mother's leaving the house. They indicated that for the first three months following childbirth, "a woman's grave is open", or that the mother should not go outdoors or stay at home alone because she is vulnerable to spirits. For this reason female family members will stay with her every day for a period following the birth.

As well as the mother's ritual uncleanness, a Turkish respondent emphasized the assistance rendered by family members during this period:

> For forty days you are not allowed to make love with your husband or to perform your daily prayer and so on. Family members come along every day to help.

[23] Ibid., 119–123 and also 137–140.
[24] Eickelman, "Rites of Passage: Muslim Rites", 399.

The assistance of family members seems to be preferred to the services of district nurses. Women who have had a baby in a hospital as an outpatient are normally assisted by their family when back at home.[25] Only 18% of Moroccan and Turkish mothers in the Netherlands make use of the services of district nurses, according to Shadid and Van Koningsveld. They attribute this low take-up to the scarce financial means of the families and their unfamiliarity with professional postnatal care services.[26] An additional explanation may be that the women would rather appeal to their sisters than to strangers who are unacquainted with the family's daily routine.

Amulets

As well as by remaining at home for forty days, a new mother may attempt to protect herself and her newborn child against evil influences by means of amulets. Turkish parents may for instance pin a medallion bearing the inscription *Maşallah* on the child's clothes, to protect him or her against the evil eye or, it was also held, against illness. The inscription *Maşallah* is also used on the sash that a Turkish boy who is to be circumcised wears, as we will see in the next chapter. A Moroccan respondent placed a small knife, some salt, and a shell under her child's mattress as a defence against the evil eye (or according to others as a defence against the *junûn*).[27] Furthermore, she preferred not to place the cradle near the bathroom because the *junûn* are supposed to be found in the vicinity of water.

A Surinamese Hindustani respondent made use of a *tawiez* (from the Arabic *ta^cwîdh*, amulet) to protect herself and her child against illness and evil influences. This amulet consisted of a Koranic text wrapped in seven layers of green cloth and placed in a stitched triangular leather pouch. Alladien points out that according to *ḥadîth* the following *du^câ'* should be recited for children or be written on a slip of paper and sewn up in a waterproof *tawiez* hung round the child's neck: "I seek refuge in

[25] Cf. Singels, "Op het raakvlak van twee geboortesystemen", 52.

[26] Shadid & Van Koningsveld, *Minderheden, hulpverlening en gezondheidszorg*, 109.

[27] Cf. also M'Erad, "La Ziadah ou naissance à Safi (Maroc)", 54: "Avec un ruban bleu, on attache au poignet droit de l'enfant, pour le préserver des Djinns et du mauvais oeil, un «guirch» (Synonyme de . . . 25 centimes hassanis), avec un peu de h'armel, de sel et d'alun. L'accouchée porte un ruban de même couleur avec les mêmes ingrédients au pied droit, si le nouveau né est du sexe masculin, au cou, s'il est du sexe féminin. On met sous l'oreille de l'enfant, toujours pour le préserver des Djinns, un sachet contenant du h'armel, de l'alun, du sel, un coquillage, un petite «mordjana» et le couteau dont on s'est servi pour lui couper le cordon ombilical."

the perfect words of God from the evil of every *shaiṭân* and reptile and from every evil eye."[28]

Some respondents also emphasized that one should remain alert, however many precautionary measures are taken. If guests pay the mother compliments on her baby, she should utter the word *Bismillah*, thus protecting her child. One should also try to avoid having negative thoughts in the baby's vicinity, for these may possibly bring harm.

2.2. Whispering in the Child's Ear and the Taḥnîk

According to the Shafi^c^ites it is recommended to whisper the call to prayer (*adhân*) in the right ear and the second call to prayer (*iqâma*) in the left ear of a child immediately after birth.[29] According to Al-Ashqar only the *adhân* is to be whispered, in the child's right ear.[30] Alladien deems it desirable to whisper the *adhân* four times in the right ear and the *iqâma* three times in the left ear.[31]

The *taḥnîk* is another rite that may be performed shortly after birth: a date is chewed to fine pulp and some of the liquid is placed into the baby's mouth after the recitation of a prayer.[32] The Malikite Ibn Rushd al-Qurṭubî refers briefly to a *ḥadîth* according to which ^c^Abdullah, the son of Abû Ṭalḥa, was brought to the Prophet on the morning following the night of his birth. On this occasion the Prophet performed the *taḥnîk*, prayed for him, and gave him the name ^c^Abdallah.[33] This *ḥadîth* additionally refers to the naming of a child as if this should also take place shortly after the birth. However, the opinions concerning the appropriate time for doing this differ, as we shall see below. Al-Ashqar, in dealing with several customs that may accompany childbirth, does not mention the *taḥnîk*.[34]

[28] Alladien, *De baby en zijn naam in de islam*, 13.

[29] Juynboll, *Handleiding tot de kennis van de Mohammedaansche wet volgens de leer der Sjâfi^c^itische school*, 150.

[30] Al-Ashqar, *Thalâth sha^c^â'ir: Al-^c^aqîqa, al-uḍḥîya, al-liḥya* (Three religious practices: The *^c^aqîqa*, the sacrifice, and the beard), 15, and also Al-Kaysî, *Morals and Manners in Islam*, 127, and Stichting Lalla Rookh, *Huwelijk, geboorte en overlijden bij moslims*, 19. Al-Ashqar is a Salafite, as we will see in the following section dealing with the *^c^aqîqa*. *Morals and Manners in Islam* and *Huwelijk, geboorte en overlijden bij moslims* are present-day guides for Muslims. The former is published by The Islamic Foundation, and the latter by the Stichting Lalla Rookh, a Surinamese Hindustani organization in the Netherlands.

[31] Alladien, *De baby en zijn naam in de islam*, 11.

[32] Al-Kaysî, *Morals and Manners in Islam*, 127, deems this practice not to be compulsory: "The second thing, though not compulsory, is to chew a date until it is fine pulp and then place some of the liquid in the baby's mouth, afterwards saying a prayer for the baby. This is known as *taḥnîk* and it was sometimes done by the Prophet."

[33] Ibn Rushd al-Qurṭubî, *Al-muqaddamât al-mumahhadât*, vol. 1, 448.

[34] Al-Ashqar, *Thalâth sha^c^â'ir*, 42.

Some religious leaders whom I interviewed indicated that they knew the custom of *taḥnîk*. However, none of my respondents actually performed it shortly after childbirth. The rite of whispering in the child's ears seems to be practiced more widely than the *taḥnîk*, though the accounts of this rite, as it took place in practice, varied substantially from respondent to respondent. People may be unacquainted with this rite or may refer only vaguely to the words to be whispered, not knowing exactly which these are: for example "*Allahu akbar* and a few words from the Koran" or "short Koranic verses".[35] Other respondents specified the words to be whispered more precisely, mentioning either only the *adhân* or both the *adhân* and the *iqâma* (*ezan* and *kamet* in Turkish). The credo (*shahâda* in Arabic, *şahadet* in Turkish) is part of the *adhân* and *iqâma*, and is also whispered separately in addition to the *adhân* and *iqâma*. A Turkish respondent, for instance, whispered the *kelime-i şahadet* and *ezan* in his child's left ear and the *kelime-i şahadet* and *kamet* in the right ear.

My respondents' unfamiliarity with this rite may be explained partially by the fact that the whispering in the child's ears is generally performed by men whereas most of my respondents were female. According to a Moroccan respondent, for example, the credo (*shahâda*) is whispered in one ear and the second call to prayer (*adhân*) in the other. Thereafter, she indicated that she was not sure about this, giving the excuse that her husband and uncle had performed this rite at the birth of her children. Prevailing custom in the countries of origin may also be relevant in explaining the variety in the formulae whispered. According to the majority of the Turkish respondents, for instance, the name of the child should be whispered in the child's ear three times after the *ezan*. To a certain extent, this was the practice in Turkey,[36] although this took place on the seventh day or a few days earlier (at least in ancient times —things may be different nowadays) whereas in the Netherlands it may take place shortly after the birth. Furthermore, in Turkey the name whispered in the child's ear is the second name whereas in the Netherlands (and possibly nowadays in Turkey as well) the distinction between the

[35] Cf. M'Erad, "Le Ziadah ou naissance à Safi (Maroc)", 49: "Le père entre dans la chambre pour voir sa femme et son enfant. Il saisit ce dernier par les oreilles et, pour qu'il grandisse dans l'Islam, lui récite quelques versets du Qoran s'il peut, et la formule de l'«adzan»."

[36] Nicolas, *Croyances et pratiques populaires turques concernant les naissances*, 115–116, and Bainbridge, *Life-Cycle Rituals of the Turks of Turkey*, 1. According to Nicolas the prayer call (*ezan*) is whispered in the child's right ear together with the child's second name, which is spoken three times, whereas according to Bainbridge the *ezan* is also whispered three times.

umbilical name and the second name has disappeared.[37] Moroccan and Surinam Hindustani respondents did not mention the child's name in connection with this rite. Rather, as we shall see in the following section, Moroccans connect the child's naming with the sacrifice performed on the seventh day.

The rite of whispering in the child's ear may be performed by the father of the child or another male member of the family. A Surinamese Hindustani respondent argued as follows: "This uncle is [ranked] higher than my husband. Therefore he [my husband] has given him [this uncle] the honour. Other people have asked my husband to perform it." Preference may also be given to someone who has been to Mecca or to a *hoca* or an *imam*, for they will certainly know the words to be recited in the child's ear.

The importance attached to the whispering of the *adhân* and the *iqâma* in the ears of the newborn child may be explained as the wish that the first words that the child hears should include the credo (which is part of the *adhân* and the *iqâma*) and consequently that Islam is the first thing that a child encounters in life. These first words confirm the child's religion: "The meaning [of this rite] is that the child is born in the house of Islam; its religion is Islam." This rite may also stress the importance of Islam for the child's future life. Suparlan argues for instance that its purpose is to summon the baby symbolically to become a good Muslim when it grows up.[38] M'Erad makes a similar point.[39] However, he also refers to Al-Zurqânî's commentary on Khalîl b. Isḥâq where it is argued that performing this rite protects the newborn child against all kinds of children's diseases.[40] I did not come across this line of reasoning in the Netherlands.

2.3. THE ᶜAQÎQA

According to the majority of Muslim scholars, it is recommendable (*sunna*) to slaughter an animal and to shave off the child's hair on the seventh day after its birth.[41] Both this sacrifice and the child's hair that has been shaven off are called *ᶜaqîqa*.[42]

[37] In section 2.4 we will return to the distinction between an umbilical name, given shortly upon birth, and a second name, given on the seventh day or a few days earlier.

[38] Suparlan, "The Javanese in Surinam", 247.

[39] M'Erad, "La Ziadah ou naissance à Safi (Maroc)", 49: "pour qu'il grandisse dans l'Islam".

[40] Ibid., 49. The reference is to Al-Zurqânî's (d. 1688) commentary on the *Mukhtaṣar* by Khalîl b. Isḥâq (d. 1365), a Malikite scholar. Cf. Brockelmann, *Geschichte der Arabischen Litteratur*, SII, 96–99 and 438.

[41] Ibn Rushd, *The Distinguished Jurist's Primer*, vol. 1, 560.

[42] Al-Ashqar, *Thalâth shaᶜâ'ir: Al-ᶜaqîqa, al-uḍḥîya, al-liḥya* (Three religious practices:

Although in dealing with the religious qualification of the *ᶜaqîqa* and the right time for its performance, scholars such as Al-Ashqar and Ibn Rushd al-Qurṭubî mention both connotations, they focus mainly on its first connotation. Likewise, asked about the *ᶜaqîqa*, most respondents referred only to its first connotation, not mentioning the second one. This does not mean that they were unacquainted with the custom of shaving the child's hair: rather, in their view, it is unrelated to the sacrifice performed for the newborn child.

Only half the Turkish respondents in my survey slaughtered an animal or intended to do so when a child was born to them.[43] Moroccan respondents in particular, but also Surinamese Hindustani respondents, seem to attach more importance to having an animal slaughtered on this occasion. Moroccans used the name *sabᶜa* or *subûᶜ*, from *sabᶜa* or "seven", rather than *ᶜaqîqa* for the festive ceremony organized on this occasion.

The importance of shaving the child's head shortly after birth was emphasized especially by Surinamese Hindustani respondents. A number of Moroccan and Turkish respondents also shaved off their child's hair, when the child was one year old or so, particularly because they believed that the child would acquire a thicker head of hair as a result.

The Religious Qualification of the ᶜAqîqa

According to the Shafiᶜites, the *ᶜaqîqa* is recommendable (*sunna*).[44] Likewise, Mâlik and his followers looked upon the performance of the *ᶜaqîqa* as *sunna*: whereas it is praiseworthy to perform this ceremony, it is not a sin to refrain from it.[45] Abû Ḥanîfa held it to be neither obligatory nor *sunna*, but optional.[46] Some scholars of earlier times, for example Al-Ḥasan al-Baṣrî and the Zahirites, attributed an obligatory character to the *ᶜaqîqa*.[47] A present-day scholar, Al-Ashqar, reaches the same conclusion.[48] However, according to him, the religious qualification of

The *ᶜaqîqa*, the sacrifice, and the beard), 9. See also Ibn Rushd al-Qurṭubî, *Al-muqaddamât al-mumahhadât*, vol. 1, 447, and Juynboll, *Handleiding tot de kennis van de Mohammedaansche wet volgens de leer der Sjâfiᶜitische school*, 150.

[43] A Turkish imam whom I interviewed estimated the number of Turks in the Netherlands who perform the *ᶜaqîqa*—here understood to mean only the sacrifice—also at 50%. This percentage seems to reflect the Hanafite view that the performance of the *ᶜaqîqa* is optional.

[44] Juynboll, *Handleiding tot de kennis van de Mohammedaansche wet volgens de leer der Sjâfiᶜitische school*, 150.

[45] Ibn Rushd al-Qurṭubî, *Al-muqaddamât al-mumahhadât*, vol. 1, 448.

[46] Al-Ashqar, *Thalâth shaᶜâ'ir*, 10; Ibn Rushd, *The Distinguished Jurist's Primer*, vol. 1, 560, and Zwemer, "The ᶜAkika Sacrifice", 238.

[47] Al-Ashqar, *Thalâth shaᶜâ'ir*, 10.

[48] Ibid., 13 and 15. Al-Ashqar's treatise on the *ᶜaqîqa* is illustrative of his Salafite

the two elements of the *ᶜaqîqa* differs. Whereas he looks upon the sacrifice as obligatory, shaving the child's hair is in his view *sunna*.[49]

The religious qualification attributed to the *ᶜaqîqa* depends on the traditions on which scholars rely. Al-Ashqar refers, for instance, to the following traditions, which are put forward in favour of its obligatory character: "For a boy one has to perform the *ᶜaqîqa*, therefore shed blood for him [perform a sacrifice for him] and take away the pain from him",[50] and "Each boy pledges his *ᶜaqîqa*, which is slaughtered for him on his seventh day, his head is shaven and he is given a name".[51] Additionally, Al-Ashqar refers to traditions concerning the Prophet's performance of the *ᶜaqîqa* for his grandsons, Al-Ḥasan and Al-Ḥusayn, and to the Prophet's command to sacrifice two identical sheep for a boy and one sheep for a girl.[52]

Those who favour the obligatory character of the *ᶜaqîqa* argue also that if the *ᶜaqîqa* on behalf of a newborn child has not taken place on the seventh day, the child is obliged to perform the *ᶜaqîqa* on his or her own behalf when he or she has come of age. This alludes to a tradition according to which the Prophet, after his prophethood had been revealed to him, performed the *ᶜaqîqa* on his own behalf. Mâlik disagreed with this opinion, questioning whether, during the lifetime of the Prophet, anyone could be found who performed the *ᶜaqîqa* on his own behalf in the days of Islam, if it had not been performed for him in the days of the *Jâhiliyya*.[53] According to Ibn Rushd al-Qurṭubi, the *ᶜaqîqa* is rather a practice taken over from the *Jâhiliyya*, be it that in the *Jâhiliyya* the newborn child was smeared with the blood of the sacrifice whereas in the time of Islam the child was smeared only with saffron.[54]

Those who are of the opinion that the *ᶜaqîqa* is *sunna* refer to the following *ḥadîth* concerning the birth of Al-Ḥasan: "When he was born,

stance, that is of his effort to transcend the existing different viewpoints of the law schools by going back to the prophetical *sunna*. See also Van Koningsveld, "Between Communalism and Secularism", 329 and 340.

49 Al-Ashqar, *Thalâth shaᶜâ'ir*, 15.

50 According to Ibn Rushd al-Qurṭubî, *Al-muqaddamât al-mumahhadât*, vol. 1, 449, the taking away of the pain (*imâṭatu-l-adhâ*) may be explained as refraining from what people used to do during the *Jâhiliyya*, that is smearing the baby with the sacrificial blood. However, in his view it is more likely that taking away the pain means shaving off the child's hair. Similarly, Ibn Rushd, *The Distinguished Jurist's Primer*, vol. 1, 560: "and the harm is removed (by shaving his hair)".

51 Both traditions reflect the notion of substition: the child's hair is a ransom for the pain, which would otherwise be caused to the child, but which is now taken away from it. Similarly, the *ᶜaqîqa* is performed in exchange for the child.

52 Al-Ashqar, *Thalâth shaᶜâ'ir*, 10–11.

53 Ibn Rushd al-Qurṭubî, *Al-muqaddamât al-mumahhadât*, vol. 1, 448.

54 Ibid., 447.

his mother Fâṭima intended to perform the *ᶜaqîqa* for him, consisting of two rams. Thereupon, the Prophet of God said: Do not perform the *ᶜaqîqa* for him, but shave off his hair from his head and give away as alms the weight of his hair in silver." However, in the view of Al-Ashqar, the Prophet ordered his daughter to do so, because he himself intended to perform the *ᶜaqîqa* for Al-Ḥasan, thereby referring to a *ḥadith* dealing with the Prophet's performance of the *ᶜaqîqa* for Al-Ḥasan and Al-Ḥusayn.[55]

Grounds for considering the *ᶜaqîqa* to be recommendable or, according to the Hanafites, permissible, are provided by a tradition according to which the Prophet, when asked about the *ᶜaqîqa*, said: "I do not like disobedience (*al-ᶜuqûq*)" as if he disapproved of the word, while adding, however: "If anyone wants to sacrifice for a child being born to him, he may do so." In the view of Ibn Rushd al-Qurṭubî, this tradition abrogated the earlier tradition put forward in favour of the obligatory character, which is quoted above: "Each boy pledges his *ᶜaqîqa*, which is slaughtered for him on his seventh day, his head is shaven and he is given a name."[56]

Notwithstanding the view of the Salafite Al-Ashqar, who attributes an obligatory character to the *ᶜaqîqa*, the majority view is that the *ᶜaqîqa* is *sunna*. This holds especially for actual practice, where one finds the opinion of the law schools concerning the religious qualification of the *ᶜaqîqa* clearly reflected in the behaviour of their adherents.

Moroccan respondents preferred to have an animal slaughtered for their child shortly after birth, provided they had the financial means to do so. If this was not the case, they might stress that it is not obligatory to perform a sacrifice for the birth of a child. Accordingly, Surinamese Hindustani respondents did not look upon the *ᶜaqîqa* as obligatory. They may therefore have no objection to postponing the *ᶜaqîqa* for a considerable time, even until the child's marriage, because of purely financial reasons. Turkish respondents may emphasize that you may slaughter an animal on this occasion if you wish. However, in their view, one is obliged to perform a sacrifice in the case of *kurban niyeti* (also called *adak kurban*), that is, if you have vowed beforehand to slaughter an animal if a particular event comes to pass. For example, you may have vowed to slaughter an animal for the birth of a child if your wife previously had a miscarriage or if it took a long time for your wife to become pregnant.

[55] Al-Ashqar, *Thalâth shaᶜâ'ir*, 12–13.
[56] Ibn Rushd al-Qurṭubî, *Al-muqaddamât al-mumahhadât*, vol. 1, 448.

The Sacrifice

The Koran does not contain literal references to the *ᶜaqîqa*. Al-Ashqar deals with the *ᶜaqîqa* in the light of what is also looked upon as one of the main purposes of the *ᶜibadât*, that is the Koranic encouragement to give thanks to God. Thus, his discussion of the *ᶜaqîqa* takes as a starting point that through this sacrifice one shows one's gratitude to God for the birth of a child.[57]

According to the Shafiᶜites, it is recommendable (*sunna*) to sacrifice one sheep or goat for a girl and two for a boy,[58] whereas according to the Malikites one sheep suffices regardless of the child's sex.[59] Several traditions are cited in support, such as "Anyone who wants to sacrifice for his child, let him sacrifice, for a boy two identical sheep and for a girl one sheep",[60] which favours the former viewpoint. The latter point of view is supported by another tradition, concerning the *ᶜaqîqa* performed by the Prophet on behalf of Al-Ḥasan and Al-Ḥusayn, which consisted of one ram for each of them.[61]

According to the majority of scholars, the animal to be slaughtered on this occasion is, in order of preference, a sheep, a goat, a cow, and a camel, whereas according to Mâlik the *ᶜaqîqa* is to be performed only with a sheep or goat.[62]

In practice, various meanings are attached to the *ᶜaqîqa*—here understood to mean only the sacrifice. It is considered to be a matter of thankfulness and joy. The sacrifice is made in gratitude for God's gift of a child. According to some respondents, by performing the sacrifice the believer follows the example of the Prophet, whereas other respondents refer to Ibrâhîm, who intended to offer his son for love of God, but was eventually allowed to sacrifice a sheep instead. The notion, generally connected with the sacrifice of *ᶜId al-Aḍḥâ*, that this sheep will be your celestial mount, your "ticket to paradise", is mentioned also with respect to the *ᶜaqîqa*. One also comes across the statement that the *ᶜaqîqa* is part of Islam without any further explanation: "That is according to our religion. That's the way we do things"; "That's our religion"; "Allah has ordained it thus".

[57] Al-Ashqar, *Thalâth shaᶜâ'ir*, 7–9.

[58] Juynboll, *Handleiding tot de kennis van de Mohammedaansche wet volgens de leer der Sjâfiᶜitische school*, 150.

[59] Ibn Rushd al-Qurṭubî, *Al-muqaddamât al-mumahhadât*, vol. 1, 450, and Juynboll & Pedersen, "ᶜAḳîḳa", 337.

[60] Ibn Rushd al-Qurṭubî, *Al-muqaddamât al-mumahhadât*, vol. 1, 450.

[61] Zwemer, "The ᶜAkika Sacrifice", 239, and Ibn Rushd, *The Distinguished Jurist's Primer*, vol. 1, 561.

[62] Ibn Rushd al-Qurṭubî, *Al-muqaddamât al-mumahhadât*, vol. 1, 449.

Moroccan respondents may explicitly connect the sacrifice with the naming of a newborn child (*tasmiya*). A respondent argued that, without this sacrifice, a child could not be given a name and consequently would not be made known to God. For this reason, the intention (*niyya*) for the slaughter should include the child's name: "The name of the child should be mentioned three times before the sheep is slaughtered."[63]

In Morocco, the sacrifice is usually carried out at home, so it is easy to arrange for the name of the child to be uttered before the animal's throat is cut, if this is considered important. In the Netherlands, by contrast, the law forbids the slaughter of animals on domestic premises, so it is more difficult to arrange for the *niyya*, unless the carcass is obtained directly from the abattoir. If an order for a carcass is placed with a butcher, the customer cannot be certain that the name of the child was uttered in the *niyya*. This may lead people to perform the *ᶜaqîqa* twice: once in the Netherlands on the seventh day after the birth without the certainty that the name of child was mentioned before the animal's throat was cut, and a second time during a holiday in Morocco.

Moroccan respondents emphasized that one sheep was sufficient regardless of the sex of the baby, whereas Surinamese Hindustani and Turkish respondents may sacrifice one sheep for a girl and two for a boy. Moreover, Moroccan respondents preferred rams to sheep and certainly to goats, perhaps because the *ᶜaqîqa* for Al-Ḥasan and Al-Ḥusayn consisted of rams, according to the tradition mentioned above: "A goat doesn't amount to anything, a sheep is better, and a ram means that one is really happy with the child."

Al-Kaysî emphasizes that "The rightful way is to slaughter an animal on this occasion and not to give its value in alms."[64] Nonetheless, Turkish respondents may prefer to perform the *akik kurban* in Turkey or to send money to Turkey rather than perform the *akik kurban* in the Netherlands. The widespread feeling that poverty in the Netherlands is as nothing compared to that in Turkey is an explanation for this

[63] As regards Safi (Morocco), M'Erad, "Le Ziadah ou naissance à Safi (Maroc)", 54, presents evidence for this connection between the sacrifice and the naming of the child: "Le septième jour, avant le lever du soleil, on égorge le *kabch et tsamiah* . . . (lit. mouton de dénomination). En accomplissant ce sacrifice, le père déclare donner à son enfant tel ou tel prénom." Eickelman, "Rites of Passage: Muslim Rites", 400, does not explicitly connect these two ceremonies: "The most important event in the child's life is the naming ceremony (*subûᶜ*), which ideally occurs a week after the birth of a child of either sex. . . . For boys in Morocco, the naming ceremony is always accompanied by the sacrifice of a sheep or a goat, although a blood sacrifice is often omitted in the case of girls. This sacrifice is known as the *ᶜaqîqah* ceremony."

[64] Al-Kaysî, *Morals and Manners in Islam*, 128.

preference. Who in the Netherlands are the poor and needy among whom the sacrificial meat should be distributed?

Moreover, it is argued that, unlike in the Netherlands, it is common usage in Turkey to perform the *akik kurban*.[65] This leads people to prefer Turkey to the Netherlands:

> My father-in-law [who lives] in Turkey wants to perform *kurban* when we are in Turkey. Here, in the Netherlands, this does not happen.

> Here in the Netherlands it is better to give money to the poor in Turkey instead of slaughtering a sheep and distributing it among the neighbours. The majority here does not slaughter a sheep, that is really different from Turkey.

One may also see fewer opportunities in the Netherlands for doing what one was used to doing in Turkey:

> Here, it is difficult to perform the ritual slaughter. Either you send money in the name of your family or you go to Turkey yourself [to perform the *ᶜaqîqa*]."

The Ḥukm of the Meat of the Sacrifice

The *ḥukm* of the meat of an *ᶜaqîqa* is the *ḥukm* of the meat of sacrifices with respect to eating, giving as alms, and the prohibition of sale.[66] This means that the same rules apply to the *ᶜaqîqa* as to the sacrifices on *ᶜId al-Aḍḥâ*. As far as the latter is concerned, it is agreed, among other things on the basis of two Koranic verses (22:28 and 22:36), that the sacrificer is commanded to eat (part of) his sacrifice and to give (part of) it away as charity.[67] The Malikites differed on whether the command is to perform both deeds or whether one has a choice among the two.[68] Because of the prophetical tradition "Eat, give charity, and store", other scholars deemed it desirable to divide the meat of a sacrifice, and as a consequence the meat of the *ᶜaqîqa*, into three parts.[69]

In practice, the meat of the sacrifice will generally not be reserved for one's own use. A Surinamese Hindustani respondent implicitly referred to the rule that the *ḥukm* of the meat of an *ᶜaqîqa* is the *ḥukm* of the meat

[65] This may vary according to region, for there is also evidence to the contrary. Nicolas, *Croyances et pratiques populaires turques concernant les naissances*, as well as Bainbridge, *Life-Cycle Rituals of the Turks of Turkey*, for example, do not mention the *ᶜaqîqa* at all.

[66] Ibn Rushd, *The Distinguished Jurist's Primer*, vol. 1, 562.

[67] Ibid., 527–528.

[68] Ibid., 528.

[69] Ibid., 528. Juynboll & Pedersen, "ᶜAḳîḳa", 337, state that the greater part of the meat of the *ᶜaqîqa* is to be divided among the poor, but it is recommendable to use part of the meat to offer a meal to one's own family.

of sacrifices. Another respondent however made an exception for the *ᶜaqîqa*: "In the case of religious feasts, part of the sacrificial animal has to be distributed among the poor. In the case of a birth, however, one is not obliged to do so. It of course allowed to distribute it among the poor, to thank God, but there is no need."

According to some, the meat of the sacrifice should be divided into three parts. The recipients of these portions may vary: oneself, the family, neighbours, the poor and needy. Another respondent kept to a division into two parts, as in her view part of the meat should be used for a shared meal with family and friends and the rest should be distributed among the poor. In the Netherlands this means for instance that one sheep is for the family and one for the mosque. Other respondents used the sacrificial meat exclusively for their own family and acquaintances. In this case packets of uncooked meat may be delivered to the homes of family members and acquaintances but the sacrificial meat may also be used for a shared meal at home or on the premises of a mosque. Some Turkish respondents argued that the parents should not eat the meat of the *akik kurban*.

Communal Gatherings

In dealing with the *walîma*, the festive meal organized on the occasion of a marriage, Al-Jazîrî deals also with the *ḥukm* of meals organized on the occasion of an *ᶜaqîqa*, a circumcision (*iᶜdhâr*), and a funeral (*waḍîma*).[70] According to the Shafiᶜites, it is *sunna* to organize a festive meal at every joyful event and to invite guests to it. According to the Hanafites, the invitation to an *iᶜdhâr* and the like is allowed (*jâ'iza*) when these gatherings are free of religious prohibitions.[71] The Malikites take the same view.[72]

In practice we will see that upon the birth of a child the family may receive many visitors in small groups, but also a large number of visitors together, for instance on the occasion of the *ᶜaqîqa* or *subûᶜ*. The sacrificial meat may be used for a shared meal or it may be delivered to the homes of family, friends, and neighbours. Moroccan respondents preferred the former option. They may hold a party during the weekend. On this occasion men and women will mostly not come together in one

[70] Al-Jazîrî, *Al-fiqh ᶜalâ al-madhâhib al-arbaᶜa*, vol. 3, 32. Al-Jazîrî presents an overview of the opinions of the four law schools.

[71] This does not apply to the wedding meal (*walîma al-ᶜurs*), for unlike the other meals, which are permitted (*jâ'iza*), the wedding meal is *sunna* according to Hanafite scholars.

[72] Al-Jazîrî, *Al-fiqh ᶜalâ al-madhâhib al-arbaᶜa*, vol. 3, 33, and also 35, for the opinion of the Malikites about accepting an invitation. In their view, accepting an invitation for a meal organized on the occasion of an *ᶜaqîqa* or a circumcision is permissible (*mubâḥ*).

room. Men may gather for instance in one room and women in another, or neighbours or relatives may put a second house at the disposal of the family so that the sexes can remain segregated. The festivities are similar to those for a circumcision, although the scale may be smaller. When they leave, the guests may be offered a small packet of sweets wrapped in tulle with a small card attached to it bearing the child's name. The festivities in the Netherlands resemble those in Morocco but are on a smaller scale. However, elements that are completely self-evident in Morocco are no longer so in the Netherlands. The assistance of neighbours and relatives in preparing the festivities is for instance not automatic, as it was in Morocco.

Among Turkish families it is not as customary as among Moroccans to organize a festive meal for many visitors on a single occasion. Rather, after the birth of a child, they may receive guests in small groups. In Turkey, in earlier times, the mother and her child received visitors for seven days in a beautifully made-up bed: "A stream of visitors called to offer their congratulations and bring gifts for the child—traditionally these were gold coins."[73] This may no longer occur, but visiting the mother and child may be a remnant of this tradition. It is a widespread custom on this occasion for relatives and friends to give a gold coin with a red or blue ribbon which is pinned on to a cushion or the child's cradle.

Nonetheless, some Turkish families in my sample organized a celebration either on the occasion of the *akik kurban* or when the child's first tooth appeared. The parents of a Turkish respondent, for example, organized a celebration in Turkey to mark the birth of their grandchild. On the occasion of the *kurban*, family and friends were invited to attend a religious gathering consisting of the recitation of the *mevlüt* (or rather the recitation of *Sura YaSin*), *duʿâ'* and the *Fâtiḥa*, and thereafter to join a shared meal.

A Turkish respondent indicated that the *akik kurban* is more important than the celebration on the appearance of the first tooth (*diş bulguru*), arguing that the latter is *âdet*, thereby referring to its non-Islamic character. Yet, in practice she preferred the latter to the former. Another respondent lay emphasis on the fact that, with the appearance of its first tooth, the child has become truly viable: "From now on the child begins to eat and to live. Therefore [there is] a party with pizza or another hot meal and everybody brings a present." On the occasion of *diş bulguru*, people may play a game involving a tray bearing a copy of the Koran,

[73] Bainbridge, *Life-Cycle Rituals of the Turks in Turkey*, 1–2.

a comb, a pair of scissors, and a gold coin. The object for which the child grabs indicates something about its future: he or she will be very learned, become a hairdresser, a tailor or very rich. A similar ritual is performed among the Surinamese Javanese Muslims in Surinam in the eighth *lapan* month after birth.[74]

The Appropriate Time for the ᶜAqîqa

It is *sunna* to perform the *ᶜaqîqa* on the seventh day after the birth. Even if it is performed later, however, the sacrifice remains valid.[75] Some scholars may hold to a fixed term, referring to a tradition of Ibn Wahb: "If no *ᶜaqîqa* is performed for him on his seventh day, then perform it on the fourteenth day. If it is not performed then, perform the *ᶜaqîqa* on his behalf on the twenty-first day. If this has gone by, the agreed term of the *ᶜaqîqa* has expired."[76] On the other hand, as we have seen in dealing with the religious qualification of the *ᶜaqîqa*, other scholars do not fix a term, emphasizing that one is obliged to perform this ritual when one has come of age, if it was not performed for one at birth.

There is also a difference of opinion about the moment from which to count the seven days. Some scholars begin the count on the first sunset following the birth. Other scholars count the day of the birth itself. Some of these scholars count the day of the birth if the birth took place before sunrise, others if it took place before noon, and others if it took place before sunset.[77] The Hanafite Alladien clearly reflects this discussion when he explicitly states that an Islamic day begins at sunset whereas a non-Islamic day begins at midnight. This implies, according to Alladien, that if a child was born after the *ṣalât al-maghrib* on Thursday, the birth in fact took place on a Friday according to Islam. Thus, the seventh day will be the subsequent Thursday.[78]

Accordingly, opinions concerning the appropriate time for the *ᶜaqîqa* vary in practice. As one would expect from the name of the ceremony, *sabᶜa* or *subûᶜ*, Moroccan respondents tended to perform the sacrifice shortly after the birth, that is preferably on the seventh day or else on the fourteenth or the fortieth day. One also comes across the opinion that the

[74] Van den Berg et al., "Javaans-Surinaamse rituelen", 40. A *lapan* month consists of 35 days.

[75] Juynboll, *Handleiding tot de kennis van de Mohammedaansche wet volgens de leer der Sjâfiᶜitische school*, 150, and Al-Ashqar, *Thalâth shaᶜâ'ir*, 14. From this it becomes clear that, in speaking of the rightful time to perform the ceremony, the moment of the sacrifice, rather than the moment at which the child's hair is shaved, is meant.

[76] Ibn Rushd al-Qurṭubî, *Al-muqaddamât al-mumahhadât*, vol. 1, 448.

[77] Ibid., 450.

[78] Alladien, *De baby en zijn naam in de islam*, 16.

ceremony should take place on the seventh day and that, if this is not possible, it should not be held at all.

The conviviality of parties in Morocco, thanks to the fact that more visitors attend the ceremony and the involvement of everybody around, encouraged some of my Moroccan respondents to hold the *subû^c^* twice, once in the Netherlands on the seventh day after the birth and a second time in Morocco during a holiday. Moreover, as we have seen, in Morocco one can easily ensure that the child's name is mentioned in the *niyya* of the sacrifice, which some consider important.

Surinamese Hindustani respondents do not invariably keep to a fixed term. The seventh day is preferred. In practice, the performance of the *^c^aqîqa* depends on one's financial means: "When you have money, you have to perform the *^c^aqîqa*. If this is not possible because of money, then you perform it after two or three years. If the child is born on a Thursday, then you have to perform the *^c^aqîqa* after two or three years on a Wednesday"; "It does not matter when you perform the *^c^aqîqa*, as long as you perform it before your *nikah* [i.e. your marriage]." Preference may be given to seven calendar units: "On the seventh day one sheep is slaughtered in case of a girl and two sheep in case of a boy. If you can't afford it, then you don't have to [perform it then] but it is better to do it on the seventh day, but not at any price; the seventh month or the seventh year is also right." One finds this preference for seven units of time also among the Moroccan respondents.

My Turkish respondents did not keep to a fixed term. If the *^c^aqîqa* took place in Turkey, for instance, the timing of this ritual was determined by the date of the trip to Turkey. Though the *^c^aqîqa* may be performed at any time between birth and death, as a respondent argued, the ceremony, if it is performed at all, should preferably take place as soon as possible, within a few months of the birth.

Shaving the Child's Hair

According to the Shafi^c^ites, it is also *sunna* to shave off the child's hair on the occasion of the sacrifice and to give away as *ṣadaqa* the weight of its hair in silver or if possible in gold.[79] The Malikite scholar Khalîl b. Isḥâq reasons likewise.[80] This custom of shaving the child's hair is traced back to, among other things, a tradition recorded by Mâlik b.

[79] Juynboll, *Handleiding tot de kennis van de Mohammedaansche wet volgens de leer der Sjâfi^c^itische school*, 150.

[80] Khalîl ben Ish'âq, *Abrégé de la loi musulmane selon le rite de l'Imâm Mâlek*, vol. 1, 186.

Anas: "Fatima, the daughter of the Messenger of Allah, may God bless him and grant him peace, weighed the hair of Hasan, Husayn, Zaynab, and Umm Kulthum, and gave away in *ṣadaqa* an equivalent weight of silver."[81]

Contrary to his view concerning the obligatory character of the sacrifice on the seventh day, the Salafite Al-Ashqar looks upon the shaving of the child's hair on this occasion as recommendable (*sunna*), thereby referring to the aforementioned tradition concerning the birth of Al-Hasan: "When he was born, his mother Fâṭima intended to perform the *ᶜaqîqa* for him, consisting of two rams. Thereupon, the Prophet of God said: Do not perform the *ᶜaqîqa* for him, but shave off his hair from his head and give away as alms the weight of his hair in silver."[82]

Moroccan and Turkish respondents may be familiar with this custom of shaving, but in their view it is unrelated to the sacrifice called *ᶜaqîqa*. This becomes evident for instance from the fact that the child's hair is shaven off only after a year or so and not on the seventh day. The reason for shaving the child's head is that this is believed to ensure that the child will acquire a thick head of hair. On second thoughts, a Moroccan respondent additionally referred to Islam. Even though she did not really like to shave off all her child's hair, she felt that she really should do so because of Islam. Both a Moroccan and a Turkish imam in the Netherlands emphasized the importance of the sacrifice, but were less forthcoming about shaving the child's hair, the former stressing that the health of the child is most important of all and the latter stressing that giving money to the poor is more important that shaving the child's hair.

According to Eickelman, in Morocco on the seventh day "the child's hair is cut for the first time, and alms are distributed to the poor." He explains that "the sacrifice, like the haircutting, is thought to avert evil from the child by offering a substitute sacrifice."[83] Eickelman's account is in line with Islamic law, but seems not to reflect the practice in

[81] Abdurrahman Bewley, trans., *Al-Muwatta of Imam Malik ibn Anas*, 199.

[82] Al-Ashqar, *Thalâth shaᶜâ'ir*, 15.

[83] Eickelman, "Rites of Passage: Muslim Rites", 400. Eickelman's explanation clearly reflects the notion of substitution. We have come across this notion already in a tradition referred to above, that is: "Each boy pledges his *ᶜaqîqa*, which is slaughtered for him on his seventh day, his head is shaven and he is given a name". See also Alladien, *De baby en zijn naam in de islam*, 18–19, for a prayer to be recited on the occasion of the *ᶜaqîqa*, which also reflects the notion of substitution: "O God, this is the *ᶜaqîqa* on behalf of . . . [name of the child], son (daughter) of . . . [name of the father]: its blood instead of his (her) blood, its meat instead of his (her) meat, its bones instead of his (her) bones, its skin instead of his (her) skin, its hair instead of his (her) hair. O God, I perform this [the *ᶜaqîqa*] to save him (her) from the fire [of hell]. In the name of God and God is the greatest."

Morocco. According to my Moroccan respondents, the practice in some parts of Morocco is for some or all of the child's hair to be shaved off around the age of six months. They say, however, that this ceremony is not related to the sacrifice performed shortly after the birth.

In contrast with Moroccan and Turkish respondents, Surinamese Hindustani respondents shaved off the child's hair shortly after the birth. They too believed that the child would thereby acquire a thick head of hair, but they also gave other explanations, such as that the child's hair is unclean due to contact with the mother's blood during pregnancy and delivery and, moreover, an equivalent weight in silver or gold should be given to the poor.

It is a Surinamese Hindustani custom that an aunt of the child makes a ball out of flour, the child's hair, and sometimes the umbilical cord, and that this ball is thrown into flowing water or alternatively, according to some, buried. I do not know why this should preferably be performed by the child's aunt.[84] According to one respondent, this custom is taken from the Hindus and should therefore be shunned.[85]

2.4. Naming

It is *sunna* to give a beautiful name to a child.[86] Examples of beautiful names are names composed of two parts, the first of which is *ᶜAbd*, and the second is one of the names of God (Abdullah, Abdurrahman etc.) or the name of one of the prophets.[87] Alladien explicitly rejects attempts to Dutchify or westernize Islamic names, arguing that all Muslims should be proud of their names and their religion.[88]

Asked about the name given to their child, many parents stressed the importance of giving a suitable name: "It has to be an Islamic name, it has to be mentioned in the Koran." It frequently occurs that a Surinamese Hindustani or Javanese child is given two names, of which the first is non-Islamic and the second Islamic; for instance, Ivan Wahid or

[84] In dealing with the ritual of marriage, we will see that, likewise, the paternal aunt paints the bride's hands with henna.

[85] According to the findings concerning rituals of birth among the Hindus in Surinam of De Klerk, *Cultus en ritueel van het orthodoxe hindoeïsme in Suriname*, 100, the baby's hair is shaven off within its first year. Its hair is collected by an aunt in a cup made of dough (*loî*), which is thereafter thrown into a river.

[86] Al-Ashqar, *Thalâth shaᶜâ'ir*, 15.

[87] Al-Kaysî, *Morals and Manners in Islam*, 131–132. The Hanafite Alladien, *De baby en zijn naam in de islam*, 30–37, gives a list of beautiful and meaningful names at the end of his booklet.

[88] Alladien, *De baby en zijn naam in de islam*, 29.

Yvonne Watini (Watini, or "by the fig", is taken from Koran 95:1). The second name may be given to the child immediately after the birth but also later, for instance when the child recites the Islamic credo (*shahâda*) for the first time. In daily life, one will generally be known by one's non-Islamic name, whereas in a religious context, for instance at gatherings with fellow believers, one's Islamic name will be used.

However, the practice of giving a child both an Islamic and a non-Islamic name seems to be undergoing change. A Surinamese Hindustani respondent for example gave her first child both names, but gave her younger children an Islamic name only. Alladien's rejection of attempts to Dutchify or westernize Islamic names as well as the preference for giving only Islamic names seem to be expressions of an increasing awareness of Islamic identity.

Similarly, among Turkish Muslims one comes across a distinction between an umbilical name (*göbek adı*) and a second name (*ad*). The umbilical name is an Islamic name, which is given immediately after the birth when the umbilical cord is cut. The reason for naming the child so promptly is to ensure that it has a name if it dies shortly after birth. Later the *hoca* or the father of the child whispers the second name in the child's ear together with the *ezan*. This occurs on the seventh day, according to Nicolas, or earlier. This second name is usually the name by which the child is known.[89] Nowadays, much seems to have changed, as Turkish respondents in the Netherlands no longer distinguish between the two names and in the Netherlands the child's name is whispered in its ear shortly after the birth.

The Appropriate Time for Naming a Child

It is *sunna* according to the Shafi^c^ites to give a child its name on the seventh day.[90] Mâlik is of the same opinion. They cite the *ḥadîth* "Each boy pledges his *^c^aqîqa*, which is slaughtered for him on the seventh day, his head is shaven, and he is given a name." However, other traditions, for instance those dealing with the *taḥnîk*, suggest naming the child on the day of its birth.[91] Present-day guides for Muslims reflect these different

[89] Nicolas, *Croyances et pratiques populaires turques concernant les naissances*, 115–116.

[90] Juynboll, *Handleiding tot de kennis van de Mohammedaansche wet volgens de leer der Sjâfi^c^itische school*, 150. Although it is recommendable (*sunna*) to name a child on the seventh day, according to the Shafi^c^ites it is also allowed to do this before the seventh day: "welke ceremonie echter ook vroeger (met name op de dag der geboorte) of later mag plaats vinden".

[91] Ibn Rushd al-Qurṭubî, *Al-muqaddamât al-mumahhadât*, vol. 1, 448.

viewpoints. Al-Kaysî emphasizes the necessity of naming the child as early as possible, preferably within seven days of the birth, whereas according to the Hanafite Alladien the naming should generally take place on or by the seventh day.[92]

The discussion of Islamic scholars on the appropriate time of the naming is reflected in practice. As we have seen, Turkish respondents whisper the child's name together with the prayer call (*ezan*) in its ears shortly after the birth whereas Moroccan respondents explicitly connect the sacrifice named *ᶜaqîqa* on the seventh day with naming the child. However, the name that the parents have chosen for the child may also be used before the seventh day; it is not common practice to call a male child "Muḥammad" and a female one "Fâṭimah" during this period, contrary to the assertion of Earle Waugh.[93] In Morocco, it may occur that the child's name is not chosen until the seventh day, allowing time for the family to decide on a suitable name.

This practice does not occur in the Dutch context, as a child in the Netherlands must have a name by the time its birth is registered. Dutch law stipulates that registration of birth must take place within three days of the birth. This is a much shorter time than that set out for example in the Turkish Civil Code (art. 39), which allows one month.

The strictness of Dutch law on this point does not seem to have caused many difficulties. A Turkish respondent was under the impression that a child's birth must be registered immediately after birth both in Turkey and in the Netherlands. Other respondents asked me in reply what reason there could be for delaying naming a child in view of the fact that the nurses ask for the child's name immediately upon the delivery. Moreover, a Moroccan imam explained that it is not a problem if the name of the child becomes known before the day of the *ᶜaqîqa*.

2.5. Conclusions

The transplantation from the countries of origin to the Netherlands seems to have affected the ritual of birth less than the other lifecycle

[92] Al-Kaysî, *Morals and Manners in Islam*, 131, and Alladien, *De baby en zijn naam in de islam*, 11.

[93] Waugh, "Names and Naming", 225: "The naming of a child need not occur until the moment of registration, which may be delayed for a considerable period, especially if the actual birthdate of the child is not held to be auspicious or if important family members are absent. This stay allowed the family to discuss the given name and provided the opportunity to assess the child's personality or health to determine what a given name should be. During this interim, a male child was called 'Muḥammad' and a female one 'Fâṭimah' as recommended in certain prophetic traditions."

rituals. In the following chapters, we will see that an infrastructure for the performance of circumcisions had to be developed afresh in the Netherlands. Similarly, many adaptations had to made in the rituals of marriage and death under the influence of and in response to the new surroundings. This has not happened to the same extent for the ritual of birth.

Certain developments, such as a stronger preference for a hospital delivery and a shortening of the time during which the mother and the child remain at home after the delivery, are found also in the countries of origin, especially in urban contexts. These developments may therefore be explained on the basis of the level of the local health services and the family's financial situation rather than the migrational context itself. Because of the common availability of health services in the Netherlands, for example, many Turkish women prefer to spend a few days in hospital to give birth. Similarly, in Turkey, a hospital delivery is fashionable and preferred, but the level of the health services varies locally and fewer people can afford it.

Birth ceremonies performed in the small family circle seem not to have changed much in the Netherlands. However, these ceremonies are not easily maintained because of the limited number of participants and the absence of an infrastructure in the Netherlands that transmits and maintains religious knowledge. People in the Netherlands may for instance be less familiar with the words to be whispered in the child's ear than in the countries of origin and there are moreover fewer people able to instruct them. Another example is the shaving of the child's head, which is less common in Netherlands than in Morocco.

Especially subject to change are those rituals that are bound to or dependent on a particular setting. In Surinam, for example, the *mitoni* ceremony in the seventh month of a Surinamese Javanese woman's pregnancy, including the ritual bath of the parents-to-be, takes place in the open air, enabling many people to attend. In the Netherlands, by contrast, the ceremony may be held in a bathroom. This obviously completely transforms the event: only a few people can attend the ceremony, which thus loses much of its performative character.

In the Netherlands, Moroccans in particular missed the conviviality experienced in Morocco thanks to the involvement of everyone around and the many guests who gather on these occasions. It goes without saying that, in Morocco, relatives and neighbours come round to render assistance if needed. The absence of this support network in the Netherlands made people feel lonely.

The Dutch prohibition on slaughtering animals in domestic premises did not pose any difficulties. However, this prohibition may induce people to perform the ᶜ*aqîqa* ceremony twice, because of the importance attached to uttering the child's name before the animal's throat is cut. As we have seen, it is easier to arrange for the intention (*niyya*) in Morocco because slaughtering animals at home is allowed there.

3
CIRCUMCISION

> Then We revealed to you: "Follow the religion of Abraham, a man of pure faith; he was not a polytheist."
>
> —Koran 16:123

> When his Lord put Abraham to the proof by enjoining on him certain commandments and he fulfilled them, He said: "I have appointed you a leader of the people." "And what of my descendants?", asked Abraham. He said: "My covenant does not apply to the evil-doers."
>
> —Koran 2:124

The next important transition in a Muslim boy's life is his circumcision. In Muslim countries, this ritual's occurrence is a matter of course, forming an integral part of daily life both from a practical point of view and in people's perceptions. In a migrational context, where only a minority keeps to this practice on religious grounds, this self-evident character does not survive. It is not that circumcision as such has lost any of its original significance for Muslims in the Netherlands—this is far from the truth. Nonetheless, an organizational infrastructure for the performance of the operation has had to be developed afresh. Moreover, the support network normally available in the countries of origin is lacking in the Netherlands, where neighbours are unlikely to play a role in the organization of the festivities and the conspicuity that generally surrounds this ritual in the countries of origin has to a large extent disappeared.

The present chapter deals only with male circumcision. Female circumcision is not practiced among Moroccan, Surinamese, and Turkish Muslims in the Netherlands. When at the end of the 1980s Somali refugees came to the Netherlands and confronted the country with the practice of female circumcision, it became a subject of discussion. Many articles on this subject appeared in the press, the Ministry of Welfare, Public Health and Culture published a report[1] and a symposium was held in Leiden.[2] In February 1993 the government, adopting the recommendations of the ministers of Justice and of Welfare, Public Health and Culture, banned all forms of female circumcision, regarding it an unacceptable infringement of the integrity of the human body, especially

[1] Bartels & Haaijer, *'s Lands wijs 's lands eer?*

[2] *Vrouwenbesnijdenis wereldwijd en in Nederland*, Leiden, 2 October 1992.

since it takes place when the person undergoing the operation is underage.[3]

The Dutch press occasionally carries calls to prohibit male circumcision on the same grounds.[4] This viewpoint has never gained wide acceptance in the Netherlands, however. The circumcision of Muslim boys seems to have become an established fact in Dutch society, even though its organization has still not taken full shape. The relative ease with which this ritual has become accepted may be explained above all by the fact that Jews have long been performing circumcisions on religious grounds in the Netherlands. Consequently, Dutch society was acquainted with this phenomenon and Dutch law accepted it as an intrinsic part of freedom of religion.[5]

3.1. The Religious Qualification of Circumcision

Male circumcision is generally defined as "the act of cutting off the whole foreskin that covers the glans, so that the glans is completely uncovered".[6] Male circumcision is called *khitân* or *ṭahâra* in Arabic, *sünnet* in Turkish, and *sunat* in Javanese.

In Muslim as well as in Jewish tradition, the ritual of circumcision is traced back to Abraham. Muslim tradition is almost unanimous in holding that he was the first man who, on God's instructions, circumcised himself.[7] However, one tradition does not link Abraham's circumcision with an injunction of God. According to this tradition, Abraham introduced circumcision in order to distinguish the believers, fighting on his

[3] Shadid & Van Koningsveld, *Religious Freedom and the Position of Islam in Western Europe*, 98, and Kool, "Vrouwenbesnijdenis in Nederland als moreel probleem", 76–81.

[4] For instance Mantel, "Verbied het besnijden van jongens", in *NRC Handelsblad*, 28 April 1997, and the replies of El Biyar, "Een goede besnijdenis is geen verminking", and Kater & Evers, "Besnijden is zonder risico's", in *NRC Handelsblad*, 1 May 1997.

[5] Shadid & Van Koningsveld, *Religious Freedom and the Position of Islam in Western Europe*, 96–98.

[6] Al-Sukkarî, *Khitân al-dhakar wa khifâḍ al-unthâ min manẓûr islâmî* (Male and female circumcision from an Islamic point of view), 10. See also Van Bommel, "Wat zegt de Islam over besnijdenis?", 11; Chebel, *Histoire de la circoncision*, 53; Hoffer, *Moslimbesnijdenissen in Nederland*, 11; Kaptein, "Circumcision in Indonesia", 287; ᶜAbd al-Hârî, *Aḥkâm al-ṭahâra fî al-fiqh al-islâmî*, 55; Al-Zabîdî, *Kitâb itḥâfu l-sâdati l-muttaqîn*, vol. 2, 417. Al-Sukkarî's *Khitân al-dhakar wa khifâḍ al-unthâ* is an important source for the present study. Al-Sukkarî (1940–) is currently a member of the teaching staff of the Faculty of Law at Al-Azhar University, Damanhûr, Egypt.

[7] Kister, "... And he was born circumcised ...", 10. Al-Sukkarî, *Khitân al-dhakar wa khifâḍ al-unthâ*, 11, argues that according to some historians Adam was the first man to be circumcised. Because Adam's descendants neglected their obligation, it was reconfirmed to Abraham and his descendants.

side, from the Amelikite unbelievers. This was especially important when warriors who had been slain in battle had to be buried.[8]

Muslim scholars have differing views concerning the religious qualification of circumcision. This emerges from the following statement of Ibn Qayyim al-Jawziyya:

> . . . Mâlik, Al-Shâfi^cî and Aḥmad [b. Hanbal] have said: it [circumcision] is obligatory. Mâlik is very strict in this respect, which led him to say: "It is not permitted to appoint someone who is not circumcised as an imam, neither is his testimony accepted." However, many scholars related on the authority of Mâlik that it [circumcision] is *sunna*, which brought Al-Qâḍî ^cIyâḍ[9] to say: "Circumcision is *sunna* according to Mâlik and to the scholars in general. However, in their opinion, *sunna* means that it is sinful to refrain from it." According to them, it occupies an intermediate position between obligatory [*farḍ*] and recommendable [*nadb*]. If this were not the case, [it may suffice to point out that] Mâlik clearly stated that the testimony of someone uncircumcised is not accepted, neither is it permitted to appoint him as an imam. Al-Ḥasan al-Baṣrî and Abû Ḥanîfa said: "It is not obligatory, but rather *sunna*." Similarly, Ibn Abî Mûsâ, one of the followers of Aḥmad [b. Hanbal] said: "It is a fixed *sunna* [*sunna mu'akkada*]."[10]

Even though the Koran does not mention circumcision explicitly, those who argue in favour of the obligatory character of circumcision

[8] Kister, "... And he was born circumcised ...", 11–12.

[9] ^cIyâḍ b. Mûsâ (476/1088–544/1149), one of the most celebrated figures of Malikism and pre-eminently a traditionist and *faqîh*, according to Talbi, "^cIyâḍ b. Mûsâ", 289–290.

[10] Ibn Qayyim, "Fî khitân al-mawlûd wa aḥkâmihi", 115, also quoted by ^cAbd al-Mu^cnim Ibrâhîm, *Al-furqân fî ḥukm khitân*, 18. Besides the contemporary scholar Al-Sukkarî, the Hanbalite scholar Ibn Qayyim al-Jawziyya (691/1291–751/1350) will be used as a starting point in the present study, first of all because his work presents an overview of the existing opinions concerning this subject. Moreover, in dealing with circumcision, many subsequent scholars referred to his "Fî khitân al-mawlûd wa aḥkâmihi" (On the circumcision of the newborn and its religious qualification), which has also appeared under the title *Kitâb tuḥfat al-mawdûd fî aḥkâm al-mawlûd*. On those who argue that male circumcision is a *sunna mu'akkada*, see Al-Sukkarî, *Khitân al-dhakar wa khifâḍ al-unthâ*, 46: "The majority of the scholars came to the conclusion that circumcision is a *sunna mu'akkada* for all, both men and women. The Hanafites and some Malikites took this position, and it is also a viewpoint of the Shafi^cites, Al-Ḥasan al-Baṣrî, the Zaydite Al-Murtaḍâ. Al-Nawawî said that most scholars have come to this conclusion." See also the Hanafite Al-Zabîdî, *Kitâb itḥâfu l-sâdati l-muttaqîn*, vol. 2, 417: "The opinions of the scholars concerning this subject vary. Most scholars came to the conclusion that it is *sunna* and not obligatory (*wâjib*). That is the opinion of Mâlik and Abû Ḥanîfa according to one transmission. But according to another one from him that it is *wâjib* and according to a third one from him that it is sinful to refrain from it. Some of the followers of Al-Shâfi^cî also upheld this. Al-Shâfi^cî reached the conclusion that it is absolutely obligatory. This is [also] implied by the words of the Malikite Sahnûn. Aḥmad [b. Hanbal] and some of the followers of Al-Shâfi^cî upheld that it is obligatory with respect to men but *sunna* with respect to women. . . ."

may find support for their viewpoint in the Koranic verses 16:123 and 2:124:

> Then We revealed to you: "Follow the religion (*milla*) of Abraham, a man of pure faith (*ḥanîf*); he was not a polytheist".[11]
>
> When his Lord put Abraham to the proof by enjoining on him certain commandments and he fulfilled them, He said: "I have appointed you a leader of the people". "And what of my descendants?" asked Abraham. He said: "My covenant does not apply to the evil-doers".

Circumcision is, according to this line of thinking, one of the commandments (*kalimât*) by which God put Abraham to the test, and as such it is part of the religion (*milla*) of Abraham, which the believer is ordered to follow.[12] Moreover, circumcision is in this view a sign of the covenant between God and Abraham, according to which God promised to appoint Abraham as a leader (*imâm*) of the people.[13]

Furthermore, several traditions may be put forward in favour of the obligatory character of circumcision. Some emphasize that conversion to Islam necessarily involves circumcision, such as ". . . came to the Prophet and said: 'I have become a Muslim.' He [the Prophet] said: 'Throw off the hair of unbelief [i.e. shave off your hair] and be circumcised.'"[14] and "Let him who becomes a Muslim be circumcised, even if he is old."[15] Others emphasize the implications of not being circumcised

[11] The adherents of the religion of Abraham (*dîn Ibrâhîm* or *milla Ibrâhîm*) are called *ḥunafâ'* (plural of *ḥanîf*). According to a tradition referred to by Ibn Qayyim, "Fî khitân al-mawlûd wa aḥkâmihi", 114, a *ḥanîf* is one who performs the daily prayer, performs the pilgrimage, and is circumcised: "*wa-qâla ghayru wâḥidin mina l-salaf: man ṣallâ wa-ḥajja wa-khtatana fa-huwa ḥanîf, fa-l-ḥajj wa-l-khitân shiʿâru l-ḥanîfiyya, wa-hiya fiṭratu llâhi llatî fuṭira l-nâsu ʿalayhâ*".

[12] Ibn Qayyim, "Fî khitân al-mawlûd wa aḥkâmihi", 110 and 113, and Al-Sukkarî, *Khitân al-dhakar wa khifâḍ al-unthâ*, 47 and also 13–17. Here Al-Sukkarî presents an overview of the viewpoints of Islamic scholars concerning the way Abraham was put to the test. We will see that those who defend the obligatory character of circumcision argue that "to follow the religion of Abraham" refers to circumcision, whereas those who defend its *sunna* character argue that it refers to monotheism.

[13] Ibn Qayyim, "Fî khitân al-mawlûd wa aḥkâmihi", 131–132. Here, circumcision as a sign of the covenant between God and Abraham is connected with the Koranic concept of *ṣibgha* (2:138). The *ṣibgha* of the Jews is Judaism, the *ṣibgha* of the Christians is Christianity, and the *ṣibgha* of God is Islam or *Ḥanîfiyya*. As such, *ṣibgha* is synonymous with *dîn* or *milla*. Circumcision, as a mode or manner of the Christian's baptism (also called *ṣibgha*), is a characteristic feature of Muslims, a sign of one's entry into the religion of Abraham. See also Lane, *An Arabic-English Lexicon*, IV, 1648, s.v. "*ṣibgha*".

[14] Ibn Qayyim, "Fî khitân al-mawlûd wa aḥkâmihi", 115, and Al-Sukkarî, *Khitân al-dhakar wa khifâḍ al-unthâ*, 49.

[15] Ibn Qayyim, "Fî khitân al-mawlûd wa aḥkâmihi", 115–116, and Al-Sukkarî, *Khitân al-dhakar wa khifâḍ al-unthâ*, 50.

for one's acts of worship (*ᶜibadât*), such as: "We asked the Prophet if an uncircumcised man is allowed to perform the pilgrimage to the house of God. He answered: 'No, until he is circumcised.'"[16] and "The *ṣalât* of an uncircumcised man is not to be accepted and the animal slaughtered by him may not be eaten."[17]

Further support for the obligatory character of circumcision may be found in the implications of other tenets. The question is posed for instance how it could have been allowed to uncover one's *ᶜawra* (the part of the body that must remain covered, extending in a man from navel to knees) for circumcision, if the latter had not been obligatory.[18] Moreover, one who is not circumcised is remiss in his *ṭahâra* and consequently in his *ṣalât* too. The *ṣalât* is not valid because of the dirt and urine that remain under the foreskin. Therefore, this practice, as a necessary condition for the validity of an obligatory act, must itself be obligatory.[19] Lastly, it is argued that, of all marks that distinguish Muslims from Christians (*shiᶜâr*, i.e. distinguishing marks), circumcision is the clearest, and therefore is obligatory.[20]

Those who consider circumcision to be a *sunna* or a fixed *sunna* (*sunna* (*mu'akkada*)) reason as follows. Firstly, in their view, the Koranic verse 16:123, in which the believer is ordered to follow the religion of Abraham, refers not to circumcision but to monotheism (*tawḥîd*), which also explains the addition "he was not a polytheist". Likewise, the injunction of Koranic verse 12:38 to follow the religion of the forefathers Abraham, Isaac, and Jacob is explained as the injunction not to attribute anything as partner to God.[21]

Those who favour the *sunna* character of circumcision may further dispute the credibility of the traditions put forward by their opponents. They may cite the tradition "Circumcision is *sunna* for men and a noble deed for women."[22] This tradition is attributed little credibility by those who hold that male circumcision is obligatory. Additionally, the latter

[16] Ibn Qayyim, "Fî khitân al-mawlûd wa aḥkâmihi", 116.

[17] Ibid., 116.

[18] Ibid., 117, and Al-Sukkarî, *Khitân al-dhakar wa khifâḍ al-unthâ*, 52–53.

[19] Ibn Qayyim, "Fî khitân al-mawlûd wa aḥkâmihi", 117–118, and Al-Sukkarî, *Khitân al-dhakar wa khifâḍ al-unthâ*, 53–54.

[20] Ibn Qayyim, "Fî khitân al-mawlud wa aḥkâmihi", 116–117.

[21] Koranic verse 12:38: "But I follow the religion (*milla*) of my forefathers Abraham, Isaac and Jacob. It is not ours to attribute anything as partner to God. That is part of God's bounty to us and to the people. But most of the people are not thankful." Ibn Qayyim, "Fî khitân al-mawlûd wa aḥkâmihi", 118–119, and ᶜAbd al-Munᶜim Ibrâhîm, *Al-furqân fî ḥukm khitân*, 27–28.

[22] Ibn Qayyim, "Fî khitân al-mawlûd wa aḥkâmihi", 118, and Al-Sukkarî, *Khitân al-dhakar wa khifâḍ al-unthâ*, 59.

may emphasize that the term *sunna* should not be interpreted as the opposite of obligatory, thereby referring to the tradition "One who dislikes my *sunna* does not belong to me."[23]

The numerous traditions dealing with the concept of *fiṭra* may also be put forward in support of its recommendable (*sunna*) character. *Fiṭra* is the natural disposition of mankind created by God, chosen as a *sunna* by the prophets.[24] Several practices are mentioned as belonging to the *fiṭra*, including cutting the nails, trimming the moustache, removing the hair from armpits and pubis, and circumcision.[25] These practices enhance the nature of men in its most beautiful form.[26]

Those who defend the *sunna* character of male circumcision argue that *fiṭra* means *sunna* and that therefore circumcision is not obligatory.[27] Those who take the opposite view object that some of the characteristics falling within the scope of *fiṭra* may be *sunna* or recommendable (*mustaḥabb*) and others obligatory. A case in point is the trimming of nails, which is *sunna*. However, if dirt remains under the fingernails because of their length, trimming them becomes obligatory for the validity of the *ṭahâra*.[28]

Those who favour the *sunna* character of circumcision may also argue that in the time of the Prophet many people converted to Islam but no checks were carried out to ascertain if they were circumcised. Had circumcision been obligatory, this would certainly have happened.[29]

On the basis of these and other arguments, Ibn Qayyim comes to the conclusion that male circumcision is a *sunna*, which one is obliged to follow.[30] Al-Sukkarî chooses the opinion that circumcision is obligatory.[31] This viewpoint may gain further substance in the subsequent discussions on the appropriate time for a boy's circumcision, for most Muslim scholars take the view that circumcision becomes obligatory when a

[23] Ibn Qayyim, "Fî khitân al-mawlûd wa aḥkâmihi", 123.

[24] Cf. Koranic verse 30:30: "So set your face to the religion, as a man of pure faith (a *ḥanîf*), the natural disposition coming from God, with which he endowed the people."

[25] For an enumeration of these practices, see for instance Al-Sukkarî, *Khitân al-dhakar wa khifâḍ al-unthâ*, 55, and Ibn Qayyim, "Fî khitân al-mawlûd wa aḥkâmihi", 113–114. According to Ibn Qayyim, circumcision is the most important of the practices belonging to the *fiṭra*.

[26] Ibn Qayyim, "Fî khitân al-mawlûd wa aḥkâmihi", 131. Cf. Van Koningsveld, "Between Communalism and Secularism", 333.

[27] Al-Sukkarî, *Khitân al-dhakar wa khifâḍ al-unthâ*, 56.

[28] Ibid., 58, and Ibn Qayyim, "Fî khitân al-mawlûd wa aḥkâmihi", 123.

[29] Al-Sukkarî, *Khitân al-dhakar wa khifâḍ al-unthâ*, 59.

[30] Ibn Qayyim, "Fî khitân al-mawlûd wa aḥkâmihi", 123.

[31] Al-Sukkarî, *Khitân al-dhakar wa khifâḍ al-unthâ*, 62–64.

boy reaches majority.[32] The example of a Sudanese people who wished to convert to Islam in the 1930s may also illustrate its de facto obligatory character. The Azhar, when asked what steps were required for conversion, sent them a list of conditions, which started with circumcision.[33]

My respondents considered circumcision either obligatory or a very important *sunna*. In support of their viewpoints, they attached a variety of meanings to circumcision, which closely resemble the variety of arguments cited above.

A number of respondents implicitly referred to the concept of *shiᶜâr* or distinguishing marks. In their view, circumcision is a distinctive character of a Muslim:

> You are not a Muslim, if you are uncircumcised.
>
> It belongs to us, to the Islam.
>
> Being circumcised is a sign of being one of them.

Moroccan respondents especially explained that the act of circumcision marks the transition to becoming a Muslim, thereby implicitly referring to the Koranic concept of *ṣibgha*:

> Through circumcision you start entering religion.
>
> It [circumcision] is obligatory if you want to be a Muslim. It should be celebrated like a marriage, because that person is becoming a Muslim.
>
> If something happens to your child [and he is not circumcised], then he will not come to heaven as a Muslim. As parents you have sinned.

Whereas the parents are deemed responsible for their son's circumcision, "praying and fasting will eventually be his [the boy's] responsibility."

Furthermore, circumcision is described, particularly by Turkish respondents, as marking the transition from childhood to adulthood in a physical sense:

> When you have been circumcised, you are a real guy.
>
> [If a boy is] not circumcised, he is not a man. That's a feeling inside.
>
> When a boy has been circumcised, he is a man. He is then perfect. If you have performed your military service, you are a real man.

[32] According to Ibn Qayyim, "Fî khitân al-mawlûd wa aḥkâmihi", 127, circumcision becomes obligatory when a boy reaches majority but before that time it is not obligatory. For more details, see section 3.2.

[33] Aldeeb Abu-Sahlieh, "To Mutilate in the Name of Jehovah or Allah", 586, and Bouhdiba, *La Sexualité en islam*, 213.

Some Turkish respondents also compared circumcision to other transitions, such as a girl's first menstruation, military service, and marriage:

> After having been circumcised, a boy is different, just like a woman who menstruates for the first time.

> In your heart you find it as important as marriage and military service. It simply has to take place.

Military service is compulsory for boys in Turkey and lasts eighteen months for most conscripts. It is considered an important marker in a boy's transition to adulthood. Before he leaves his native town to enter military service, he pays visits to family members and neighbours together with fellow conscripts. They present the boys with gifts of money, as in the case of a circumcision. Boys tend to marry soon after the completion of military service.

Closely connected with this is the view that circumcision marks a boy's transition to adulthood in a religious sense. A Surinamese Javanese boy may therefore be led to pronounce the profession of faith (*shahâda*) formally for the first time on the day of his circumcision. Thus, circumcision is linked with the age at which a boy has to begin observing the *ṣalât*. It is within this framework of thought that a Turkish respondent argued:

> In any case circumcision should take place before the age of fifteen. After that age, all children should pray and do all the things mentioned in the Koran.

Many respondents said that circumcision is prescribed by the Koran. Other respondents stressed that circumcision is an important prophetical *sunna*:

> Circumcision is *sünnet*, viz. something done by our Prophet, but it is an important one.

Sometimes the religious qualification of *fiṭra* is implicitly invoked:

> [Circumcision belongs to the sphere of] hygiene. It is done in this way ever since the time of the Prophet. It is a fixed custom just like the shaving or removal of hair from under the arms.

However, one also comes across the bare statement that circumcision is a fixed Islamic custom without any further explanation.

The majority of the respondents emphasized additionally that circumcision is a matter of hygiene, protecting one against all kind of diseases:

> It [circumcision] is very healthy. There is a lesser chance of getting prostate cancer.

If it were not good for health, then it would not be allowed.

It is healthy. His wife will not get cervical cancer.

Circumcision is also of importance against infections.

3.2. Age of Circumcision

Opinions concerning the appropriate time for a boy's circumcision differ. Some scholars argue that there is no determined time for circumcision, since Abraham circumcised himself after he had lived for many years.[34] Most scholars, however, indicate both a recommendable and an obligatory time. Circumcision becomes obligatory when a boy reaches majority (*al-bulûgh*), because from then on he has an obligation to fulfil the acts of worship (*ᶜibadât*), which require him to be circumcised. Before that time, circumcision is recommendable.[35] According to Al-Sukkarî, parents are free to choose a suitable moment for their son's circumcision between the seventh day after the birth and the boy's majority.[36]

By contrast, the Shafiᶜite Al-Mâwardî, who likewise distinguished between the recommendable and obligatory time for circumcision, favoured the seventh day after the child's birth, or else the fortieth day or the seventh year of his life.[37] Other scholars also gave preference to the seventh day, and referred thereby to a prophetical tradition according to which the Prophet circumcised his grandsons Al-Ḥasan and Al-Ḥusayn on the seventh day of their life.[38] Al-Ḥasan al-Baṣrî and Mâlik b. Anas disagreed with this practice: they argued that the seventh day is the day of circumcision prescribed for the Jews and that Muslims should distinguish themselves from Jews rather than imitate them.[39] Accordingly, in a tradition recorded by the Shafiᶜite traditionist Al-Bayhaqî, it is argued that Muslims should delay circumcision: "Abraham circumcised Isḥaq on the seventh day and

[34] For the age of Abraham when he was circumcised, variously reported as eighty, one hundred and twenty, one hundred and thirty, thirty, and seventy, see Kister, "... And he was born circumcised ...", 10–11; Al-Sukkarî, *Khitân al-dhakar wa-khifâḍ al-unthâ*, 92, and also Ibn Qayyim, "Fî khitân al-mawlûd wa aḥkâmihi", 107–111.

[35] For instance, Al-Sukkarî, *Khitân al-dhakar wa-khifâḍ al-unthâ*, 95, and Ibn Qayyim, "Fî khitân al-mawlûd wa aḥkâmihi", 127.

[36] Al-Sukkarî, *Khitân al-dhakar wa-khifâḍ al-unthâ*, 95.

[37] Ibid., 92.

[38] Ibid., 93. ᶜAbd al-Hârî, *Aḥkâm al-ṭahâra fî al-fiqh al-islâmiyya*, 55, thereby refers to Al-Ḥâkim and Al-Bayhaqî, who trace this tradition back to Aisha and not to the Prophet.

[39] Al-Sukkarî, *Khitân al-dhakar wa-khifâḍ al-unthâ*, 93–94, ᶜAbd al-Muᶜnim Ibrâhîm, *Al-furqân fî ḥukm khitân*, 56, and Ibn Qayyim, "Fî khitân al-mawlûd wa aḥkâmihi", 130.

Ismâᶜîl when he reached majority. The circumcision of Isḥâq became the *sunna* of his descendants and the circumcision of Ismâᶜîl the *sunna* of his descendants."[40]

According to Mâlik, the practice in his town, Medina, was that a boy was circumcised when he started to lose his milk teeth[41] or, according to another source, around the age of seven.[42] This corresponds approximately to the opinion of Al-Layth b. Saᶜd, who related that it is recommendable (*mustaḥabb*) to perform circumcision between the ages of seven and ten.[43] A further argument for this viewpoint may be found in another tradition, according to which a father should command his children to perform the *ṣalât* from the age of seven and beat them for not performing it from the age of ten.[44] This presupposes that a boy has already been circumcised by the latter time.

According to Al-Nawawî, the majority of the Shafiᶜites took the view that it is permitted to perform a boy's circumcision when he is young. Among them, according to Al-Nawawî, one also comes across the viewpoint that a boy's guardian (*walî*) is obliged to have him circumcised before he reaches majority as well as the viewpoint that it is prohibited to have this done before he reaches the age of ten.[45] A *ḥadîth* concerning the circumcision of Ibn ᶜAbbâs may be quoted to underpin this latter viewpoint: this *ḥadîth* states that in the Prophet's time a boy was not circumcised before he reached the age of distinction [*ḥattâ yudriku*], the age at which he is held responsible for his actions.[46] The *ḥadîth* cited above concerning the age at which a boy is punishable for not observing

[40] Ibn Qayyim, "Fî khitân al-mawlûd wa aḥkâmihi", 130. Here, Ibn Qayyim also refers to another tradition, according to which Ismâᶜîl was circumcised when he was thirteen years of age.

[41] Ibid., 130.

[42] Al-Sukkarî, *Khitân al-dhakar wa-khifâḍ al-unthâ*, 91.

[43] Ibid., 91, Ibn Qayyim, "Fî khitân al-mawlûd wa aḥkâmihi", 130, and ᶜAbd al-Muᶜnim Ibrâhîm, *Al-furqân fî ḥukm khitân*, 57.

[44] Ibn Qayyim, "Fî khitân al-mawlûd wa aḥkâmihi", 128, and Al-Sukkarî, *Khitân al-dhakar wa-khifâḍ al-unthâ*, 91 and 93.

[45] ᶜAbd al-Muᶜnim Ibrâhîm, *Al-furqân fî ḥukm khitân*, 57.

[46] Thus ᶜAbd al-Harî, *Aḥkâm al-ṭahâra fî fiqh al-islamiyya*, 55. Ibn Qayyim, "Fî khitân al-mawlûd wa aḥkâmihi", 127–128, tried to determine the exact meaning of "*ḥattâ yudriku*" by quoting several traditions which state that Ibn ᶜAbbâs was already circumcised when he was either ten, thirteen or fifteen. This brought him to the conclusion that "*ḥattâ yudriku*" means "before he reached majority". However, according to Al-Sukkarî, *Khitân al-dhakar wa khifâḍ al-unthâ*, 93, the *sinn al-idrâk* stretches approximately from the age of seven to the age of ten, when circumcision nearly becomes obligatory.

prayer may also be adduced in favour of this viewpoint. It is argued that the pain of circumcision is harder to bear than the pain of a blow for not observing prayer, and it is therefore more appropriate to delay the former.[47]

Of the sons of my respondents, six were below three years of age, fourteen were between three and seven, and six boys were seven or older at the time of their circumcision. I came across no parents who favoured the seventh day after the birth for their son's circumcision. Even Surinamese Hindustani parents, in whom I expected a preference for having their son circumcised immediately upon birth, had the operation performed between the ages of two and four.[48]

Most of the Moroccan boys among my respondents' families were below five at the time of their circumcision. This agrees with the findings of David Hart concerning the Rif, the Northern region of Morocco from where most of the Moroccans in the Netherlands originate: he found that circumcision was performed between the ages of three months and four years.[49] Turkish boys in my sample were on average older than Moroccan boys, being circumcised generally between the ages of three and seven.

Whereas some Surinamese Javanese respondents stated that there is no fixed time for circumcision, some also indicated that in practice, in the Netherlands as well as in Surinam, a boy is often circumcised at an advanced age, that is between the ages of eight and twelve. Annemarie de Waal Malefijt noted that in Surinam circumcision takes place at any time between the ages of ten and sixteen, but in any case before marriage.[50] According to Suparlan, the Surinamese Javanese circumcise their sons between the ages of six and sixteen. Interestingly, he further observed that, according to Javanese culture, a boy

[47] Al-Sukkarî, *Khitân al-dhakar wa-khifâḍ al-unthâ*, 93. However, Ibn Qayyim, "Fî khitân al-mawlûd wa aḥkâmihi", 128, stated: "My opinion is that the *walî* is obliged to have the boy circumcised before his majority, so that he reaches majority circumcised, because one cannot fulfil one's [religious] obligations without it." Moreover, if a father is supposed to command his children to perform the *ṣalât* from the age of seven and chastize them for not performing it from the age of ten, how then, Ibn Qayyim asks, can fathers refrain from having their sons circumcised even though they have already reached majority?

[48] My expectation was based on, for instance, Hoffer, *Moslimbesnijdenissen in Nederland*, 14, and Shadid & Van Koningsveld, *Religious Freedom and the Position of Islam in Western Europe*, 97, who describe the preference among Surinamese Muslims for having a boy circumcised during the first week of his life as reflecting the prevailing practice in Surinam.

[49] Hart, *The Aith Waryaghar of the Moroccan Rif*, 119.

[50] De Waal Malefijt, *The Javanese of Surinam*, 143.

should be circumcised between the ages of thirteen and fifteen.[51] These outcomes more or less reflect the Shafi^{c}ite position presented above.

A variety of justifications were put forward for performing a boy's circumcision when he is young (i.e. below three): "then he will not be aware of it", "he will forget it all the sooner", and "the younger he is, the less the pain". Other respondents, however, deemed it better to wait until a boy is able to understand at least a little of what is happening to him. One respondent preferred to wait until her son became aware of his circumcision, or there is no sense in celebrating and giving him presents on this occasion, she argued. Another respondent had his two- and five-year-old sons circumcised at the same time. It took the younger longer to recover than the elder because the latter "was more open to reason". This experience led him to the conclusion that a boy should not be too young. Ibn Qayyim's expression "*ḥattâ yudriku*", or "before he reaches majority", was also cited implicitly. One respondent argued that a boy's circumcision should in any case take place before the age of fifteen: "After that age, all children should pray and do all things mentioned in the Koran."

The more advanced age of Surinamese Javanese boys may be explained by the fact that, according to Javanese custom, the time for a boy's circumcision is considered to have come only when he asks his parents for it to be done. De Waal Malefijt presents evidence of a similar attitude in Surinam: "Boys can, supposedly, not be circumcised against their will (hence the custom that on the day of the circumcision the boy asks his parents for it). But some seem to be rather afraid, and in that case it is better to wait. He is then mostly shamed into it; the parents say: you are probably a Creole boy, because you are not circumcised."[52] A further explanation of the fact that boys in Surinam are circumcised at more advanced ages was offered by another respondent: "People had to save up a long time because of the party organized on the occasion of a circumcision." The financial argument was also put forward by Surinamese Javanese parents in the Netherlands.

Just before his circumcision, a Surinamese Javanese boy may also be prompted to pronounce the *shahâda* for the first time. His transition from childhood to adulthood in a religious sense is thereby explicitly

[51] Suparlan, "The Javanese in Surinam", 254.
[52] De Waal Malefijt, *The Javanese of Surinam*, 145.

marked. If a boy is too young to utter the *shahâda* at the time of his circumcision, the formula may be whispered in his ear before the operation. Later, when the time has come for him to begin praying, he himself formally pronounces the *shahâda*.

3.3. The Organization of the Operation

Muslims in the Netherlands have the choice between having their sons circumcised in the Netherlands and in their countries of origin. From the beginning of their presence, the majority of the Surinamese Muslims had the operation done in the Netherlands. In the period immediately following the family reunifications in the 1970s, many Turkish and Moroccan Muslims favoured their country of origin for performing the operation. As long as the ties with the country of origin are strong, performing the operation there has the obvious advantage of the presence of family and friends to participate in the festivities to follow.[53]

Even though today circumcisions may still take place in the country of origin, the number of parents choosing to have their sons circumcised in the Netherlands is on the increase. Some parents in my sample who had their eldest child circumcised in Turkey or Morocco preferred the Netherlands in the case of a younger child. They may consider that performing the ritual in the Netherlands obviates the need to devote special attention to the child during holidays because of his circumcision and leaves more time free for their family in Morocco or Turkey.[54]

In cases where the Netherlands is preferred, parents had until recently only the choice between a hospital and a professional circumciser (called *hajjam* in Morocco, *sünnetçi* in Turkey, and *dukun sunat* or *tjallak* by Surinamese Javanese Muslims). Whereas Surinamese Muslims in Netherlands mostly have the operation done in a hospital, Turkish and Moroccan Muslims make use of both options. On the basis of figures of the Stichting Informatiecentrum Gezondheidszorg, an information service on medical care in the Netherlands, Niek van den Dungen concludes that about 6,000 circumcisions are performed in hospitals each

[53] Shadid & Van Koningsveld, *Religious Freedom and the Position of Islam in Western Europe*, 97. For a previous discussion of the organization and celebration of the circumcision, see Dessing, "The Circumcision of Muslim Boys in the Netherlands".

[54] See also Van den Dungen, "Masallah: Een exploratief onderzoek naar de ontwikkeling van moslimbesnijdenissen onder Turkse migranten in Nederland", 10 and 47, which also contains detailed information on the reactions in Dutch society on the performance of Muslim circumcisions in the Netherlands.

year.[55] He found that there are some five professional circumcisers in the Netherlands, who perform an estimated few hundred circumcisions in total per year.[56]

Before 1987, the operation in a hospital generally involved an overnight stay, whereas more recently the operation has increasingly taken place in out-patient departments.[57] The normal practice in hospital is that a surgeon or an urologist treats the boy under general anaesthesia. The foreskin is drawn over the glans and clipped in a pincer, or an instrument is inserted between the glans and the foreskin in order to protect the glans, after which the foreskin is cut off with a scalpel or surgical scissors. The blood vessels are cauterized to stop the bleeding and both ends of the skin are sutured. The boy's parents are not allowed to attend the operation.

Where parents opt for a professional circumciser, the operation will be performed at home or on the premises of a mosque or in a public hall. Professional circumcisers have usually acquired their skills from experience and mostly have no medical qualifications. The Dutch state does not recognize such circumcisers as competent to perform the operation. The Dutch Public Health Inspectorate takes the view that any interference with the human body falls within the competence of qualified medical practitioners. In practice, however, this body does not supervise circumcisions performed by professional circumcisers, acting only in the case of complications reported to it.[58]

A professional circumciser may use local anesthesia.[59] As well as the techniques mentioned above used by medical specialists, professional circumcisers may use the cauterization technique, which consists of cauterizing the foreskin at the desired place, after which it can easily be removed. One Turkish circumciser successfully applies this technique. He regularly visits both Germany and the Netherlands, where he sometimes treats more than fifty boys at one time. These group circumcisions usually take place in a room adjacent to a mosque.[60]

[55] Ibid., 34–36 and 48. Nederlands Centrum Buitenlanders, "Regulering besnijdenissen bij jongetjes in Nederland: Projectverslag", 9, estimates the number of circumcisions performed in the Netherlands per year at 7,000 to 10,000. It is not clear whether this estimate includes circumcisions performed by professional circumcisers.

[56] Ibid., 31. It is not clear whether these five circumcisers are of Turkish origin or come from different countries. The number of circumcisions performed in the Netherlands by professional circumcisers based in Germany has not been registered, according to Van den Dungen, and is therefore not included in his estimate.

[57] Ibid., 34–36.

[58] Ibid., 31.

[59] Ibid., 15.

[60] Shadid & Van Koningsveld, *Religious Freedom and the Position of Islam in Western Europe*, 97, and Hoffer, *Moslimbesnijdenissen in Nederland*, 31.

In my research I came across two sets of parents who had their sons circumcised by a professional circumciser in the Netherlands, one at home and the other on the premises of a mosque. In the former case, the parents eventually opted for a circumcision at home because of the waiting list at the hospital. They wanted to have the operation done quickly, because relatives from Morocco were staying in the Netherlands at the time.[61] This preference for a professional circumciser may be explained on the basis of prevailing practice in Morocco and Turkey, where most of the circumcisions are performed by professional circumcisers.

According to Van den Dungen, parents seem increasingly to prefer a hospital to a professional circumciser for circumcisions, mostly because a hospital operation is considered safer from a medical viewpoint.[62] Furthermore, in most cases health insurance companies cover the costs of circumcisions performed in hospital. This is not the case when a circumcision is performed by a professional circumciser outside a hospital. On the other hand, a circumcision by a professional circumciser may be experienced as more intimate and less clinical, since it takes place in familiar surroundings in the presence of family members who participate in various ways throughout the process. One relative will hold the child, while others will encourage him or may try to distract him.

All Dutch health insurance companies cover the costs of hospital circumcisions performed on medical grounds, such as in the case of phimosis (tight foreskin). This uniformity of policy does not extend to circumcisions performed on religious grounds. The Ziekenfondsraad, the Dutch Medical Insurance Board, has taken the position that the latter must also be covered. The Board argued that it is difficult to decide whether a circumcision has really taken place on medical grounds alone. Moreover, in their view, the outcome that must at all costs be prevented is that a boy suffers complications because of medical incompetence, in which case

[61] The fact that I came across this only twice is perhaps due to a bias in the data collection. A children's hospital in The Hague and the Al-Gitaan foundation in Rotterdam brought me into contact with parents who had their sons circumcised there. Nevertheless, my findings agree with the estimates of Van den Dungen. According to him, as we have seen, approximately 6,000 circumcisions are performed in hospitals each year, and a few hundred circumcisions are performed by professional circumcisers; in my research, twenty-one respondents had their sons circumcised in hospital or by Al-Gitaan; two respondents had used a professional circumciser.

[62] Van den Dungen, "Masallah: Een exploratief onderzoek naar de ontwikkeling van moslimbesnijdenissen onder Turkse migranten in Nederland", 5 and 48. Similarly, in the exhibition catalogue *De buren vieren feest: Geboorte, overgang en huwelijk bij Antwerpse bevolkingsgroepen* (The neighbours are celebrating: Birth, transition, and marriage in Antwerp population groups), 121, it is argued that in urban contexts in Turkey as well as in Western Europe the operation is increasingly performed by a doctor in a clinic.

hospitalization will be compelled on medical grounds and the costs incurred will be much higher than those of an out-patient treatment.

Although the advice of the Medical Insurance Board is not binding, insurance companies in the public health sector usually comply with it. Insurance companies that deal with both the public and the private sector (such as Zilveren Kruis Zorgverzekeraar) often fall into line with the public health sector, which in this case means that they too cover the expenses of circumcision on religious grounds irrespective of the type of insurance held. Some private insurance companies cover the costs of a circumcision on religious grounds, others do not. In all cases, however, insurers stipulate that the operation takes place in a hospital.

New Organizational Developments in the Netherlands

Modalities for the performance of circumcisions alternative to the hospital setting and the professional circumciser have recently been developed in the Netherlands at the local level. These attempt, in varying degrees, to take the social and religious character of the operation into account.

One might expect Muslims in the Netherlands to have followed the precedent established by the Jewish community in offering professional training for circumcisers, consisting of both medical and religious instruction. Jewish circumcisers (*mohel*, plural *mohaliem*) who have completed this training comply with established medical standards and their performance of the operation is sanctioned by the Dutch government. The Jewish community in the Netherlands has thereby created the option of circumcision in familiar surroundings by a professional circumciser, alongside the possibility of circumcision in a hospital by a medical specialist.

Up to now the Muslim community has not reached a similar solution at a national level. New approaches to the performance of circumcisions have been explored at a local level only. New initiatives were launched in Rotterdam in 1994 and in Utrecht in 1997. In The Hague the matter is still being negotiated. The course of these initiatives appears to be determined by the opinion of the parties involved concerning the question whether circumcision should be considered a medical act or first and foremost a religious and social act. What follows is a brief description of the local initiatives in Rotterdam, Utrecht, and The Hague, and the standpoint of the initiators with respect to this question.

Rotterdam

In 1994, a foundation named Al-Gitaan was established in Rotterdam by three partners: the Stichting Platform Islamitische Organisaties

Rijnmond (SPIOR), a platform of Islamic organizations in Rotterdam and environs, the Sophia Children's Hospital, and Zilveren Kruis Zorgverzekeraar Rijnmond, a health insurance company.[63] The original aim of Al-Gitaan, as stated in its first brochure, was "to organize group circumcisions in a few centrally situated locations in Rotterdam, where many Muslim families live". Al-Gitaan aimed to bring together families that have similar views about the concomitant festivities, so that they can celebrate the circumcision of their sons together after the operation. In practice, however, Al-Gitaan performs circumcisions on one boy at a time at a single location in Rotterdam, and, mostly, no circumcision celebrations are held on its premises after the operations.

Al-Gitaan performs between 350 and 400 circumcisions per year.[64] The operations are performed on Saturdays, every week or once per fortnight. Originally the operations took place on the premises of Centrum Santoso, a Surinamese Javanese organization, but since January 1999 they have been performed on the premises of Thuiszorg, a public institution that organizes home care. The board of Al-Gitaan decided to move to the latter location after comments by many parents that they found the premises of Centrum Santoso, which used to be a school building, not suitable for the performance of circumcisions. Al-Gitaan rents several rooms in the building owned by Thuiszorg, including an operating room that Al-Gitaan has outfitted with medical equipment, and uses Thuiszorg's waiting room.

The operating room is equipped to perform circumcisions on one patient at a time. The other boys and their families must await their turn in an adjacent waiting room. The boy is given a hypnoticum (Dormicum) shortly before the operation and a local anaesthetic (Lidocaine) on the operating table. Each operation takes approximately half an hour. As soon as the operation is completed, most parents return home with their child immediately: they mostly celebrate their son's circumcision with their family and friends on another date.

Despite the demand, Al-Gitaan appears reluctant to develop its activities further, such as by performing circumcisions in other locations. A Turkish organization in Rotterdam asked Al-Gitaan to come to its premises for the collective circumcision of a number of their boys, so

[63] *Gitaan* is a variant transcription of *khitân*, i.e. "circumcision" Initially the foundation used the transcription Chitaan. Due to the fact that Chitaan was sometimes incorrectly pronounced as *shaitân*, i.e. devil, the foundation decided to adopt the transcription Gitaan.

[64] Al-Gitaan performed 328 circumcisions in 1995, 333 in 1996, 319 in 1997, 350 in 1998, and 408 in 1999.

that the subsequent festivities could take place in their familiar surroundings. Even though this request matched the original intentions of Al-Gitaan very well, the foundation did not feel prepared to take this step and refused. They expected difficulties in creating a sterile room and in transporting their equipment.

The establishment of Al-Gitaan served the interests of the three founding parties. The participation of SPIOR guaranteed that circumcision was regarded as not only a medical act but also, or especially, a religious act with social aspects. The importance attached to the religious aspects is revealed, for example, by the fact that the surgeon pronounces the word *Bismillah* or "In the name of God" at the moment at which the foreskin is cut off. Furthermore, Al-Gitaan allows parents to attend the operation, whereas in a hospital they would normally be barred from the operating theatre.

The foundation of Al-Gitaan was also in the interests of the Sophia Children's Hospital. This hospital, which had previously performed many circumcisions for religious reasons, announced in 1991 that it was no longer prepared to perform circumcisions other than for medical reasons.[65] The foundation of Al-Gitaan constituted a medically sound response to the ever-increasing demand for circumcisions in Rotterdam and environs, relaxing the pressure on the Sophia Children's Hospital.

Lastly, the health insurance company benefited from the reduction of the costs of circumcision. An out-patient circumcision in a hospital costs a private insurance company around *f*1,100 (*f* = Dutch guilder; *f*1 = euro 0.45), including preliminary tests and a medical check-up.[66] The cost of a circumcision by Al-Gitaan has tentatively been fixed at *f*450. This sum is refunded to insured persons by Zilveren Kruis Zorgverzekeraar Rijnmond, except for *f*75 (*f*85 since September 1999) to be paid by the policyholder.

[65] According to Van den Dungen, "Masallah: Een exploratief onderzoek naar de ontwikkeling van moslimbesnijdenissen onder Turkse migranten in Nederland", 38, the specialist staff of the departments of child urology and child surgery of the Sophia Children's Hospital and the Academic Hospital sent a letter to all general practitioners of Rotterdam and environs requesting them not to refer anyone for circumcision on religious grounds from August 1991 onwards. In doing so, they declared themselves willing to perform circumcisions only on medical grounds. Their standpoint does not necessarily imply that they have moral objections to circumcisions performed on religious grounds.

[66] The Dutch Centre for Immigrants, Nederlands Centrum Buitenlanders, "Regulering besnijdenissen bij jongetjes in Nederland: Projectverslag", 11, mentions that parents received a bill of *f*2,500 for the circumcision of their son in a hospital. The Centrum voor Gezondheid en Maatschappelijke Dienstverlening (CGM), a health support organization in Rotterdam, ibid., 17, estimates the costs of a circumcision in a hospital at *f*3,500.

Utrecht

Utrecht has seen the development of another option for the performance of circumcisions. This development was initiated by several partners: the Nederlands Centrum Buitenlanders (NCB), a Dutch centre for immigrants, ANOVA, a health insurance company, the local GG & GD or health authority, the Wilhelmina Children's Hospital, and the Districts Huisarten Vereniging (DHV), an organization of general practitioners. The parties agreed that circumcision is a relatively simple operation that can very well be performed in surgeries of general practitioners and similar locations outside hospitals. The parties aimed to lower the costs of the operation, involve general practitioners, use local anaesthesia, and make their services more accessible than those of a hospital.[67]

After difficult negotiations relating to among other things the financing of the project by ANOVA and the involvement of general practitioners, the GG & GD in Utrecht started a pilot project "Besnijdenissen van jongetjes in Utrecht" on its premises on 5 April 1997. The circumcisions are performed there twice a month on Saturdays by a surgeon or urologist and an assistant. As in the operations performed by Al-Gitaan, the boys are given a hypnoticum beforehand and a local anaesthetic on the operating table. However, in Utrecht, an alternative circumcision technique, employing the Taraklamp, is used. The Taraklamp is a device inserted between the glans and the foreskin. By a clipping mechanism, the Taraklamp blocks the blood-supply to the foreskin and compresses it at the right place. The foreskin is then cut off. The Taraklamp is removed after four days.

The operation takes about twenty minutes and the parents are allowed to attend the operation. As in Rotterdam, the operating room is equipped to perform circumcisions on one patient at a time. The other boys and their families must await their turn in an adjacent waiting room. The word *Bismillah* is pronounced at the moment at which the foreskin is cut off. The GG & GD charges parents holding the relevant insurance policy with ANOVA *f*75 for the operation, and ANOVA covers the rest of the cost. Persons with no such insurance are charged *f*325. The costs of the operation are fixed at *f*620.[68]

The Utrecht initiators also planned to recruit general practitioners in the city to follow a training programme to enable them to perform

[67] Ibid., 25–26.

[68] Schmitz, "Rituele besnijdenis van jongens in Nederland", 122.

circumcisions in their own practice. Originally, Al-Gitaan too had aimed at engaging general practitioners in its project, but only two GPs became involved. The rest of the Al-Gitaan medical staff is composed of either medical students or employees of the Sophia Children's Hospital. By enabling GPs to perform circumcisions in their surgeries, the Utrecht project aimed to prevent waiting lists for hospital circumcisions building up. The Rotterdam solution has not succeeded, it was argued in Utrecht: in Rotterdam there is still a waiting list, which has now been transferred from the hospitals to Al-Gitaan. Eight general practitioners followed the training programme, consisting of a theoretical introduction to the technical and cultural aspects of circumcision and a practical course. The latter involved sitting in on operations on the premises of the GG & GD, where the Taraklamp was not yet used, and performing five circumcisions under supervision. Upon completing the programme, the GPs received a certificate authorizing them to perform the operation in their own practice. Several of these GPs now perform circumcisions in their practice once in a while. One of the GPs who followed the programme considered attending a further course at the GG & GD to learn how to use the Taraklamp in order to apply this new technique in his practice.

In the Utrecht project, circumcision is seen first and foremost as a medical act, and not a religious and social one. This means, among other things, that according to the Utrecht initiators it is not relevant whether the general practitioner performing the operation is a Muslim. By contrast, Al-Gitaan regards it as more important that the practitioner be a Muslim, though they do not impose this as a strict requirement. Moreover, the Utrecht initiatiors do not feel responsible for the concomitant festivities, which are considered a private matter. The Utrecht initiators do not intend to organize group circumcisions either. In Morocco, they argue, group circumcisions are performed only if the family is poor or if the boy is an orphan, or in the case of circumcision in remote villages for which a circumciser of a neighbouring town is specially invited. If group circumcision is not done "at home", why then aim for it in the Netherlands, it is asked.

The Hague

Two organizations in The Hague, Stichting ter Ondersteuning van de Gezondheidszorg en Maatschappelijke Dienstverlening in Den Haag-centrum (STIOM), a support organization of general practitioners in the city, and Stichting Haags Islamitisch Platform (SHIP), an organization similar to Rotterdam's SPIOR, have discussed alternative ideas. A STIOM delegation paid a visit to Al-Gitaan to gather information but returned disappointed. In their view, the procedures of Al-Gitaan closely resembled those of a hospital, whereas they aimed to perform the operation in a less clinical setting in the midst of the child's family. This turned out to be impossible, if only because the hypnoticum that Al-Gitaan administers proves effective only in quiet surroundings.

In a meeting in November 1996, SHIP and STIOM were not able to reach agreement concerning a possible alternative. STIOM feared that few of their general practitioners would become involved if an approach like that of Al-Gitaan were chosen, and that they would therefore not reach their main aim of improving relations with patients with an Islamic background by performing circumcisions in a less clinical setting. Moreover, SHIP was internally divided about which alternatives were acceptable to the majority of the Muslim community in The Hague. SHIP and STIOM therefore decided to explore possibilities for improving practice in hospitals. At the same time, SHIP committed itself to continue searching for an alternative acceptable to all parties which would take medical, religious, and social aspects into account as well as meeting the needs of the entire Muslim community in The Hague. Up to now, however, initiatives like those in Rotterdam and Utrecht have not got off the ground.

The establishment of a foundation like Al-Gitaan in The Hague would certainly have jeopardized an important source of income for hospitals in that city. Unlike the Sophia Children's Hospital in Rotterdam and the Wilhelmina Children's Hospital in Utrecht, hospitals in The Hague were willing to improve their services in order to prevent a possible decline of the number of their patients. One hospital, for example, considered permitting parents to attend the operation, while another was planning to organize group circumcisions. The results of this have yet to be seen.

The Operation in the Countries of Origin

In Morocco and Turkey, parents either make use of the services of professional circumcisers, or have the operation done in a hospital or clinic by a medical specialist. In Morocco, collective circumcisions may be organized during *mawâsim*, the annual feasts at the grave of a saint.[69]

There are more professional circumcisers in Morocco and Turkey than in the Netherlands, so it is easier and more straightforward to appeal to their services.[70] The choice between the possibilities depends

[69] For a description of a collective circumcision, see Reysoo, "Een collectieve besnijdenis in Noord-West Marokko", 42–50.

[70] Van den Dungen, "Masallah: Een exploratief onderzoek naar de ontwikkeling van moslimbesnijdenissen onder Turkse migranten in Nederland", 56.

also on the financial means of the family: the fee charged by a professional circumciser is generally lower than that of a medical specialist. The available infrastructure may also play a role. Turkish respondents for instance presented evidence that in urban contexts in Turkey the operation is performed in a hospital or clinic whereas in villages it is carried out by a *sünnetçi*.

The operation in a hospital or clinic in Turkey and Morocco seems however to have a less clinical character than in the Netherlands. This is above all because family members are often allowed to attend the operation. In this respect, the procedures of Al-Gitaan and Utrecht resemble the operation in a hospital or clinic in Turkey or Morocco. Moreover, according to some Moroccan respondents, passages from the Koran may be recited during the operation.

The preference of Surinamese respondents in the Netherlands for a hospital reflects prevailing practice in Surinam. In Surinam nowadays the operation is performed in a hospital or clinic and not at home by a professional circumciser, as was common among Surinamese Muslims in former times.

3.4. Circumcision Festivities

The *ᶜidhâr*, *iᶜdhâr* or *ᶜadhîr* is the festive meal organized on the occasion of a circumcision.[71] According to the Shafiᶜites, it is *sunna* to organize a festive meal at every joyful event and to invite guests to it. According to the Hanafites, the preparation of a meal on account of a circumcision is allowed (*jâ'iza*), provided the gathering accords with religious prohibitions, such as that against the consumption of alcohol. The Malikites also take this view, while further explaining that these meals are neither recommendable (*mustaḥabb*) nor obligatory (*wâjib*).[72]

Kister indicates: "According to tradition, some of the Companions of the Prophet spurned attending such parties, while others arranged parties and even invited singers to comfort the circumcised boys and to alleviate their pain. According to an utterance attributed to the Prophet he recommended to arrange a party on the occasion of circumcision, *walîmatu l-iᶜdhâr*."[73] According to one tradition, ᶜUmar b. al-Khaṭṭâb consented to

[71] Ibn Ṭûlûn, *Faṣṣ al-khawâtim fîmâ qîla fî al-walâ'im*, 60. For the religious qualification of this meal, Ibn Ṭûlûn refers only to his Shafiᶜite teacher, who deems it recommendable (*mustaḥabb*).

[72] Al-Jazîrî, *Al-fiqh ᶜalâ al-madhâhib al-arbaᶜa*, vol. 3, 33.

[73] Kister, "... And he was born circumcised ...", 29.

singing and tambourines on the occasion of weddings and circumcisions only.[74]

In practice, the circumcision of a boy is almost always celebrated, although the scale of the festivities will vary according to the family's financial resources. A shortage of money, but also lack of space or personal reasons, such as a recent bereavement in the family, may induce the family to invite only a few guests. The circumcision and the festivities surrounding the operation usually take place in the same country. It may also occur, however, that parents choose to hold two parties, one in the Netherlands and one in their country of origin, or to have the operation done in the Netherlands and organize a party in their country of origin at a later date.

Celebrations in the Netherlands

In the Netherlands, a boy's circumcision is celebrated either at home, or in a hall or on the premises of a religious organization. Moroccan respondents preferred a party at home while Turkish respondents made use of all these options. The Surinamese Javanese parents whom I interviewed celebrated their son's circumcision at the weekly gathering of their organization at the weekend.

In the Netherlands, celebrations usually took place within a month of a boy's circumcision, mostly during a weekend, but in some cases on the day of the circumcision itself.[75] The latter is more likely if the operation takes place in familiar surroundings, that is at the parental home by a professional circumciser or on the premises of a religious organization. For example, a Surinamese Javanese family celebrated their son's circumcision on the premises of their organization on the day on which he was circumcised there by Al-Gitaan. They felt able to do this because they were familiar with the venue: even though Moroccan and Turkish boys were also circumcised in that building by Al-Gitaan, their families preferred to go home immediately after the operation.

The celebrations in the Netherlands generally take one day, not including the preparations that may take place in a small family circle, such as painting the boy's hands and feet with henna. Only once did

[74] According to Ibn Ṭûlûn, *Fass al-khawâtim fîmâ qîla fî al-walâ'im*, 62, a fourteenth-century Shafiᶜite jurist argued on the basis of this tradition that playing the tambourine at a circumcision is recommendable (*mustaḥabb*).

[75] According to the exhibition catalogue *De buren vieren feest: Geboorte, overgang en huwelijk bij Antwerpse bevolkingsgroepen* (The neighbours are celebrating: Birth, transition, and marriage in Antwerp population groups), 121, the party will be held later if the operation is performed by a doctor in a clinic.

I come across celebrations that extended over more than one day. A Turkish respondent gave a henna party restricted to women on the evening before her son's circumcision, and a party for both men and women on the following day.

Festive Dress

In the Netherlands, when a boy is circumcised, either at home or by Al-Gitaan, he will nearly always arrive for the operation dressed in festive clothes. However, if the operation takes place in a hospital, parents sometimes consider it better to postpone dressing their son in festive clothes until the celebrations, for fear of lack of understanding or negative reactions among doctors and nursing staff. A Turkish respondent had her son circumcised in the Netherlands; only later at his circumcision feast in Turkey was he dressed festively. It seemed to her that she had done everything in reverse order compared to the custom in Turkey, where a boy will appear in his festive clothes on the days preceding his circumcision.

A Moroccan boy often wears white, being dressed in a *la^{c}bâya*, a loose, shirtlike garment, with a *jellâba*, a loose, shirtlike garment with a hood, over it. He will wear a *tarbûsh* or fez on his head and *bilgha* (slippers) on his feet, and sometimes a *silham* (cape) or a *sirwâl* (kind of trousers). One may also see the typical green velvet suit from Fez, consisting of trousers and a waistcoat over a white shirt. The day before the circumcision, the boy's hair is cut and his hands and feet may be painted with henna. Henna protects the child against evil influences and is also considered beautiful.

A Turkish boy may wear a red or blue *sünnetpelerini*, a cape trimmed with artificial down, dark trousers with a white shirt, and a *şapka* on his head, and hold an *asâ*, a kind of sceptre, in his hand. He also wears a sash bearing the inscription *Maşallah* or 'What God wills', known as *Maşallah kuşağı*. According to the majority of my Turkish respondents, *Maşallah* means something like 'good luck' and is meant to protect the child against evil influences.

Unlike a Moroccan or a Turkish boy, a Surinamese Javanese boy circumcised in the Netherlands will not wear any special clothes for a circumcision. In Surinam, such a boy will be dressed in a *sarong*, but in the Netherlands this festive attire has fallen into disuse.

Celebrations at Home

The majority of the Moroccan and Turkish respondents held a party at home. Men and women generally did not mingle at these parties. Men gathered for example in the living room, while women joined together in the bedrooms. Alternatively, if a second house had been put at the disposal of the boy's family by neighbours or relatives, women would be received in one house and men in the other. However, if only a few guests had been invited, men and women might come together in one room. There may also be separate parties for women and men alone. One Turkish mother, for instance, invited only women because, as a single parent, she bore the responsibility for the upbringing of her children alone.

Whereas a Turkish circumcision party in a hall consists primarily of dancing to music, a communal meal, present-giving (*takı*),[76] and often the consumption of alcohol, a party at home consists primarily of Koran recitation and the singing of religious songs (*ilahi*), followed by a communal meal.[77] From a religious point of view, a party at home may be preferred for its modest character. A Turkish family, for example, had the opening sura (*Al-Fâtiḥa*) and sura *Yasin* (36) recited, the latter repeated forty times, four times by ten women, after which they sang *ilahi*. The religious part of the celebration was followed by a communal meal consisting of pastries, salads, and cheese rolls. Another family had invited male and female *hoca*s, who recited the Koran in the men's and women's room respectively.

Moroccan respondents also stressed the importance of Koran recitation on this occasion. "The Koran", one of them said, "must be recited for one or two hours. Thereupon they [men] eat and drink. Men do not dance." However, I came across Koran recitation twice only. This may be explained by the fact that there are not as many professional Koran reciters in the Netherlands as in Morocco, which makes it more difficult to find one. On the other hand, it may be that Koran recitation took place more often than I have observed, because this is a men's affair, and, as a woman researcher, I mainly spoke with women and joined them when attending a party.

76. For a description of the *takı*, see the discussion of wedding parties in the Netherlands in section 4.3.

77 Some respondents mistakenly called this religious part *mevlüt*, thereby meaning Koran recitation. In fact "*mevlüt*" denotes the recitation of the best-known of the *mevlüt* poems in Turkey, written by Süleyman Çelebi around 1400. The *Shorter Encyclopaedia of Islam*, s.v. "Mawlid", gives the following definition of *mawlid*: "panegyrical poems of a very legendary character, which start with the birth of Mujḥammad and praise his life and virtues in the most laudatory fashion".

The social part of Moroccan parties usually consists of dancing to music and a meal. Whereas according to Turkish respondents a choice to hold a party at home generally implies a choice for Koran recitation and against music and dancing, among my Moroccan respondents one does not exclude the other. Koran recitation is often called a men's affair and dancing a women's affair. Female guests, dressed festively in *tekshiṭa* or *kandura*, may dance to recorded music or make their own music, beating drums and singing.

Customarily, in the course of the evening Moroccan tea is served and home-made biscuits are presented, wrapped in cellophane so that they may be taken home. At the end of the evening, meals are served in the men's room and in the women's room. The menu generally includes chicken with olives and almonds as a first course followed by meat with prunes. Both dishes are served with bread and lemonade and there is fresh fruit to conclude the meal.

Celebrations in a Public Hall

Among Turkish respondents in particular, the question whether a circumcision party should be held at home or in a rented hall proved a subject for lively discussion. The choice in favour or against a hall depends above all on the family's financial means. Religious considerations are a further factor in the choice. A party in a public hall involves dancing to music and may bring with it the consumption of alcohol. Moreover, men and women will come together in one room, although they may prefer to sit in family groups or with men gathering on one side of the room, in the passageway or at the bar.

A Turkish man explained his choice not to hold a party in a hall as follows: "You have to offer service. It costs 4,000 or 5,000 guilders. Everybody is going to drink whisky. . . . Just the recitation of the Koran and no party [in a hall] is best from a religious point of view." His wife added: "If you are sociable, then you give a party [in a hall]. That is what I wanted. But in any case, you have to agree with each other." Another Turkish woman, who opted not to hold a party in a hall, argued that such a party is not compatible with religion. However, her daughter said that they would have given such a party if they had been able to afford it.

Several hundred guests may be invited to a Turkish party in a rented hall. One party that I attended started at two o'clock in the afternoon. Whereas in Turkey a boy may be dressed festively on the days preceding his circumcision, in this case he appeared in his festive clothes only at the party, which was held a few days after the operation. For most of the party the guests danced to the music hand in hand, with the person at the head of the line flapping a brightly coloured handkerchief. Dinner was served at about seven o'clock. After dinner the guests congratulated the boy, his parents, and the co-parent (*kirve*),[78] and presented the boy with gifts, mainly consisting of money. The guests left shortly afterwards, at about nine o'clock.

I heard from one of my respondents that at a circumcision party that she attended a bed beautifully made up with embroidered bedclothes, bedspread, and balloons was placed in the hall as if the boy had been circumcised on that day, even though this was not the case. This practice is a remnant of earlier times, when visitors came to congratulate a boy immediately upon his circumcision, while he was lying in a bed beautifully made up for the occasion. A similar Turkish practice of room decoration is found in the case of a mother receiving visitors after having given birth, or in the display of a bride's trousseau in the wedding room.

Celebrations on the Premises of a Religious Organization

When a Turkish boy is circumcised by a professional circumciser (*sünnetçi*) on the premises of a mosque, a bed will be prepared beforehand in one of the rooms, where he can lie down for a while after the operation. In most cases parents will take their son home as soon as possible after the operation to rest, postponing the celebrations to another day.

Only Surinamese Javanese families among my respondents celebrated their son's circumcision on the premises of Centrum Santoso on the day of the circumcision, which was carried out there by Al-Gitaan. The day may go as in the following example. An hour or so before the circumcision, a Surinamese Javanese boy and his family came to the prayer hall of their organization, which is in the same building as Al-Gitaan. The imam began by wishing the boy well and by reciting the opening sura of the Koran and the sura *Al-ᶜAsr* (103). Then the boy formally pronounced the Islamic profession of faith (*shahâda*) for the first time by repeating the imam's words. After that, he shook the hand of all those present. For the following twenty minutes, a second imam gave a speech (called *dawa* or *nazikhat*) explaining the meaning of the event. He said that

[78] *Kirvelik* is a form of ritual co-parenthood established through circumcision and practiced in Eastern Turkey and in Southern Turkey, according to *De buren vieren feest*, 121. According to Magnarella & Türkdoğan, "Descent, Affinity, and Ritual Relations in Eastern Turkey", 1626 and 1628, the sponsor, who usually holds the child while he is circumcised, is called *kirve*. The sponsor shares responsibility for the boy's circumcision expenses, training, well-being, and marriage. In return the boy reciprocates with the loyalty, obedience, respect, and affection that he owes to his own father.

circumcision is *sunna*, that Abraham too was circumcised, and that circumcision is performed for reasons of hygiene. All this took place in the presence of some ten people, among whom were the boy's parents and other relatives. More relatives would probably have been invited to attend the ceremony if part of the building had not been rented out to Al-Gitaan for the afternoon.

About forty more people had been invited to the evening event. For some forty-five minutes the gathering, which took place in a hall next to the prayer hall, had a religious character, starting with a welcome speech by the boy's father followed by Koran recitation. Then, several men gave short speeches (*dawa* or *nazikhat*), each lasting about ten minutes. A prayer (*duʿâ'*) concluded the religious part of the evening. Up to then the boy had been asleep. As soon as he awoke, everyone gathered to congratulate him and to offer him presents of money. From then on the gathering had an informal character, with people sharing a meal and conversations in small groups. The party came to an end with the *ṣalât al-maghrib*. The evening thus closely follows the pattern of a *slametan*, which normally consists of a formal address, a prayer and Koran recitation, and a meal, as we have seen in chapter 2.

Celebrations in the Countries of Origin

In the countries of origin, the festivities generally take place on the day of the circumcision, although there are many exceptions. Among the Aith Waryaghar (Morocco), according to David Hart, the festivities generally come to an end with the operation: musicians and women are invited to attend a party with dancing on the evening preceding the operation.[79] According to a Turkish respondent, parties are no longer held in her birthplace as they used to be, and if there is a party, it will be given before the operation and not afterwards. According to *De buren vieren feest*, by contrast, in urban contexts in Turkey the operation is increasingly performed by a doctor in a clinic and the party is held later.[80]

In the countries of origin one frequently comes across parties that last longer than one day. The duration varies according to the financial position of the family: "The more money, the more party." Irrespective of whether a circumcision party is held, in certain parts of Turkey a boy will appear in his festive clothes on two or three days and everyone in

[79] Hart, *The Aith Waryaghar of the Moroccan Rif*, 121.
[80] *De buren vieren feest*, 121.

the neighbourhood knows that on the third day or so he will be circumcised.

In Surinam, according to De Waal Malefijt, a Surinamese Javanese circumcision feast consists of a *slametan* on the evening before a boy's circumcision and a *slametan* on the day itself. This may be followed on subsequent evenings by performances, such as a shadow play with puppets (*wajang*) and horse dances (*jaran képang*), depending on the wealth of the family.[81] If a family refrains from these performances, for either financial or religious reasons, the celebrations will last one or two days only.

Celebrations in Morocco, Surinam, and Turkey take place either at home or in a rented hall, and one can again distinguish a religious and a social part. In Morocco the religious part is called *ṭalba* or *ṣadaqa*.[82] In Turkey a *mevlüt* recitation may be held. The religious part of a Surinamese Javanese boy's circumcision in Surinam may consist of the boy's formal pronouncement of the *shahâda*, a visit to his relatives' graves, and a *ṣadaqa* or *slametan*.[83]

Religious Part

Religious scholars (*ṭalba*) seem to be invited to circumcision parties for Koran recitation more often in Morocco than in the Netherlands. Some respondents made the point that in Morocco the Koran is recited on a pilgrim's return from Mecca, on the occasion of a circumcision, on the birth of a baby, and on the third and fortieth days following a death. Another respondent contended however that a Koran recitation takes place following a death, but not on the occasion of a circumcision. Thus, prevailing practice may vary locally or according to the religious convictions of the family. Just as in the Netherlands, in Morocco Koran recitation is considered to be a men's affair: "*Al-ṭalba* [Koran recitation] is especially for men. Women are there just a little bit."

In Turkey, men may recite the *mevlüt* together with a *hoca* either shortly before or on the day after a boy's circumcision: "Women were in another room but they could hear the recitation." In Eğirdir, according to Nancy Tapper and Richard Tapper's findings:

> . . . the joyful life-cycle ceremonies of circumcision and marriage may be begun with a *mevlûd* performed by men. The temporal orientation of these

[81] De Waal Malefijt, *The Javanese of Surinam*, 144–145.

[82] *Ṭalba*, the plural of *ṭâlib* (student), is sometimes understood to mean the Koran recitation performed by these religious scholars.

[83] For a discussion of these terms, see section 2.1.

> latter services is enhanced in various ways: they are held in private houses early in the morning and are attended by few men, but are followed by a lavish ceremonial meal in which all invited guests, perhaps several hundred, will partake.[84]

Some of my Turkish respondents preferred to give a party in a hall (*salon*) because they wished to invite many guests. In such cases it may also be argued that only old people will come to *mevlüt*. A party in a *salon* was supposed to be more popular. In some instances, the two were combined, the *mevlüt* being recited at home in the afternoon and the party being given in the evening in a hall: "Those invited to the *mevlüt* were not exactly the same ones as those invited to the party. One knows who prefers what and that is taken into account."

Descriptions of the ritual of circumcision among Surinamese Javanese Muslims in Surinam mention several religious ceremonies apart from the formal pronouncement of the *shahâda*. Parsudi Suparlan gives for example the following account:

> The Javanese traditionalists and some of the moderate reformists still follow the ritual prescribed in Javanese culture in circumcising their boys, i.e., a ritual within the family in which the boy, accompanied by his father or by one of his immediate elder relatives if his father has died, pays a visit to all his relatives' graves, especially those of his grandparents, and *njekar* (offers flowers) and *ngirim donga* (sends Islamic incantations, i.e., *Surat Al Fatihah* and *Qulhu*) to them as taught by the one who is accompanying him at the graves.
>
> At home a *sadjen* offering is made, and the varieties of food and things offered in this *sadjen* are almost the same as those offered in the *sadjen* for the occasion of the *slametan tetesan*. . . .
>
> On the following day, right before he is about to be circumcised, a boy is led in pronouncing the *kalimat sahadat* (the creed of Islam) by the doctor who will circumcise him. In case the boy is not to be circumcised by a Muslim doctor, the boy is led in pronouncing the creed of Islam by a *kaum* during the *slametan* which is held the evening before he will be circumcised. After the circumcision, the parents usually have a feast in the evening.
>
> For the reformists, the most important circumcision event is when the boy recites the creed of Islam. No *sadjen* offering or *slametan* are made by the reformists. A few of them, however, held a small party in the form of eating together with the guests in the evening of the day of circumcision.[85]

[84] Tapper & Tapper, "The Birth of the Prophet: Ritual and Gender in Turkish Islam", 77.

[85] Suparlan, "The Javanese in Surinam", 254–255. His distinction between traditionalists and reformists accords with the distinction between westward-prayers and eastward-prayers mentioned above (see section 2.1). *Sadjèn*, according to De Waal Malefijt, *The Javanese of Surinam*, 131, is ceremonial food offerings to the spirits, but not eaten communally as in the case of *slametan*.

De Waal Malefijt also mentions a boy's visit to the cemetery. Moreover, according to her findings, a *slametan* is held twice: once on the evening before the circumcision, in the boy's absence, and once on the evening of the day of the circumcision, in which the boy takes part.[86] However, these accounts date back to the end of the 1950s and the beginning of the 1970s, and much may have changed since then.

For example, the influence of the eastward-prayers has nowadays further increased in Surinam. This may be shown among other things by the greater interest attached to pronouncing the *shahâda* on the occasion of a circumcision and by attempts to sober down the festivities. The family of a Surinamese Javanese respondent, for example, used to organize only a *ṣadaqa*, consisting of Koran recitation, *duᶜâ'*, edification (*nazikhat*), and a communal meal, on festive occasions such as circumcisions and marriages. They refrained from all practices associated with the westward-prayers, including shadow plays with puppets (*wajang*) and horse dances (*jaran képang*).

Social Part

The social element of the circumcision celebrations usually consists of eating and drinking and sometimes of dancing to music or performances, such as *wajang* and *jaran képang* (Surinam). Additionally, the boy may appear in festive clothes on the days before his circumcision (Turkey). He may be paraded through the streets in festive clothes on horseback or in a car (Morocco and Turkey). Henna may be applied to his hands and feet on the evening before the circumcision (Morocco and Turkey). This conspicuity that goes with the ritual of circumcision in the countries of origin has to a large extent disappeared in the Netherlands.

In certain parts of Turkey, irrespective of whether a circumcision party is held, a boy dresses in festive clothes for two or three days before the operation, visiting uncles and aunts and kissing their hands. They will offer him encouragement and give him some money or another treat. Everyone knows that, on the third day or so, the boy will be circumcised.

A boy may also be paraded through the streets on horseback or in a horse-drawn cart. It seems that the former practice does not occur throughout Morocco: Oujda, Marrakesh, Meknes, Rabat, Tangier, Casablanca, and Taza were mentioned by respondents as places where

[86] De Waal Malefijt, *The Javanese of Surinam*, 144–145.

the practice occurs, and El Hoceima and Nadur as places where it does not. A boy may also be driven around in a car with a sounding horn. In Turkey a panel may be affixed to the numberplate with the inscription *azıcık ucundan*, or "a small piece of the tip". Cars carrying children may follow and in Turkey musicians may play music at the door of the house on the boy's return. In Morocco the boy on horseback may be accompanied by men playing the oboe (*ghîthâ*) and beating drums (*thibâl*).[87]

In Morocco the boy's hands and feet may be painted with henna on the evening before his circumcision. Many guests may be invited to this event but it may also take place in the presence of only a few family members. Henna parties on the occasion of a boy's circumcision seem less widespread in Turkey. However, Konya is mentioned by respondents as a town where henna parties are organized on the evening before a circumcision.

In Turkey, if a party is held in a hall, musicians may be invited to entertain the guests. In Morocco, there is often live music (*shikhât* or *jûqq*), sometimes only for the female guests, but it may also occur that a band is invited to parties where men and women mingle. In these cases only young girls dance to the music. It may also occur that women make their own music at such events.

Some Moroccan women in the Netherlands cherish the memory of parties in Morocco to which only women are invited. A Moroccan woman surprised her mother by organizing such a party on the occasion of her younger brother's circumcision. The party took place in Morocco during the summer holidays, ten months before the boy's circumcision in the Netherlands. Another Moroccan respondent was also planning to hold a party in Morocco for women only, to celebrate the birth of the child that she was expecting and the circumcision of her son, which had been performed in the Netherlands.

In Surinam, it occurred that theatrical performances, such as *wajang* or *jaran képang*, were held in the evening two or three days after the circumcision.[88] A family may refrain from these performances for

[87] Hart, *The Aith Waryaghar of the Moroccan Rif*, 119–120, calls these musicians *imdhyazen*. According to Le Coeur, "Les Rites de passage d'Azemmour", 135: "Des *meddahiyat*, des musiciens, avec *tebal* et *gheita*, les enfants des écoles pour qui le père a demandé une demi-journée ou un jour entier de congé, accompagnent le cortège."

[88] Thus De Waal Malefijt, *The Javanese of Surinam*, 145. On the horse dance (*jaran képang*), see Gooswit, "Jaran képang, beheerste bezieling", 8. She places the *jaran képang* performances within the cultural framework of the Javanese religion (*Agama Djawa*). They are associated with the Surinamese Javanese westward-prayers because, among other things, *sadjèn* offerings for the spirits are made on the occasion of these performances and incense is burnt, which is also typical of the westward-prayers. Furthermore, a possible visit to the graveyard where the spirits are believed to reside may accompany the performances. Eastward-prayers therefore prefer to refrain from these performances.

financial or religious reasons, as we have seen. One Surinamese Javanese respondent stated for instance that when she was young her family used to organize *jaran képang* on the occasion of a circumcision, whereas for religious reasons her husband's family preferred to give a *ṣadaqa* only.

3.5. CONCLUSIONS

In the Netherlands the ritual of circumcision has changed in many respects, especially because the self-evident character that marks the ritual in the countries of origin has vanished in the Netherlands. The importance attached to circumcision and the age at which the operation is performed seem to have remained the same. I had expected that in a migrational context, where only a small minority of the population observes the practice, Muslims would have increasingly emphasized the distinguishing character (*shiᶜâr*) of circumcision. My fieldwork findings did not confirm this. New developments are to be found mainly in the field of the organization and celebration of circumcisions.

We have seen that until recently the circumcision of Muslim boys living in the Netherlands either took place in a hospital or, to a far lesser degree, was performed in familiar surroundings by a professional circumciser in the Netherlands or in the countries of origin. The increased use of hospitals for circumcisions represents an important shift in comparison with the countries of origin, particularly Morocco and Turkey, where in the majority of cases the operation is done by a professional circumciser and less frequently in a hospital or a clinic by a medical specialist.

Apart from the fact that in the Netherlands the number of people making use of the services of a hospital for circumcision has increased in relative terms, a number of respondents further indicated that the operation in a hospital or clinic in Morocco or Turkey has a less clinical character compared to the Netherlands, which indicates that the character of a circumcision in a hospital has changed in the Netherlands.

A major change arising from the Dutch migration context is the development of local alternatives to the three possibilities mentioned above for the performance of circumcisions: in a hospital or by a professional circumciser in the Netherlands, or in the countries of origin. The decision of some hospitals in Rotterdam and the Wilhelmina Children's Hospital in Utrecht no longer to perform circumcisions on religious grounds has made the need for alternatives in these cities more pressing than in The Hague. In contrast with the situation in Rotterdam and

Utrecht, hospitals in The Hague turned out to be quite willing to adapt their services, for fear of losing patients and consequently an important source of income. Even though the results have still to become evident, it is clear that the development of local alternatives will generally prompt hospitals in the Netherlands to review their position.

Another characteristic typical of circumcision in the Dutch context is that health insurance companies cover the costs of the operation if they are performed in a hospital, by Al-Gitaan, or, in Utrecht, on the premises of the GG & GD. This is not the case in the countries of origin, where people bear all costs themselves regardless of where it is performed.

Within the organizational framework gradually coming into existence in the Netherlands several interested parties may be expected to influence further developments. The hospitals' fear of losing business, combined with the wish of insurance companies to reduce the costs of circumcision, suggests that the negotiating position of Muslim organizations is probably strong. One may expect that the local initiatives pioneered in Rotterdam, Utrecht, and The Hague will eventually produce some arrangement that will be adopted on a larger scale in the Netherlands. As a consequence, a new organizational infrastructure for the performance of circumcisions will gradually unfold itself also at a national level. This is a unique situation which is typical of the Dutch migration context and differs greatly from the situation in the countries of origin.

The self-evident character of the celebrations of the circumcision ritual in the countries of origin does not persist in a migrational context, where only a minority keeps to this practice. The celebrations in the Netherlands, which sometimes only dimly recall the celebrations in the countries of origin, express this lack of self-evidence in several ways.

Some customs, widespread in the countries of origin, have for instance partly or completely disappeared in the Netherlands. Many respondents cherished the memory related to their countries of origin, especially the parading of a boy through the streets on horseback or in a car shortly before his circumcision, a form of conspicuous behaviour that rarely or never occurs in the Netherlands. In the Netherlands, parents tend to dress their son festively on his circumcision feast and not, as is customary especially in Turkey, on the days preceding his circumcision, thus publicly announcing his circumcision.

Moreover, certain services, which are commonly available in the countries of origin, are less easy to come by in the Netherlands, where, for instance, there are not as many professional Koran reciters and professional musicians as in Morocco. These circumstances compel

Muslims in the Netherlands to improvise. They will either recite the Koran themselves or play a recorded Koran recitation cassette, or may simply omit this element altogether.

The different housing in the Netherlands also has an impact on the character of the festivities. Shortage of space, often combined with a lack of financial means, has caused Muslim families living in the Netherlands to celebrate circumcisions on a modest scale. Moreover, Dutch houses are less suited to the separate reception of men and women. As a consequence, as we saw, men may gather in the living room and women in the bedrooms on this occasion, they may be received in separate houses, or may be invited to parties at different times.

Finally, in the Netherlands the operation and its celebration are often separated in time. This applies to a much smaller degree to the countries of origin, and Turkey and Morocco in particular, where operation and celebration form a unity, especially when the operation is performed by a *sünnetçi* or a *hajjam* in the familiar surroundings, as is mostly the case. The involvement of everyone around, rendering assistance as a matter of course whenever needed, makes it easier to arrange a party on the day itself. However, if the operation is performed in a clinic or a hospital, whether in the Netherlands or in the countries of origin, the celebrations will often be postponed to a later date. One may therefore wonder whether an increased medicalization of the operation goes hand in hand with a separation of operation and celebration.

4
MARRIAGE

> Marriage is a lawful pact between a man and a woman to unite and remain together in a permanent manner, its aim being integrity and chastity and the growth of the population of the nation by the founding of a family under the care of the husband, based on stable foundations, and requiring the contracting parties to bear its burdens in trust, peace, affection and respect.
> —*Mudawwana*, art. 1, trans. Dawoud S. El Alami and Doreen Hinchcliffe

Among Muslims in Turkey, Morocco, and—although to a lesser extent—Surinam, marriage has always been considered the only legitimate form of cohabitation. The basis for this can be found in the fundamentals of Islamic learning, according to which the aim of marriage is to legitimize sexual relations between the partners. Without the legal channeling of these relations in the framework of marriage, chaos (*fitna*) would arise in society, leading ultimately to its decline.[1]

The family, which is based on marriage, thus forms the cornerstone of society. The family serves four main purposes: it ensures reproduction, gives coherence to society, ensures the development of love and affection between husband and wife, as well as between parents and children, and provides a moral framework that regulates sexual relations and protects honour.[2]

Islamic law schools hold different viewpoints regarding the religious qualification of marriage: according to most Shafiᶜites marriage is permitted, according to most Malikite and Hanafite scholars marriage is recommended, according to the Hanbalites and some Hanafite scholars marriage is an obligation for every Muslim, and according to some Shafiᶜite scholars marriage belongs to the collective duties of the Muslim community (*farḍ kifâya*). This means that if the obligation of marriage is fulfilled by a sufficiently large number of individuals, others are excused from it.[3]

The transplantation of the ritual of marriage to the Dutch context has affected it in several ways. Unlike in the case of the other lifecycle rituals, the marriage legislation of the country of origin has remained influential, since many Muslims in the Netherlands have not taken Dutch

[1] Buskens, *Islamitisch recht en familiebetrekkingen in Marokko*, 38.
[2] Shadid & Van Koningsveld, *Moslims in Nederland*, 111–112.
[3] Ibid., 12.

nationality and prefer to contract marriages under the law of their country. In order to understand how this preference affects the ritual of marriage in practice, it is necessary to examine the marriage legislation of Morocco, Turkey, and Surinam.

This chapter begins with a discussion of the proposal of marriage. Section 4.2 treats the Islamic prescriptions pertaining to the contracting of a marriage, the marriage legislation of Morocco, Turkey, and Surinam, and the influence of this legislation on the marriage practice of migrants from these countries in the Netherlands. In section 4.3 there follows a description of the marriage festivities.[4]

4.1. Proposal of Marriage

The engagement or *khiṭba*, which is prior to and distinguishable from the conclusion of marriage, is recommendable according to Islamic law.[5] The acceptance of a marriage proposal does not oblige the contraction of the marriage and places no commitment on either party.[6]

A marriage proposal is valid only if two conditions are met. The first is that there must be no permanent or temporary impediments to a marriage between the parties. If there were a permanent impediment, a proposal would be pointless, since the marriage would never be allowed. If the impediment is temporary, for example in the case of a widow whose waiting period (*ᶜidda*) has not yet expired, a suitor is allowed to drop hints before the end of the waiting period in order to make his interest known.[7] The second condition is that no proposal from another suitor has been accepted or is under consideration.[8]

[4] For a previous treatment of Islamic marriage law and present-day marriage legislation in Morocco, Turkey, and Surinam, see Dessing, "Continuïteit en verandering in de huwelijkssluiting bij Marokkaanse, Turkse en Surinaamse moslims in Nederland".

[5] Linant de Bellefonds, *Traité de droit musulman comparé*, vol. 2, 29 and 40. The information on marriage under Islamic law presented in this chapter is based mainly on volume two of this work, which deals with marriage and marriage dissolution according to Islamic law. Linant de Bellefonds gives a comparative survey of the viewpoints of the four law schools, classifying his subject according to Hanafite principles.

[6] Ibid., 33–34.

[7] Reference is made to Koran 2:235. On this basis, by analogy, it is also argued that it is allowed to drop hints to make known one's interest in marriage to a woman who has been definitely repudiated but whose waiting period has not yet expired. According to Jordens-Cotran, "Het Marokkaanse huwelijks- en het Nederlandse internationaal huwelijksrecht (I): De verloving of khitba", 220, the Hanafites take the view that dropping hints is allowed only during the waiting period of a widow and not during the waiting period of a definitely repudiated woman.

[8] Linant de Bellefonds, *Traité de droit musulman comparé*, vol. 2, 30–32.

When a marriage proposal is accepted, as a legal effect, the intending husband is allowed to see the face, hands, and feet of the woman. According to the Malikites, however, the intending husband is allowed to see only her face and hands. Moreover, according to the Hanafites, Shafi^c^ites, and Hanbalites, it is permitted for the intending husband and wife to talk with each other as often as is deemed necessary, provided that a member of the woman's family is present. It is prohibited for fiancés to meet without a third person present. They are entitled to do so only when married. The following *ḥadîth* is adduced in support: "When a man and woman who are not married to each other isolate themselves, the devil will be their partner."[9]

According to Moroccan respondents, the term *yakhṭub* means "he proposes". Once the proposal has been accepted, the parties are deemed to be *makhṭûb* or *lamlek*, or "engaged" (*khuṭuba* means "engagement"). Turkish respondents called the official acceptance of a proposal *söz kesme* and the subsequent celebration of this event *nişan*.[10] Surinamese Hindustani respondents, like Surinamese Hindus, used the word *chekái* for engagement.[11]

In practice an engagement, and especially an engagement party, seems not to play an important role among Surinamese Hindustani Muslims. Only one pair of Surinamese Hindustani fiancés in my sample marked their engagement by going out for dinner. On that occasion the man gave his fiancée a ring. The two families may nevertheless attach great importance to informal talks during which they may reach detailed agreements about the amount of the bridal gift, the number of guests to be invited to the wedding party, the place of the wedding, and the division of the wedding party costs.

According to my Moroccan and Turkish respondents, once the two parties have reached an agreement about marriage after more or less informal talks, there always follows an official proposal of marriage at

[9] Ibid., 32–33.

[10] Krüger, "Grundzüge des türkischen Verlöbnisrechts", 316, defines *söz kesme* as follows: "Dasselbe gilt grundsätzlich hinsichtlich eines anderen traditionellen türkischen 'Verlöbnisses', des sog. 'söz kesimi' (etwas feste Absprache). Hierbei handelt es sich nämlich um eine Vereinbarung zwischen den *Eltern* der beiden Kinder, daß diese einander heiraten werden. Ein wirksames Verlöbnis kommt durch eine derartige Abrede jedoch nicht zustande, weil Stellvertretung bei Verlobung und Heirat nach geltendem türkischen (anders als nach islamischem) Recht ausgeschlossen ist." According to the Turkish respondents, *söz kesme* is not an agreement between parents only: generally the future couple is closely associated with the negotiations. According to them, *söz kesme* means to accept the proposal officially.

[11] Mungra, *Hindoestaanse gezinnen in Nederland*, 123.

the girl's home. In the case of several couples in my sample, the couple itself took the first steps towards getting acquainted. They may have met several times, possibly without their parents' knowledge. When it becomes clear in such a case that the pair wish to marry, they inform their parents. The subsequent official proposal of marriage gives the families the opportunity to get to know one another, and aims to make the couple's intentions public.

Other couples in my survey, however, did not know one another at the time of the official proposal of marriage. One Turkish woman associated with the *Milli Görüş*, for example, had a conversation with her future husband only once before *söz kesme*, or official acceptance of the proposal of marriage. This conversation lasted about forty-five minutes and took place in the presence of the girl's mother. In this case, moreover, the official proposal of marriage was not considered sufficient to legitimize meetings of the couple. My respondent argued that only the conclusion of marriage before an imam (*imam nikâhı*) allows the intending husband and wife to talk with one another, and even then it is considered recommendable that a third person continue to chaperone their meetings until the wedding party has taken place. The *ḥadîth* mentioned above, "When a man and woman who are not married to each other isolate themselves, the devil will be their partner", was cited in support.

A proposal of marriage may take place in the presence of many members of both families. This is usually the case when all issues have been settled during earlier informal talks. When the sides have met only few times before, by contrast, the proposal may take place in a small family circle. In such a case an imam or a mutual acquaintance may make the proposal, since the parents' unfamiliarity with one another would oblige them to begin with conventional light conversation, whereas acquaintances of the girl's family may broach the subject more easily. Acquaintances of the husband and wife may accompany the intending husband too if his parents do not live in the Netherlands. One Turkish woman, for example, received her future husband's proposal in the presence of acquaintances who had mediated between them (*aracı*, plural *aracılar*) and in the absence of his parents.

The intending husband attends the official proposal of marriage in most but not all cases. One Turkish respondent, for example, received a proposal from her suitor's parents. She decided to accept the proposal only after having been given the opportunity to talk with her prospective husband for a while at a later time. It may occur that the girl too is absent when the proposal is received. She may for example leave the room where the two families have gathered after having poured the tea.[12]

To become better acquainted with the girl, in Turkey *görücüler* ("those who take a look"),[13] consisting of a number of women of the boy's family, visit the girl's home shortly before the official proposal to observe the potential fiancée closely. "It's like a full-dress rehearsal", a Turkish respondent explained, "because if these women agree, men of the boy's family will come to propose".

According to Moroccan and Turkish respondents, the girl's side does not usually accept a proposal of marriage immediately upon its being made. Mostly the girl's parents ask to be allowed to consider the proposal for one or two weeks. During this period they may ask their daughter for her opinion or make inquiries into the boy's family, or merely allow the time to pass, considering that an immediate acceptance would suggest that the girl is in little demand.

The *Mudawwana* ("collection"), the Moroccan codification of Islamic family law and law of inheritance, deals with *khiṭba* in book 1, articles 2 and 3. The *Mudawwana* defines engagement as a promise of marriage and explicitly distinguishes engagement from marriage.[14] This implies that the agreements that the two parties may have reached during the engagement do not have the same status as the stipulations of a binding marriage contract.[15] The *Mudawwana* states that as a rule the

[12] Gailly, *Een dorp in Turkije*, 132–133, describes the marriage negotiations between two families in Turkey at the end of the 1970s, when the girl joined the visitors only at the beginning of the gathering to pour out tea.

[13] Dirks, *La Famille musulmane turque*, 52, mentions *görücü* in dealing with family life before Atatürk: "Après l'échange des première formules de politesse, la candidate arrive, apportant le café; la coutume exige que ce soit la jeune fille elle-même, et non une servante, qui le serve en cette occasion. Pendant que les 'visiteuses' sirotent leur café (elles essaient de le faire le plus lentement possible), elles observent à la dérobée la jeune candidate, la font rire pour voir si elle a de belles dents, la font parler pour voir si elle a de l'esprit; après quoi, la jeune fille peut se retirer." See also ibid., 62 and 68, and Gailly, *Een dorp in Turkije*, 132–140, esp. 133. Gailly describes in detail the negotiations for an engagement in Turkey in 1978–79. The *görücü* is in this case a woman who searches for a suitable candidate for marriage and who mediates between the two families.

[14] For Moroccan marriage legislation I use the Dutch translation of the *Mudawwana* by Berger and Kaldenhoven: *De Mudawwanah: Marokkaans wetboek inzake personen-, familie- en erfrecht*. For the text of the Turkish Civil Code I use the German translation by Bergmann & Ferid, *Internationales Ehe- und Kindschaftsrecht*, s.v. "Türkei". The Turkish Civil Code deals with engagement in articles 82 to 87. Article 82 stipulates among other things "Das Verlöbnis wird durch das Eheversprechen begründet" (ibid., 97. Lieferung, 22), and article 83 "Das Verlöbnis gibt kein Klagerecht, die Eheschließung zu erzwingen" (ibid., 116. Lieferung, 23).

[15] Jordens-Cotran, "Het Marokkaanse huwelijks- en het Nederlandse internationaal huwelijksrecht (I): De verloving of khitba", 219. See also Lahrichi, *Vivre musulmane au Maroc: Guide des droits et obligations*, 53: "La récitation d'un verset du Coran (Fatiha)

opening sura of the Koran, *Al-Fâtiḥa*, is recited on this occasion and the two parties present each other with gifts in accordance with prevailing custom. By this, the *Mudawwana* means that the recitation of the opening sura on this occasion has become a tradition, but Moroccan law does not oblige either of the parties to perform it.[16] According to Leila Jordens-Cotran, the *Fâtiḥa* is usually recited by a male family member or by an imam who has been asked to recite on this occasion.[17] Only one Moroccan respondent mentioned the recitation of the opening sura on this occasion. According to my findings, it occurs more frequently that an imam or the couple's parents call for God's help in a more general way, such as by pronouncing the formula, "Let us hope that God will make them happy".

Some Turkish and Moroccan respondents celebrate the acceptance of a marriage proposal with an engagement party. Yerden concluded that Turkish youngsters in the Netherlands attach little weight to an engagement party. He reports that, mostly, a small, intimate party will be given on this occasion.[18] However, my findings do not fully support Yerden's claim. One respondent sent out invitations for her engagement party; another party occupied two rooms in which male and female guests were received separately. One Turkish respondent organized an engagement party, in many respects similar to a wedding party, in a sports hall. These examples suggest that not all Turkish engagement parties in the Netherlands have a small and intimate character.

The exchange of rings may have an important place in engagement parties. In Turkish engagement parties, it occurred that a kind of master of ceremonies attempted to cut a red ribbon that bound together the fiancés' rings with scissors that he seemed at first, as a conceit, to find to be blunt. He thereupon prompted the onlookers to donate money, because he would succeed in cutting the ribbon only when he felt that enough money had been collected.[19] Moroccan couples may exchange milk and dates as a welcoming ritual before exchanging rings.

Generally the fiancés, particularly the fiancée, are festively dressed on this occasion. Turkish respondents expected the fiancé to buy his fiancée

durant la cérémonie de fiançailles n'équivaut qu'à une bénédiction divine et n'entraîne aucun lien juridique entre les fiancés qui peuvents donc librement rompre leurs fiançailles de part et d'autre."

[16] Jordens-Cotran, "Het Marokkaanse huwelijks- en het Nederlandse internationaal huwelijksrecht (I): De verloving of khitba", 219.

[17] Ibid.

[18] Yerden, *Trouwen op z'n Turks*, 87.

[19] For a similar ritual in Turkey, see Gailly, *Een dorp in Turkije*, 140.

an engagement dress.[20] A Moroccan fiancée was dressed in *tekshiṭa* with a collar of pearls and a small crown with a veil of tulle on her head. Her hair was done up and she wore colourful make-up. However, the attire on this occasion is usually modest by comparison to the wedding attire.

4.2. Contracting of Marriage

Linant de Bellefonds, relying on classic Islamic authors, defines (a contract of) marriage (*nikâḥ*) as a contract that obliges a man to pay a woman a bridal gift (*mahr*, *ṣadâq*) and to provide for her living (*nafaqa*),[21] thereby acquiring the right to be legitimately intimate with her.[22] This definition lays emphasis on the legal effects of marriage. Our main focus is on marriage formalities, that is the time and place of consent and the guardianship (*wilâya*) as conditions for the formation of a marriage, and the presence of witnesses as an essential condition for the validity of the marriage. The bridal gift, which is a legal effect of marriage according to the majority of law schools, will also be discussed in view of its importance in the preliminaries and the conclusion of marriage itself. Other legal effects, such as the husband's obligation to provide for his wife's living (*nafaqa*) and the rights and duties of both husband and wife, are left aside here, because they are not important for the ritual of marriage itself.

According to Islamic law, marriage consists of the exchange of consent by the intending husband and wife or by their guardians in the presence of two witnesses.[23] Islamic law requires neither the presence of a registrar or a religious authority nor the drawing up of a written document on this occasion. Nevertheless, these institutions and forms of registration have gained significance in present-day marriage legislation of Muslim countries. In Morocco, for example, the Minister of Justice appoints qualified, professional witnesses (*ᶜudûl*). These officials put in writing what they have seen and heard as professional witnesses and register marriages concluded before them in the marriage register of the competent court.

[20] Ibid.

[21] On *nafaqa*, see Linant de Bellefonds, *Traité de droit musulman comparé*, vol. 2, 259–262. The *nafaqa* consists of food, clothing, housing, servants, and medical costs. The *nafaqa* is closely related to the husband's right to be intimate with his wife, but also to other rights of the husband, such as his right to determine where to live, to forbid his wife to leave their house without his permission, to forbid her to receive visitors, to take her with him on travels, and to admonish her. When a woman denies her husband his rights, in certain cases she loses her right to *nafaqa*, ibid., 287–295.

[22] Ibid., 23.

[23] Ibid., 39.

Islamic law treats marriage contracts as part of the subject of *mu^câwaḍât* or contracts on the basis of "do ut des", which also include transfer of ownership in buying and selling.[24] According to Islamic law, agreement of the parties in itself does not suffice to conclude such contracts: the following three conditions apply too. The first states that the exchange of consent, that is offer and acceptance (*ijâb wa qabûl)*, must take place during a single meeting of the two parties arranged specifically to this end (*ijâb wa qabûl fî majlis waḥid*). The meeting (*majlis*) opens when an offer is made and comes to an end when the parties separate. The acceptance of an offer must take place during the *majlis*. Separation is defined as a motion carrying the parties out of one another's earshot, but also as any gesture or act that could be interpreted as separation according to custom.[25] The Hanafites, says Linant de Bellefonds, take a stricter line. In their view, the *majlis* is over as soon as one of the parties utters a remark unrelated with the offer. This is for example the case when, after the offer has been made, one of the parties utters a comment about the weather without the proposal's having been accepted, or one of the parties assumes a different posture from which it may be concluded that the offer is withdrawn or rejected.[26]

According to the majority of the law schools, the order in which the intending husband and the guardian (*walî*) of the intending wife express their consent to marriage is not material. The first act is called *ijâb* and the second *qabûl*. In practice, however, according to Linant de Bellefonds, especially in non-Hanafite countries, the guardian (*walî*) of the prospective wife makes the offer (*ijâb*), which is thereupon accepted by the prospective husband (*qabûl*).[27]

The second condition for the validity of *ijâb wa qabûl* is that the offer and acceptance must correspond fully. This condition applies particularly to the amount of the bridal gift or marriage settlements. If, for example, the conclusion of marriage is made subject to the payment of a certain sum of money, and the intending husband consents to the marriage but proposes a lesser sum, no marriage has been concluded.[28]

According to the Hanbalites, who are less strict than the Hanafites, Malikites, and Shafi^cites with regard to marriage settlements, it is permitted to insert stipulations in a contract of marriage on condition that

[24] Ibid., 24.
[25] Ibid., 43–44.
[26] Ibid., 44.
[27] Ibid., 45.
[28] Ibid.

these stipulations are not contrary to the *sharîᶜa*. For example, the obligations of paying a bridal gift (*mahr*) or providing for the wife's living (*nafaqa*) cannot be abrogated, because both are legal effects of marriage under Islamic law. However, it may be stipulated that the intending husband will not take a second wife. If he contravenes this stipulation, his wife has the right to ask for the dissolution of the marriage.[29]

Sharṭ al-simâᶜ, the third condition for the validity of offer and acceptance, prescribes that the statement of each of the contracting parties must be audible. This condition has recently been interpreted as prescribing that the contracting parties must have understood one another.[30]

Guardianship

According to classical *fiqh*, there is no minimum age of marriage, even though a marriage of a child may not be consummated until the child has reached puberty. If either the bride or groom is underage, a *walî mujbir* or enforcing guardian represents his ward at the marriage conclusion. The *walî mujbir* is entitled to give a child in marriage without the child's consent.[31]

If the groom is of adult age and sound mind, his personal or warranted consent is an essential condition for the validity of the marriage under Islamic law.[32] According to the Shafiᶜites, Malikites, and Hanbalites, however, the bride's consent, whether in person or by warrant, has no legal validity, even if she has reached adulthood or has been married several times before. In order for the contract to be valid, she must be represented by a guardian (*walî*) for the pronouncement of either the *ijâb* or the *qabûl*.[33] In contrast, the Hanafites hold that it is recommendable for a bride who has reached adulthood to make use of a *walî*, but she is not obliged to do so.[34]

The Shafiᶜites, Hanbalites, and—with some reservations—Malikites consider the right of *jabr*, i.e. the right of the *walî mujbir* to force his ward to marry, to apply not only to minors but also to a virgin (*bikr*) who has reached adulthood.[35] By contrast, the Hanafites take the position that an adult woman, whether a virgin or not, cannot be forced to

[29] For more information, see ibid., 89–96.
[30] Ibid., 46.
[31] Ibid., 48.
[32] Ibid., 48.
[33] Ibid., 49 and 53.
[34] Ibid., 53.
[35] Ibid., 60–61.

marry.[36] According to all the schools, it is recommendable (*mustaḥabb*) to ask the opinion of a virgin before giving her in marriage. A virgin, says a *ḥadîth*, should make her consent to a marriage known by remaining silent; if she does not consent, she must make this known explicitly.[37] The bride's consent to a marriage is required if she has been married before.[38]

Presence of Witnesses

The presence of two witnesses (*shâhid*, plural *shuhûd*) is a necessary condition for the validity of a marriage. According to the Hanafites, Shafiᶜites, and Hanbalites the witnesses must be present at the conclusion of the marriage itself, when offer and acceptance are exchanged. In support, they cite the *ḥadîth*, "Every marriage concluded without four persons being present, that is the *walî* (of the bride), the suitor and the two witnesses, is but fornication." This *ḥadîth* is generally considered weak, however.[39]

According to the Malikites, who also consider the presence of witnesses to be a condition for the validity of marriage, their presence has the function primarily of contributing to the publicity of the marriage. In this line of thought, if a long time elapses between the conclusion of a marriage and its consummation, the presence of witnesses is required not at the marriage conclusion but rather at the moment when the bride leaves the parental home to start married life. Accordingly, if the witnesses in a marriage are asked to observe secrecy, the marriage has no existence in law because the witnesses have not served the need for which they were required.[40]

The Bridal Gift in Islamic Law

The bridal gift, which the Hanafites mainly call *mahr* and the scholars of the other law schools mainly *ṣadâq*, is an essential aspect of marriage. The husband's obligation to pay his future wife a bridal gift is based on, among other things, the Koran and numerous *ḥadîth*s, such as Koranic verse 4:4: "Give women their bridal gift as an absolute bequest; but if they choose to please you with a part of it, dispose of it with joy and happiness."[41]

[36] Ibid., 62.
[37] Ibid., 79–80.
[38] Ibid., 49.
[39] Ibid., 51 and 100.
[40] Ibid., 100–101.
[41] Ibid., 199.

According to the Hanafites, Shafi^c^ites, and Hanbalites, *mahr*, on a par with *nafaqa* (the husband's obligation to provide for his wife's living), is a legal consequence of marriage (*ḥukm*). This implies that a marriage contract is considered valid even if it does not make mention (*bi dûn tasmiya*) of a *mahr*. However, in the view of these schools, it is recommendable (*mustaḥabb*) that mention of the bridal gift is not omitted when a marriage is concluded. Similarly, a marriage contract containing the stipulation that no *mahr* will be paid is valid, but the stipulation concerning the *mahr* is null and void and an appropriate *mahr* is due. Half the appropriate *mahr* is payable if the wife is repudiated before marriage consummation.[42]

According to the Malikites, on the other hand, the *mahr* is an essential condition for the validity of a marriage (*rukn*). They therefore take the position that a marriage contract containing the stipulation that no bridal gift will be paid is null and void. If, however, consummation has taken place, such a marriage contract is no longer deemed null and void and an appropriate *mahr* is due.[43]

In the case of a *mahr musammâ*, or negotiated bridal gift, the spouses or their guardians agree the amount of the bridal gift. The Hanbalites and Shafi^c^ites stipulate no lower limit for the *mahr musammâ*, whereas the Hanafites and Malikites do. All four law schools take the view that there is no upper limit, but it is usually stressed that it is recommendable (*mustaḥabb*) that the amount should be reasonable.[44]

If the amount of the bridal gift is not explicitly stipulated at marriage conclusion or if the stipulation concerning the bridal gift is invalid for any reason, a *mahr al-mithl*, or appropriate bridal gift, is due. As Linant de Bellefonds puts it:

> Le dot d'equivalence (mahr al-miṯl) est établie, compte tenu de l'origine familiale de la femme dotée . . . et par comparaison avec la dot que les femmes pourvus des mêmes qualités morales et physiques qu'elle-même ont coutume de recevoir. Il convient donc de prendre en considération de très nombreux éléments d'appréciation: âge, beauté, fortune, intelligence, éducation, facilité d'élocution, piété, vertu, mais aussi le fait que la mariée est vierge ou a déjà été mariée, et le nombre de ses mariages antérieurs. La liste de ces éléments de comparaison est plus ou moins longue suivant l'école considérée. . . .[45]

[42] Ibid., 202.
[43] Ibid., 203.
[44] Ibid., 207–208.
[45] Ibid., 214.

Three law schools, since they do not regard the bridal gift as an essential condition for the validity of a marriage, permit payment in instalments on condition that the entire amount is paid at the latest when the marriage comes to an end, for example because of death or repudiation. If the payment dates are not agreed beforehand, the prevailing usage is that a first instalment is paid at marriage conclusion and the remainder at the end of the marriage.[46]

Present-Day Marriage Legislation

Dutch private international law takes nationality as a point of departure for marriage legislation. This implies among other things that a Dutch registrar possesses the exclusive right to conclude a marriage between two Dutch citizens resident in the Netherlands. A consulate marriage is recognized under Dutch law only if it involves a marriage between two citizens of the consulate's country or a marriage between a citizen of the consulate's country and a citizen of a third country, on condition that this third country recognizes such a marriage. A consulate marriage that involves a Dutch citizen is not recognized in the Netherlands. Rules for the competence of persons to marry are laid down in their national law.[47]

The Dutch parliament has recently abrogated the rule that a foreign citizen must renounce his or her original nationality in order to take Dutch nationality. This measure is relevant particularly to Moroccans in the Netherlands, who under Moroccan law cannot renounce Moroccan nationality. Although the number of naturalizations of Moroccans and Turks has increased in the last few years, more than 50% of Moroccans and approximately 30% of Turks still do not have Dutch nationality. By contrast, most Surinamese have taken Dutch nationality.[48]

Islamic prescriptions concerning marriage have been implemented in varying degrees in the national marriage legislations of Morocco, Turkey, and Surinam. These marriage legislations determine to a large extent the marriage practice of Moroccan, Turkish, and Surinamese Muslims in the Netherlands, as we shall now see.

[46] Ibid., 218–219.

[47] Rutten, *Moslims in de Nederlandse rechtspraak*, 28–30.

[48] According to official statistics, 128,600 Moroccans and 102,000 Turks did not have Dutch nationality in 1999: Centraal Bureau voor de Statistiek, "Niet-Nederlanders naar nationaliteit" (Non-Dutch nationals according to nationality), updated on 4 May 2000, http://www.cbs.nl/nl/cijfers/kerncijfers/sbv0610b.htm, consulted on 20 December 2000.

Moroccan Marriage Legislation and Its Influence on the Marriage Practice of Moroccans

Up to 1958, marriage in Morocco was regulated by Malikite law as laid down in *fiqh* books.[49] In 1957 and 1958 the *Mudawwana* ("collection"), the Moroccan codification of Islamic family law and law of inheritance, which in content is strongly influenced by Malikite *fiqh*, was promulgated.[50] The first of the six books of the *Mudawwana* deals with engagement and marriage. Unlike the Turkish and Surinamese civil codes, the *Mudawwana* does not distinguish between a registry-office marriage and a religious marriage, or a marriage in accordance with Islamic prescriptions.[51] On the contrary, being largely based on Malikite law, the *Mudawwana* incorporates Islamic prescriptions concerning marriage.[52]

Many years of discussion led in 1993 to a revision of the *Mudawwana*, bringing changes in the regulations concerning guardianship, the husband's obligation to provide for his wife's living (*nafaqa*), and polygamy, among other areas.[53] The *Mudawwana*, unlike Surinamese and Turkish marriage legislation, admits polygamy, though this was subjected to stricter regulation in the 1993 revision.

In accord with Islamic law, the *Mudawwana* (articles 4 and 5) regards marriage as a private law agreement between two parties established through offer and acceptance during a single meeting. A necessary condition for the validity of a marriage is, according to the *Mudawwana*, the presence of two *ᶜudûl* (singular: *ᶜadl*)—qualified, professional witnesses

[49] Buskens, *Islamitisch recht en familiebetrekkingen in Marokko*, 36.

[50] Ibid., 46.

[51] By analogy with a church wedding, one may think that the conclusion of marriages in accordance with Islamic prescriptions takes place in the prayer hall of the mosque. However, this is hardly ever the case. Rather such a marriage conclusion will take place either elsewhere in a mosque or at home in the presence of only a few people.

[52] For Moroccan marriage legislation I use the Dutch translation of the *Mudawwana* by Berger and Kaldenhoven: *De Mudawwanah: Marokkaans wetboek inzake personen-, familie- en erfrecht*. For more information concerning Moroccan marriage law, see among others Buskens, *Islamitisch recht en familiebetrekkingen in Marokko*, and idem, "De recente hervorming van het Marokkaanse familierecht"; Jordens-Cotran, "Het Marokkaanse huwelijks- en het Nederlandse internationaal huwelijksrecht (I): De verloving of khitba", idem, "Het Marokkaanse huwelijks- en het Nederlandse internationaal huwelijksrecht (II): De verloving in het Nederlandse internationaal familierecht", and idem, "Enkele wijzigingen van de Marokkaanse familiewetgeving"; *De wenselijkheid van een bilateraal verdrag tussen Marokko en Nederland over conflicten aangaande het Internationaal Familierecht*, especially the contribution of Boele-Woelki, "Bipatridie in het Nederlandse Internationaal Huwelijks- en Echtscheidingsrecht en de gevolgen daarop van een eventueel bilateraal verdrag met Marokko".

[53] For a discussion of these changes, see Buskens, "De recente hervorming van het Marokkaanse familierecht", and idem, *Islamitisch recht en familiebetrekkingen in Marokko*, 74–75 and 77–82.

appointed by the Minister of Justice—at the meeting. These officials issue a written report of the proceedings and are charged with drawing up a marriage certificate.[54] This certificate, signed by the *ᶜudûl* and homologated by the *qâḍî*,[55] is registered in the court's marriage register and a copy of it is sent to the Registry Office.[56] This illustrates how the presence of two witnesses, a condition for the validity of marriage under Islamic law, has been incorporated and formalized in present-day Moroccan family law. The viewpoint of the Malikites that, if a long time elapses between marriage conclusion and its consummation, the presence of witnesses is required not at the conclusion of a marriage but when the bride leaves her parental home to start married life, is not reflected in the *Mudawwana*.

According to the *Mudawwana*, the minimum age for marriage is eighteen for a man and fifteen for a woman.[57] In keeping with Malikite law concerning guardianship, a bride's personal consent at the meeting has no legal validity. She must be represented by a *walî* at the conclusion of her marriage. However, since the 1993 revision, the *Mudawwana* requires the bride to sign an official register containing the details of the marriage agreement in evidence of her consent.[58] According to Léon Buskens's findings, this implies in practice that the bride briefly enters the room where the groom, the *walî*, and the *ᶜudûl* are gathered to make her consent known to the *ᶜudûl* and to sign the register.[59] The documentary film *In het huis van mijn vader* by Al-Ouazzani shows a Moroccan bride attending the entire marriage ceremony including the exchange of offer and acceptance between groom and *walî*, but playing no active part in it.

Moreover, since 1993 a bride who has reached adulthood and whose father has died has had the right to conclude a marriage without the intermediation of a guardian. Another effect of the 1993 revision has been to rescind the right of *jabr*, the right of the father to compel his daughter to marry.

[54] Buskens, *Islamitisch recht en familiebetrekkingen in Marokko*, 290.

[55] Concerning the role of the *qâḍî*, see Buskens, *Islamitisch recht en familiebetrekkingen in Marokko*, 249. The *qâḍî* is appointed to supervise the *ᶜudûl* in his jurisdiction. His supervision consists of homologation of deeds written by the *ᶜudûl*, his involvement in its registration and his inspection of the offices of the *ᶜudûl*. In present-day Morocco separate *qâḍî*s are appointed for the administration of justice and the supervision of *ᶜudûl*, according to Buskens, ibid., 268. For more information on the *khiṭâb* or homologation by a *qâḍî*, see ibid., 262–276.

[56] For administrative formalities, see the *Mudawwana*, articles 41–43.

[57] *De Mudawwanah: Marokkaans wetboek inzake personen-, familie- en erfrecht*, 34–35.

[58] Buskens, "De recente hervorming van het Marokkaanse familierecht", 65.

[59] Ibid., 66.

The terms *mahr* and *ṣadâq* (bridal gift) are used interchangeably in the *Mudawwana*.[60] Consistent with the Malikite viewpoint, Moroccan marriage legislation deems mention of the composition and the amount of the bridal gift during the meeting (*majlis*) an essential condition for the validity of a marriage.[61] It is permitted to prepay all or part of the bridal gift during the *majlis* or to postpone payment. The bridal gift must be settled in a lump sum or partly on the consummation and is claimable in its entirety upon death or upon consummation.[62] Moroccan law fixes neither a lower nor an upper limit to the bridal gift.[63]

Consummation of marriage or the wife's invitation to it obliges a husband to provide for his wife's living. The *nafaqa* consists of housing, food, clothing, and nursing.[64] The 1993 revision of the *Mudawwana* determines the extent of the *nafaqa* more precisely, relating the *nafaqa* among other things to the husband's income and the level of consumer prices.[65]

Half of the Moroccans living in the Netherlands have only Moroccan nationality and marriages among them normally take place either at the Moroccan consulate in the Netherlands or in Morocco. Since these marriages are concluded in accordance with the *Mudawwana*, and consequently to a large extent also in accordance with Malikite prescriptions, there is no need of a religious wedding alongside a civil wedding, as there is among Surinamese people in the Netherlands and Turkish people both in Turkey and the Netherlands.

If one of or both the prospective spouses have Dutch nationality, Dutch registrars possess the exclusive power to conclude a marriage between them. To have a marriage concluded by a registrar in the Netherlands recognized in Morocco, as is required if the couple intends to visit Morocco together as husband and wife, they must undergo a consulate marriage as well. Although the number of Moroccans who have dual nationality has increased in the last few years, I came across no marriages between Moroccans concluded before a Dutch registrar in my fieldwork.

At the Moroccan consulate in the Netherlands the stipulations of the *Mudawwana* are not always strictly followed. One respondent, for example, married at the consulate in the presence of both partners' parents

[60] *De Mudawwanah: Marokkaans wetboek inzake personen-, familie en erfrecht*, 38.
[61] See the *Mudawwana*, article 5, subsection 3.
[62] Ibid., article 20.
[63] Ibid., article 17, subsection 2.
[64] Ibid., article 117.
[65] Buskens, "De recente hervorming van het Marokkaanse familierecht", 82.

and only one consular official, and thus without the two *ᶜudûl* required by the *Mudawwana*. The bride was asked if she agreed with the amount of bridal gift; subsequently the intending husband and wife merely signed a form, without the groom and the *walî* explicitly having had to exchange the *ijâb* and *qabûl* beforehand. This practice is in all likelihood exceptional and, according to my respondents, would certainly not occur in Morocco.

In the Netherlands as well as in Morocco, the marriage festivities take place mostly two to six months after the conclusion of a marriage contract.[66] A marriage conclusion in accordance with Moroccan family law is in the view of my respondents required on the grounds of the religious character of the ceremony. Nonetheless, the moment at which people believe that the marriage has come into being is when the wedding celebrations and the consummation of marriage have taken place. It is only after the festivities, and not immediately after the consulate marriage or a wedding before the *ᶜudûl* in Morocco, that a couple starts to live together. Whereas the number of people attending a marriage conclusion is usually small, many guests are invited to the wedding party. The wedding party thus contributes to making the marriage public.[67]

Turkish Marriage Legislation and Its Influence on the Marriage Practice of Turks

In 1926 the Turkish Civil Code—adopted with few changes from the Swiss Civil Code—came into force. Among other things, this abolished polygamy. Article 93 stipulates that before being allowed to marry a second time, one must prove the dissolution of any earlier marriage. The

[66] Rude Antoine, *Le Mariage maghrébin en France*, 66, presents similar evidence with regard to the Moroccans living in France.

[67] Cf. Mir-Hosseini, *Marriage on Trial: A Study of Islamic Family Law*, 175: "In social practice there are two phases to a marriage, both intertwined with the Shariᶜa rules. The first phase is known, both in Iran and Morocco, as *ᶜaqd* (literally, contract); it consists of a small ceremony during which the marriage contract is drawn up. The second phase is the wedding celebration, known as *ᶜurs* in Morocco and *ᶜarusi* in Iran. It marks the social recognition of the contract made during the first stage, allowing the consummation of the marriage and the establishment of a marital home. . . . The distinction between these two stages, especially the time interval, was clear-cut until recently. Now they seem to be in the process of amalgamation, especially among the middle classes. The *ᶜaqd* is often conducted in the afternoon, in the presence of the notaries; and the wedding celebration in the evening. This is more evident in Iran, where the *ᶜaqd* is acquiring more importance at the expense of the *ᶜarusi* stage, whereas in Morocco the *ᶜurs* stage is still associated with the public announcement of the union, giving it social legitimacy."

introduction of the Turkish Civil Code also instituted the *resmî nikâh*, or civil wedding before a registrar, alongside the *imam nikâhı*, or marriage in accordance with Islamic prescriptions in the presence of an imam or a *hoca*. Turkish law thus distinguishes a civil wedding from a religious wedding. It stipulates moreover that the *imam nikâhı*, if concluded, must take place after the *resmî nikâh*.[68]

The introduction of the *resmî nikâh* in Turkey has met with severe difficulties. According to statistics of the Turkish Ministry of the Interior, 15% of marriages in 1988 took place before an imam only.[69] In response, the Turkish government on several occasions issued regulations promoting the registration of nonmarital bonds as marriages, most recently in 1991, aiming particularly to register marriages that had been concluded before an imam only.[70]

The preference of many Turks for an *imam nikâhı* and their unwillingness to conclude a *resmî nikâh* have been officially attributed chiefly to the complexity of civil wedding procedures and the high minimum age of marriage stipulated for the *resmî nikâh*.[71] The Turkish government

[68] For the text of Turkish marriage law, I use the German translation by Bergmann & Ferid, *Internationales Ehe- und Kindschaftsrecht*, s.v. "Türkei". For more information on Turkish marriage legislation, see Öztan, "Das türkische Familienrecht unter besonderer Berücksichtigung der Familienrechtsnovelle"; Örücü, "Turkish Family Law: A New Phase"; Nicolasen, "Gewijzigd Turks familierecht"; Ansay, "Die Eheschliessung der Türken in der Bundesrepublik Deutschland"; Krüger, "Änderungen im türkischen Familienrecht", and idem, "Grundzüge des türkischen Verlöbnisrechts"; Zevkliler, "Die neuen Formvorschriften im türkischen Eheschließungsrecht".

[69] Öztan, "Das türkische Familienrecht unter besonderer Berücksichtigung der Familienrechtsnovelle", 30. Tekeli, "Introduction: Women in Turkey in the 1980s", 19 nn. 4 and 19, presents data gathered by PIAR Marketing Research between 1985 and 1989. In 1987, 78.6% of the population indicated that both a civil and a religious ceremony are required, 17.6% that a civil ceremony suffices, and 3% that a religious ceremony suffices. Kulu Glasgow, "Het huwelijk in Turkije", presents yet other figures: 10% of the Turkish population performs a civil wedding only, 8% perform marriages before an imam only, and 80% of the population perform a civil and a religious ceremony. In Eastern Turkey, however, the latter percentage is much lower (66%); 20% of the population in this region performs only a religious ceremony.

[70] Ansay & Krüger, "Gesetz Nr. 3716 vom 8. 5. 1991 über die Registrierung von außerehelichen Verbindungen als Ehen und von nichtehelich geborenen Kindern als eheliche Kinder", 87, n. 2: "Im türkischen Text 'birleşme' (= Verbindung); gemeint sind alle außerehelichen Gemeinschaften; vornehmlich die durch sog. Imam-Ehen begründeten Gemeinschaften, die zivilrechtlich Nichtehen sind."

[71] See for example Jäschke, "Die 'Imam-Ehe' in der Türkei", 187–193, especially 187–188: "Nach der Begründung zu dem Gezetz von 1945 gibt es für die 'ehelosen Verbindungen' (*nikâhsız birleşmeler*) juristische, verwaltungsmässige, gesellschaftliche und wirtschaftliche Gründe, die aber alle von dem Kultur- und Niveau-Problem des Einflusses einer alten Gewohnheit überragt werden", an argument which he further elaborates

therefore simplified the procedures that seemed to form a hindrance to the conclusion of *resmî nikâh*, making adjustments among other things in the field of the marriage announcement and no longer requiring the future husband and wife to submit a medical certificate before marriage.[72]

Şeriat law, which applied before the introduction of the Turkish Civil Code, stipulated no minimum age for marriage. When the Civil Code came into force, it was common for marriages to proceed even if the spouses had not reached the required age. Sometimes, the spouses' birth dates would be antedated. This practice prompted the Turkish legislative authorities in 1938 to reduce the minimum age for marriage from eighteen to seventeen for men and from seventeen to fifteen for women.[73]

Articles 97–111 of the Turkish Civil Code deal with marriage announcement and conclusion. The conclusion of a *resmî nikâh* must take place before the mayor, his representative, or the municipal chairman (*muhtar*) in the presence of two witnesses, men or women of at least eighteen years of age. The bride and groom must attend the ceremony in person and simultaneously; a guardian cannot attend in their place. The presiding official enters the marriages in a marriage register and sends a written acknowledgement to the *nüfus* register (which also registers births and deaths). The couple receives an authenticated marriage certificate. The conclusion of the *imam nikâhı* may take place only when the newlyweds are able to present this certificate.

The bridal gift is not established in the Turkish Civil Code and consequently does not feature in the *resmî nikâh*. The settlement of a bridal gift normally forms part of the conclusion of an *imam nikâhı*, but as such it is not statutorily guaranteed. The rule is that, if no marriage settlement is made beforehand with regard to property, the couple have no community of property.[74]

Articles 151–169 deal with marriage effects. The husband is stipulated to be the head of the family. He determines their place of residence and makes suitable provision for his wife's and children's living. A wife

by means of eight points. See also Öztan, "Das türkische Familienrecht unter besonderer Berücksichtigung der Familienrechtsnovelle", 30: "Seit dem Inkrafttreten des tZGB gibt es ernsthafte Bemühungen, die Imam-Ehe abzuschaffen und zurückzudrängen. Nach den wenigen bislang durchgeführten Untersuchungen sind es insbesondere die genannten Formalitäten, die eine Eheschließung nach dem geltenden Recht erschweren."

[72] Öztan, "Das türkische Familienrecht unter besonderer Berücksichtigung der Familienrechtsnovelle", 32

[73] Turkish Civil Code, article 88, and Öztan, "Das türkische Familienrecht unter besonderer Berücksichtigung der Familienrechtsnovelle", 28.

[74] Turkish Civil Code, article 170.

must advise her husband and assist him to keep the marriage thriving. She uses his family name and is in charge of the housekeeping. A bill revising these articles was defeated in 1984, but it was ruled in 1990 that a woman no longer needs the permission of her husband to follow a profession.[75]

The number of people attending a civil marriage ceremony in Turkey may vary from a few family members to a hundred or so guests, who, as Nancy Tapper describes, customarily receive perfume and sweets after the ceremony.[76] One Turkish respondent married at a registry office in Turkey four days after the wedding party. The civil ceremony had to be held at their parents' place of birth, some distance away. Because of the distance, they travelled with only a few family members. Their parents did not attend the civil ceremony, which probably indicates that they did not consider this ceremony important from a religious and social point of view. The bride did not wear a white bridal gown. Most brides wear white, if many guests are expected to attend the *resmî nikâh*.[77]

It is not usual for a Turkish bride to be dressed in white at a consulate marriage in the Netherlands. The number of people attending the civil ceremony at the Turkish consulate in the Netherlands is often smaller than at a *resmî nikâh* in Turkey. A Turkish bridal couple went to the consulate with about 25 people, a number larger than that attending most such ceremonies. The consulate was unprepared for such a large number. The guests added some chairs in a row facing the table and chairs for the bride and groom. After the ceremony the couple presented sweets to the guests, as is customary in Turkey. The family thus attempted to recreate the atmosphere of the ceremony which they had experienced in Turkey. However, they were somewhat disappointed at the informal and haphazard character of the ceremony; the bridal couple was amazed to be asked to act as witnesses for the couple marrying after them.

The *imam nikâhı* often takes place in the presence of only a few people and normally takes no longer than five or ten minutes. Besides the exchange of consent and the settlement of the bridal gift, it may consist of *duᶜâ'* and Koran recitation. Both the future husband and wife may be asked to give their consent three times and a written document may be drawn up. Some couples expected that at the conclusion of the *imam nikâhı* they would have to answer questions about the credo, the pillars of

[75] Öztan, "Das türkische Familienrecht unter besonderer Berücksichtigung der Familienrechtsnovelle", 37.

[76] Tapper, "'Traditional' and 'Modern' Wedding Rituals in a Turkish Town", 151.

[77] Ibid., 147.

Islam or the thirty-two obligations, but this often turned out not to be the case. Some respondents explained this by saying that the *hoca* is considerate of the bride's shyness. The *imam nikâhı* may take place at the bride's or at the groom's home, or on the premises of a mosque. One bridal couple for example went to the mosque shortly before their wedding party.

Though Turkish law stipulates that the civil wedding ceremony must precede the religious ceremony, this precept is not strictly followed either in the Netherlands or in Turkey. The interests and meanings attached to each of these ceremonies seem to determine the order in which they are held and the number of people attending. Some Turkish respondents performed the *imam nikâhı* in a very early phase of their acquaintanceship, long before the *resmî nikâh*. Others performed the *imam nikâhı* several times and more or less in secret, mostly before the conclusion of the *resmî nikâh*. Yet another group of Turkish respondents concluded the *imam nikâhı* after the *resmî nikâh*, and not always in a small circle. These three possibilities will now be discussed.

Holding to a stricter religious point of view concerning sexual segregation, a number of Turkish respondents, particularly those associated with the *Milli Görüş*, favoured concluding an *imam nikâhı* shortly after the acceptance of a marriage proposal. Referring to the *ḥadîth*, "When a man and woman who are not married to each other isolate themselves, the devil will be their partner", they argued that a boy and a girl are not allowed to talk with one another until they have married and therefore the *imam nikâhı* must be planned in an early phase of their acquaintance to legalize their relationship. One Turkish respondent for example spoke with her future husband only once for forty-five minutes in the presence of her mother before the *imam nikâhı*. This pattern of behaviour seems to be characteristic of the Dutch context in particular, for the same respondents of the *Milli Görüş* indicated that it is unusual in Turkey to conclude the *imam nikâhı* as early as the acceptance of the marriage proposal (*söz*) or the engagement (*nişan*).

It is noteworthy that this stricter view concerning sexual segregation has no consequences for the bride's presence at the conclusion of the *imam nikâhı*. Like the majority of the Turkish brides, the *Milli Görüş* brides gave their consent in person, not being represented by a *vekil* (i.e. *walî*) at the conclusion of the *imam nikâhı*. Some Turkish brides among my respondents were represented by their father at the marriage conclusion, because of discipline or because of the presence of men, but these women did not belong to the *Milli Görüş*.

It also occurred in my sample that the conclusion of the *imam nikâhı* took place several times and more or less in secret for protection against evil influences. One Turkish respondent for example performed the *imam nikâhı* three times: the first time at the engagement, the second time two weeks before the wedding when the two families went shopping together, and the third time shortly before the wedding night. In this case the *resmî nikâh* took place only after the wedding celebrations. This couple explained their behaviour from the fact that a person attending the *imam nikâhı* may cause the breakdown of the marriage by, for example, keeping his or her fingers crossed: "One knot is enough for an unsuccessful marriage". To make sure that their marital bond would hold securely, they repeated the religious ceremony twice. They also minimized risks by not announcing the ceremony and by allowing only a few people to attend. As a result it occurred that for example only an imam and three or four family members attend the couple's exchange of consent.

The repetition of the *imam nikâhı* and the secrecy observed on these occasions harmonizes strikingly with the stricter view of the Hanafites concerning the moment at which the meeting (*majlis*) is over. We have seen that this law school argues explicitly that the *majlis* comes to an end when one of the parties makes a remark unconnected with the offer or when one of the parties assumes a different posture, thereby suggesting that the offer is withdrawn or rejected. However, no Turkish respondent mentioned the Hanafite viewpoint in explanation of this pattern of behaviour. They instead explained it on the basis of a fear of evil influences.

Besides the official explanations mentioned above for the unwillingness of a substantial part of the Turkish population to conclude a *resmî nikâh*—complexity of procedures and an excessively high minimum age for marriage—the fear of evil influences is also cited in explanation of the existing preference for an *imam nikâhı*. As Gotthard Jäschke found:

> Allerdings scheint ein grosser Teil der Landbevölkerung nur darum an der Imam-Ehe festzuhalten, weil sie an die wundertätige Kraft (*baraka*, *bereket*) der Einleitungsworte (*hutbe*) und der Schlussgebetes (*dua*) glauben when nicht sogar krasser Aberglaube . . . wie z.B. Abwehr von Zauber (Knoten im Taschentuch usw.) dabei mitspielt.[78]

Jäschke's explanation for the popularity of the *imam nikâhı* to the neglect of the *resmî nikâh* on the basis of the salutary influence of sermon and prayers is not entirely convincing, because it does not

[78] Jäschke, "Die 'Imam-Ehe' in der Türkei", 192.

account for the fact that many couples omit to perform the latter ceremony. Similarly, neither ignorance nor backwardness of the Turkish population can fully account for the great number of marriages concluded before an imam only.[79] The reference to knots in handkerchiefs, bearing a strong resemblance to my findings, may nevertheless indicate that the fear of evil influences plays a role in the marriage practice of Turks in Turkey.

Another possible explanation of the secrecy observed at the *imam nikâhı* is the introduction of secular family law in Turkey, though my Turkish respondents did not mention this explanation either. According to this line of thinking, the *imam nikâhı* has remained the only accepted form of marriage in the eyes of the majority of the Turkish population since the introduction of secular family law, but many henceforth held the religious ceremony in secret for fear of punishment. The *resmî nikâh* has eventually become accepted, but the custom of concluding an *imam nikâhı* in secret remained.

An inquiry established by the Turkish Ministery of Justice in 1942 into the reasons for the preference for imam marriages presents some evidence for this assumption. An interviewee says: "Es ist nicht recht, die Türken einer Freiheit zu berauben, die die Juden, Armenier und Griechen geniessen, oder sie zu heimlichen Handlungen zu veranlassen."[80] Krüger says that "Weite Teile der Bevölkerung—insbesondere auf dem Lande und in den Kleinstädten—leisten seit Jahrzehnten offenkundig *passiven* Widerstand gegen das rezipierte Familienrecht",[81] without further elucidating the nature of this opposition. Similarly, Bergmann and Ferid state: "Der Abschaffung der Mehrehe und insbesondere die Einführung der Zivilehe, dh der nichtreligiösen Eheschließung vor dem staatlichen Zivilstandsbeamten, wurden nicht gänzlich vom Volk und dem Islam verhafteten Kreisen angenommen."[82] This probably also explains why particularly people associated with the *Milli Görüş* prefer to conclude the *imam nikâhı* in a very early phase of their relationship, long before the *resmî nikâh*.

[79] Dirks, *La Famille musulmane turque*, 76, regards ignorance as the primary cause for the preference for an *imam nikâhı*: "Il y a diverses raisons à cette persistance de l'ancien usage à la campagne. L'ignorance en est presque toujours la cause première: le paysan qui se marie selon la tradition croit s'être conformé aux formalités obligatoires et ne se considère pas coupable."

[80] Jäschke, "Die 'Imam-Ehe' in der Türkei", 200.

[81] Krüger, "Fragen des Familienrechts", 288.

[82] Bergmann & Ferid, *Internationales Ehe- und Kindschaftsrecht*, s.v. "Türkei", 116. Lieferung, 11.

The religious ceremony does not always take place in secret. Several couples in my sample held an *imam nikâhı* in the presence of about twenty people. One bridal couple holding an *imam nikâhı* at home sat with their parents and the imam in one room, while the rest of the company witnessed the ceremony from the adjoining room separated by connecting sliding doors. At the end of the ceremony the bridal couple went round kissing the hands of those attending the ceremony. The ceremony thus did not have a secret character.

The time of the conclusion of the *imam nikâhı* varies in these cases from two months before the wedding party to shortly before or after the wedding party. One couple held an *imam nikâhı* at home immediately after the *resmî nikâh* at the consulate. The conclusion of the *resmî nikâh* moreover seems to have become more important for these respondents. "Marriage at the consulate is more important, because then you have to sign", one explained. The importance attached to *resmî nikâh* also showed itself in the fact that in the majority of these cases comparatively many people attended this ceremony at the consulate.

Surinamese Marriage Legislation and Its Influence on the Marriage Practice of Surinamese

The marriage regulations concerning Muslims (*Huwelijksbesluit Mohammedanen*) and Hindus (*Huwelijksbesluit Hindoes*) came into force in Surinam in 1941 on the initiative of governor Johannes Coenraad Kielstra. These regulations were passed in response to the then current Muslim and Hindu practice of contracting marriages only before a religious leader and not before a registrar. The Surinamese Civil Code did not recognize these marriages and the children born from them were thus considered illegitimate. The *Huwelijksbesluit Mohammedanen* recognized marriages contracted in accordance with Islamic law on condition that certain rules were followed. These prescribed for example that the religious ceremony take place before an officially registered religious leader, who is responsible for the registration of marriages contracted before him.[83]

[83] For the text of Surinamese marriage law I use Zevenbergen, *De Surinaamse huwelijkswetgeving in historisch en maatschappelijk perspectief*, appendices B and D. For more information on Surinamese marriage legislation, see Prins, "Een Surinaams rechtsgeding over een moslimse verstoting", and idem, "Twintig jaar praktijk van de Aziatische huwelijkswetgeving in Suriname"; Adhin, "Surinamisering van het huwelijksrecht", and idem, "Ontstaan en ontwikkeling van de z.g. Aziatische huwelijkswetgeving"; Buschkens & Zevenbergen, "Surinaams huwelijksrecht: streven naar eenheid in verscheidenheid"; Hoefnagels, "Huwelijks- en concubinaatsvormen in Suriname"; Oedayrajsingh Varma & Ahmad Ali, *Surinaams familierecht*; Kraan, *Hoofdlijnen van het Surinaamse huwelijksvermogensrecht*.

A revision of Surinamese marriage law proposed in 1973 was intended to offer every Surinamese citizen, and not only Hindus and Muslims, the choice between a civil marriage before a registrar and a religious marriage before a *huwelijksbeambte*, a member of a religious community who is authorized by the state to conclude such a marriage.[84] This revision was also intended to harmonize the Surinamese Civil Code and the marriage regulations concerning Muslims and Hindus regarding the minimum age for marriage. It would have the effect of raising the minimum age for marriage for Muslims.[85] This proposed revision never came into force, and the *Huwelijksbesluit Mohammedanen* still applies in Surinam to marriages among Muslims.[86]

The *Huwelijksbesluit Mohammedanen* does not regulate marriage law exhaustively. Where it does not explicitly amend the Surinamese Civil Code, the latter is deemed to apply.[87] What precisely a marriage in accordance with the teachings of Islam requires regarding witnesses, guardianship, and the bridal gift is not elucidated in the regulations. This implies that the *huwelijksbeambte* determines the contents and course of the religious ceremony. Much of the legal practice of these marriages is consequently unknown.

The *Huwelijksbesluit Mohammedanen* bar men under the age of fifteen and women under the age of thirteen from marriage. Under the Surinamese Civil Code the minimum age of marriage is eighteen for men and fifteen for women; under the 1973 revision, which never came into force, the minimum age is seventeen for men and fifteen for women.[88]

Thus in Surinam the *Huwelijksbesluit Mohammedanen* made it legally possible to conclude a marriage in accordance with Islamic law that is

[84] Zevenbergen, *De Surinaamse huwelijkswetgeving in historisch en maatschappelijk perspectief*, 99–101.

[85] Oedayrajsingh Varma & Ahmad Ali, *Surinaams familierecht*, 35.

[86] Tweede Kamer der Staten-Generaal, vergaderjaar 1995–1996, 24709, no. 3, 4. Zevenbergen, *De Surinaamse huwelijkswetgeving in historisch en maatschappelijk perspectief*, 99, suggests a number of explanations for the fact that this revision still had not come into force at the end of the 1970s, even though the Colonial Government had adopted this law in 1973. The reasons that he suggests, such as the absence of implementing orders and of the definite results of the proceedings of the legislative committee, are not convincing because today, more than twenty years after its adoption, still nothing has changed in this respect. The marriage regulations concerning Muslims and Hindus and a substantial number of articles of the Surinamese Civil Code will expire when the 1973 revision comes into force.

[87] Oedayrajsingh Varma & Ahmad Ali, *Surinaams familierecht*, 29.

[88] Kraan, *Hoofdlijnen van het Surinaamse huwelijksvermogensrecht*, 61.

on certain conditions valid under the Surinamese Civil Code too. Things are otherwise in the Netherlands, where the conclusion of marriages in accordance with the teachings of Islam is not accepted as valid under Dutch law. If either or both partners have Dutch nationality, as is mostly the case among the Surinamese in the Netherlands, the bridal couple must conclude a civil marriage before a Dutch registrar at a town hall in order to be legally married.

In practice most Surinamese Hindustani couples in the Netherlands consequently conclude the marriage twice, once in an Islamic manner and once before a Dutch registrar at a town hall. Some couples hold a wedding party including a religious ceremony (*nikah*) to legalize their relations from a religious point of view, thus allowing cohabitation, but postpone the civil ceremony for some time, for example for financial reasons.

Among my Surinamese Hindustani respondents, as among my Turkish respondents, the order in which the religious and the civil ceremony should be held turned out to be a point of discussion. If they hold both ceremonies, some couples opt to hold the religious ceremony (*nikah*) at the bride's home just before the civil ceremony at the town hall. Such couples argue that if the bride and groom are not yet married they are not allowed to sit next to each other, as occurs at the civil ceremony. Only when the *nikah*, the religious ceremony, has taken place, are they allowed to do so. Other couples hold the *nikah* at the beginning of the wedding party. If such couples also hold a civil ceremony, this mostly takes place a day or so earlier.

On the occasion of the religious ceremony (*nikah*), a Surinamese Hindustani bride is normally dressed in a *silwar*, a knee-length top complemented with loose trousers, or a *sari*, a cloth swathed around the body; the groom normally wears a high-necked suit without a lapel and a *pagri* on his head with or without garlands before his face. Some respondents took the view that it is reprehensible to decorate the *pagri* with garlands because this custom was adopted from the Hindus. If the *nikah* takes place at the beginning of the wedding party, the bride and groom will change clothes at the end of the ceremony. At the civil ceremony and at the wedding party the bride will be wearing her white bridal gown and the groom will change his high-necked suit for a suit with a lapel and will remove his *pagri*.

Wherever the religious ceremony takes place, at the bride's home or in a hall, the bride and her family await the arrival of the groom and his family. Thus, if the *nikah* is held in a hall at the beginning of the wedding party, the bride and her family will be the first to arrive. The groom and his family announce their arrival by letting off fireworks in the street outside the hall. Thereupon men of the bride's family go out towards the groom and his family to welcome them. Women of the bride's family welcome the groom into the hall by offering him a drink, called *sharbat* or *paan*. According to some respondents, *paan* is not a drink but a kind of chewing tobacco which may also be offered on this occasion. This corresponds with Speckmann's findings concerning the marriage of Hindustani Muslims in Surinam: "Before the bridegroom sits down he is presented with sweetened water, betel leaves and some money by the female members of the bride's family."[89]

Both male and female guests attend the religious ceremony if it takes place at the beginning of a wedding party in a hall. However only men —including the groom, religious leaders, called *mawlana* or *mijadji*, the fathers of the bride and groom, other male family members, and male witnesses—sit at a table that is placed in the front of the hall. If the *nikah* takes place at the bride's home a day or so before the wedding party, the ceremony is attended only by the men of the two families, who also sit together at a table prepared for the meal immediately following the religious ceremony.

A Surinamese Hindustani bride gives her consent in person but not in the presence of all the guests. During the entire ceremony the bride stays in a separate room. At the beginning of the religious ceremony two witnesses (*gawah*s), mostly one from the bride's and one from the groom's side, are officially appointed. It is agreed who will ask the bride's and groom's consent. This honourable job of *wakil* or representative is not necessarily fulfilled by the imam. Instead, a family member of the groom for example may be appointed to ask the bride's consent. If such is the case the imam stays with the groom while the *wakil* asks the bride for her consent. Sometimes, the imam asks the groom for his consent at that moment, but mostly he awaits the return of the *wakil* before opening the official part of the religious ceremony.

The *wakil* accompanied by the witnesses invites the bride to profess her faith by saying or repeating the *kalma*s, the main articles of faith, or only the first *kalma*, that is the *shahâda*.[90] She is then asked to give her consent to marriage three times, to make sure that her agreement is genuine. Finally the bride mentions the amount of the bridal gift to be paid by

[89] Speckmann, *Marriage and Kinship among the Indians in Surinam*, 147.

[90] The Stichting Lalla Rookh, *Huwelijk, geboorte en overlijden bij moslims*, 12, reports to the contrary that the bride and groom sometimes still pronounce the *kalma*s at the religious ceremony (*nikah*), even though this occurs increasingly rarely. From this it may be inferred that the importance of reciting the *kalma*s has again increased in the last ten years.

the groom. Once, when I attended this part of the ceremony in the bride's room, there was some confusion about the significance of the proceedings. When the *mawlana* left for the official part of the ceremony after having gained the bride's consent, the bride wondered, "Am I married now?"[91]

The *wakil* and the two *gawah*s return to the groom's room where the official part of the ceremony begins. This part, taking about thirty minutes, normally consists of Koran recitation, a sermon, *du*ᶜ*a'*, and sometimes also the singing of *milaad* (religious songs). In the course of this ceremony the groom too repeats the *kalma*s or only the first *kalma*. Some of my Surinamese Hindustani respondents explained the great importance attached to the recitation of the *kalma*s on this occasion by referring to the fifth *kalma* where the believer asks for God's remission of sins known and unknown. The recitation of this *kalma* thus enables the bridal couple to start married life with a clean slate. The groom then too expresses his consent to marriage three times. He gives his assent to the amount of *mahar*, or bridal gift, requested by the bride. His witness will immediately hand over the *mahar* in cash to the bride.

As we have seen, the order in which the *walî* of the bride and the intended husband express their consent to marriage is generally deemed to be of no importance according to Islamic law, the first being called *ijâb* and the second *qabûl*. According to my Surinamese Hindustani respondents, however, the *wakil* is the one who makes the offer (*ijâb*) both to bride and groom, and the spouses put forward their acceptance (*qabûl*) of the offer.

The *mawlana* continues by giving official notice of the marriage, announcing among other things the names of the partners and the amount of bridal gift agreed earlier. This may be followed by a sermon delivered by the *mawlana* or *mijadji* about the rights and duties of the husband and wife.

In most cases the ceremony is carried out in Urdu, although Surinamese Hindustani Muslims seem increasingly to prefer to use the Dutch language because many young persons of their community do not understand Urdu. One respondent stressed that before the groom starts to repeat the *kalma*s and to express his consent, he should be informed

[91] The findings of Speckmann, *Marriage and Kinship among the Indians in Surinam*, 147, deviate in certain respects from what is described here. According to Speckmann, the bride is not asked to recite the *kalmas*. In her presence only prayers are said constituting a kind of 'act of contrition'. Moreover, according to his findings, the witnesses together with the father of the bride, in his capacity as *walî* and not as *wakil*, ask the bride to give her consent to marriage.

about the rights and duties of marriage. He therefore argued that the ceremony must begin with a sermon in Urdu or Dutch concerning the rights and duties of husband and wife. Only then should the groom be asked to repeat the *kalmas* and to consent. In these cases a sermon in Arabic, being a short version of the sermon delivered earlier in Urdu or Dutch, and a *duᶜa'* may conclude the ceremony.

If the ceremony is held at the bride's home, normally the marriage conclusion takes place only in the presence of male members of both families. Women of the groom's family usually remain at their home. As soon as the religious ceremony is over, the bride's family present the groom and male members of both families with a meal. In a hall, by contrast, sweets may be presented at the end of the religious ceremony to all those attending.[92] In this case the groom and male members also partake of a meal together, but not until the end of the evening when all guests have been offered a meal.

The Bridal Gift

What form does the bridal gift (*mahr*, *ṣadâq*, *mihir* or *dain mahar*) take? Who pays for the wedding rings? Who pays for the wedding party? These are matters for negotiation between the two families shortly before or after the acceptance of a proposal. Nowadays it is the view and practice that the bridal gift comes into the possession of the bride and not, as often occurred in earlier times, of her family. It may be argued that, for all the social provisions and the relative prosperity of the Netherlands, the bridal gift is a form of social security for the bride in the event of divorce or the death of her husband. The ever-increasing amount of the bridal gift gives rise to discussions. People may ask ironically whether the bride was made of gold, and the amount of the bridal gifts may prompt imams in their Friday sermons to exhort people to make marriage conclusion easy and to be moderate in their demands concerning the bridal gift. Some people consequently opt for a token payment; in other cases the amount of the bridal gift is related to expenses connected with marriage, such as the cost of the wedding party, the furnishing of the couple's future home, the gold and other presents given to the bride and her family, and the trousseau that the bride

[92] Speckmann, *Marriage and Kinship among the Indians in Surinam*, 148, presents similar evidence concerning the Surinamese Hindustani Muslims in Surinam: "Finally, the *maulvi* leads the company in prayer, and afterwards gives a brief exposition of the marital duties of both parties. *Sew* or *gula*—a kind of doughnuts—are then offered to the guests."

brings into the marriage. However, there was no discussion among my respondents that a bridal gift must be given.

The contracting of a marriage under Moroccan family law requires the amount of the bridal gift to be specified. The husband is thus legally bound to pay the bridal gift. In contrast, the payment of the Surinamese Hindustani *mahar* and the Turkish *mihir* cannot be enforced by legal process. In the case of Turkish marriages the amount of the bridal gift may be mentioned only at the conclusion of *imam nikâhı*. The amount of the bridal gift may be put down in writing during the ceremony, which make one feel honour-bound to pay it. Nevertheless, its payment is not statutorily guaranteed because the bridal gift is not mentioned in the *resmî nikâh*. During the religious ceremony of Surinamese Hindustani marriages the bridal gift is also explicitly agreed. However, in Surinam, where such a marriage is recognized as legally valid, the bride has no legal means to demand payment if the groom fails to pay the agreed bridal gift.

In Turkish marriages, preference is given either to money (a sum of the order of *f*50,000 payable in the case of divorce), to gold or to a combination of forms (for instance an amount of gold, a sum of money for the furnishing of the future home, and an air ticket to Saudi Arabia enabling the intending wife to perform the *hajj*). The addition of the provision "payable in the case of divorce" was meant above all to discourage divorce, for the respondent concerned would not be able to gather a sum of this magnitude. The preference for gold is explained partly by worries concerning inflation affecting the Turkish lira. Other respondents preferred gold because they felt that a bridal gift consisting of money gives the bride the impression that she is being sold. The variety of views concerning the form of the bridal gift perhaps indicates that the meanings attached to its payment have gradually changed.

Moroccan respondents, generally giving greater preference to a bridal gift consisting of money, suggested that the sum should be between *f*500 and *f*10,000. However, related expenses were in many cases also drawn into the negotiations. The future husband is for instance expected to provide for the bridal gift and the furnishing of the couple's future home. However, if the bride receives a considerable sum as a bridal gift, she too is expected to invest in equipping their future home. In Meknes, for example, a girl who receives about *f*6,000 is also expected to provide for some larger items, such as a couch. A double-income couple may furnish their future home together. In these cases the bridal gift will often be lower, for example about *f*1,000.[93] The bridal gift may be used to increase the trousseau. The bride may for example spend her bridal gift on clothing (bridal dress, underwear, and so on) or on household goods: "blankets, glasses, and other things a man does not think about". Some respondents said that a Moroccan girl particularly in the Netherlands is encouraged to invest her bridal gift in gold.

Surinamese Hindustani respondents seem to prefer a token payment. Couples mentioned bridal gifts varying from *f*125.25 to *f*500 to be paid in cash during the religious ceremony itself. A gift from the future husband to his wife on their wedding day consisting of a suitcase containing clothes for dressing the bride from top to toe, such as a dress or two-piece suit, underwear, nightwear, shoes, a bag, a chain, a bracelet, earrings, a ring, and make-up, is sometimes also considered part of the bridal gift. One Surinamese Hindustani respondent emphasized however that the bridal gift consists only of money. The suitcase was in this case also considered to be part of the game "because it is a feast and you have to please on this occasion". But the suitcase was deliberately delivered to the bride's home on the day before the *nikah* to stress that it was not part of the bridal gift.

Many Surinamese Hindustani families in my sample reached agreement beforehand about the contents of the bridal gift,[94] relating this to the payment for the wedding party and wedding rings and the amount of money to be given to the groom at the wedding party. One couple for example agreed beforehand that the money that would be given to the groom before he sat down to dinner at the wedding party would be used for the honeymoon trip and to equip the couple's future home.

[93] For more information on the *ṣadâq* in Morocco, see Elaroussi, "Pratiques du mariage au Maroc", 123–126, and Naamane-Guessous, *Au-delà de toute pudeur*, 77–83.

[94] Speckmann, *Marriage and Kinship among the Indians in Surinam*, 147–148, also distinguishes the *mahar* from the gift consisting of clothing and indicates that the bridal gift may be agreed beforehand: "Meanwhile she has already received a gift from her future husband, consisting of several articles of clothing and ornaments. The bride is expected to ask the bridegroom a bride price (*mahar*), a sum of money to be named by herself, though often it has been agreed upon between the two families before the wedding takes place." Furthermore, he points out that, if the groom agrees to the *mahar* asked by the bride, "He may then immediately hand the sum of money involved to the *maulvi* who passes it on to the father of the bride. Often only one part of the money is given; but in any case the balance has to have been paid if the couple should subsequently get divorced." In the Netherlands it seems no longer to be common usage to pay the bridal gift in instalments as the *mahar* has become more or less a token payment. Moreover, the groom's witness immediately hands over the *mahar* to the bride and not to her father.

4.3. Marriage Festivities

When a marriage is contracted, a small festive gathering may be held, but most such celebrations are modest compared to the festivities that follow at a later time when a couple actually starts to live together. The latter festivities normally last two or three days and include a henna evening and a wedding party. Islamic law does not deal with these events in much detail, but nevertheless gives some information on the religious qualification of the festivities, their time and duration, and singing and dancing on this and similar occasions.

The term *walîma* refers to the meal that is organized on the occasion of a wedding (*ṭaᶜâm al-ᶜurs*). *ᶜUrs* or wedding relates to marriage contracting (*ᶜaqd*) as well as to marriage consummation (*dukhûl*). However, by *walîma al-ᶜurs* Islamic jurists mean particularly the meal that is organized on the occasion of marriage consummation (*dukhûl*). The meals held on other festive occasions bear other names, such as *ṭaᶜam al-imlâk*, upon contracting of marriage, and *'iᶜdhâr*, to celebrate a circumcision.[95]

According to the majority of the law schools, organizing a *walîma* on the occasion of marriage consummation is a fixed *sunna* (*sunna muᶜakkada*). Only the Malikites take the viewpoint that holding such a meal is recommendable (*mandûba*) but neither obligatory nor *sunna*.[96] According to the Malikites, the *walîma al-ᶜurs* must be held just before or just after marriage consummation. The Hanafites are of the same opinion and additionally hold the view that guests are welcome from the meal following the consummation to the next day. The Hanbalites take the view that the *walîma* may be held at any time from the moment at which the marriage is contracted to the termination of the wedding. According to them there is no objection to the common practice of holding the *walîma* shortly before marriage consummation. A *walîma* lasting longer than two days is in their view reprehensible (*makrûh*). The Shafiᶜites hold the opinion that the appropriate time for the *walîma al-ᶜurs* begins when a marriage is contracted, but that it should take place preferably after marriage consummation (*dukhûl*).[97]

In practice, both in the Netherlands and in the countries of origin, the wedding celebrations mostly took place before the wedding night and not after it. All the Surinamese Hindustani respondents whom I interviewed celebrated their marriage in the Netherlands. This also holds for

[95] Al-Jazîrî, *Al-fiqh ᶜalâ al-madhâhib al-arbaᶜa*, vol. 3, 32. See also Ibn Ṭûlûn, *Fass al-khawâtim fîmâ qîla fî al-walâ'im*, 39–40.

[96] Al-Jazîrî, *Al-fiqh ᶜalâ al-madhâhib al-arbaᶜa*, vol. 3, 32–33.

[97] Ibid., 33–34.

the majority of my Turkish respondents, whereas, according to the findings of Yerden, Turkish migrants in the Netherlands prefer to celebrate the marriage during holidays in Turkey to bring family members and friends together.[98] Half of my Moroccan respondents celebrated or intended to celebrate their marriage in Morocco. The choice to celebrate one's marriage in the country of origin depends firstly on the degree of closeness of the relations with the country of origin. One Turkish respondent, for example, preferred Turkey because her future husband and his family lived in Turkey. Another argument for choosing the country of origin is that certain services, commonly available in the country of origin, are less easy to come by in the Netherlands. This consideration is especially strong among Moroccan respondents, who preferred Morocco for this reason:

> The atmosphere there [i.e. in Morocco] is different. The hall is bigger, the bands are nicer and the celebrations take three days: the henna party with the next of kin, the big feast day and the day bride and groom come together. The *neggafa*s offer a lot more to choose from.[99] A marriage in Morocco may easily go on until seven o'clock in the morning.

In the Netherlands the festivities may last two or three days. In Surinamese Hindustani marriages a *nikah*, i.e. the religious ceremony of contracting a marriage, is held on these days either at the bride's home or in a hall or on the premises of a mosque. In the case of Turkish marriages an *imam nikâhı* is concluded either on these days or long before the actual wedding celebrations. Moroccan couples mostly contract their marriage at the Moroccan consulate two to six months before the festivities, and usually start to live together only after the wedding party.

In the following subsections the wedding celebrations will be described in four main phases: the religious gathering called *ṣadaqa* or *kitaab*; the henna party including the visit to the bathhouse; the wedding party; and the welcoming of the bride at the groom's home. My information on the wedding celebrations in the Netherlands is based largely on my fieldwork. Information on the countries of origin available from respondents is in the majority of cases more limited. Many Surinamese newlyweds for example were often unable to compare the Netherlands

[98] Yerden, *Trouwen op z'n Turks*, 97.

[99] A *neggafa* or dresser accompanies the bride during the wedding. Her services, for which she is paid, consist of helping the bride change her clothes during the wedding party and doing the bride's make-up. She brings with her attributes of all kinds such as bridal dresses and make-up but also litters on which to carry the bride around and present her to the wedding guests. At the henna party she may also paint the bride's hands and feet with henna.

to Surinam because they had grown up in the Netherlands and had visited Surinam only once.

The Ṣadaqa or Kitaab

Surinamese Hindustanis as well as Moroccans in the Netherlands may organize a gathering with a religious character on the occasion of a wedding. The Surinamese Hindustani and Moroccan respondents named such a gathering *kitaab* (or book, referring to the Koran recitation that may take place on this occasion) and *ṣadaqa* (or charitable gift) respectively. Turkish respondents mostly did not organize a religious gathering in the Netherlands before the wedding party. In Turkey, however, a wedding day may begin with a religious gathering consisting of the recitation of Süleyman Çelebi's *mevlüt* poem.[100]

In the case of Surinamese Hindustani marriages, a *kitaab* may be organized at the groom's home one or two days before the wedding party. The religious part of this gathering takes about an hour. Religious leaders (*mawlana*s and *mijadji*s) and family members who are closely associated with mosque activities may lead this ceremony. At a *kitaab* ceremony of Surinamese Hindustani Muslims that I attended, eight men who led the ceremony were sitting together at a table that was placed on one side of the living room. About twenty-six male and female guests of the groom's family attended the ceremony seated in rows facing the table.

The *kitaab* mostly consists of Koran recitation and the singing of *milaad* or *naath*.[101] The ceremony is concluded with a variation on a benediction named *Selaam*,[102] sung standing, and with the recitation of the opening sura of the Koran (*Al-Fâtiḥa*) and the saying of a prayer (*du*ᶜ*â'*). This part of the ceremony was called *al-khatam al-sharif*.[103] The *mawlana*s and the *mijadji*s usually start with the singing of the *Selaam*,

[100] See Tapper, "'Traditional' and 'Modern' Wedding Rituals in a Turkish Town", 77.

[101] For a collection of these songs, see Alladien, *Mohammed: De genade der werelden, de roem der werelden*. *Milaad* are songs sung on the birthday of the Prophet (the *Mawlud*) but also on other occasions. These songs were sometimes called *naath* by respondents.

[102] See Alladien, *Mohammed: De genade der werelden, de roem der werelden*, 67 and 196–202, for variations on the *Selaam*. According to Alladien, the *Selaam* begins and ends with the following refrain: "Peace be upon you, oh Prophet, peace be upon you, oh messenger of God, peace be upon you, oh beloved, the blessings of God be with you."

[103] Apart from the recitation of the *Fâtiḥa* and the beginning of sura *Al-Baqara* (2), this conclusion may also consist of the recitation of four suras which start with *Qul*, i.e. "Say", namely *Al-Kâfirûn* (109), *Al-Ikhlâs* (112), *Al-Falaq* (113) and *Al-Nâs* (114), and finally a *du*ᶜ*â'*. The recitation of these suras beginning with *Qul* three times was supposed to have the same weight as the recitation of the Koran as a whole.

when the groom's family place opened bottles of lemonade and sweets on the table. They thus indicate that the ceremony has to come to an end. They set the table with uncovered food and drink "so that the *du^c^â'* goes into the food". The guests stand because the Prophet is believed to walk in at this moment. Some respondents rejected this custom as superstition. Other respondents rejected the custom of placing the bottles of lemonade opened on the table, but considered the recitation of *al-khatam al-sharif* on this occasion and standing at the end of the *kitaab* to be a *sunna* of the Prophet. After the *kitaab* the guests are served a meal.

The bride's family may also organize a *kitaab*, either simultaneously with the *kitaab* at the groom's house or earlier. The family of a Surinamese Hindustani bride for example held a *kitaab* on a Saturday, one week before the wedding. On the following Thursday, shortly before the wedding day, a henna party was organized at the bride's home while a *kitaab* was held at the groom's.

Among Surinamese Hindustani Muslims it occurred that more religiously oriented family members attended only the *kitaab* and *nikah* ceremony. They may have decided not to come to the wedding party, if they expected dancing to music to take place which they shunned on religious grounds. In dealing with the ritual of circumcision we saw that, similarly, Turkish Muslims in Turkey sometimes offer their guests a *mevlüt* performance in the morning and a party in a hall in the evening; some guests take part in the *mevlüt* ceremony but prefer not to join the party.

The Moroccan respondents whom I interviewed seem not to have organized a *ṣadaqa* in the Netherlands, even though most stated that everyone organizes a religious gathering both in Morocco and the Netherlands on such occasions. One Moroccan respondent for example said that in principle, in Morocco as well as in the Netherlands, people invite religious scholars (*ṭalba*) for Koran recitation on the day of marriage contracting, although in Morocco *ṭalba* are easier to find. The same respondent indicated however that her family did not invite *ṭalba* on the day of her marriage contracting at the consulate because, as she explained, her wedding passed off rather chaotically. A *ṣadaqa* may nevertheless have been held more often than I observed, since a *ṣadaqa* is a men's affair and as a woman researcher I spoke mainly with women and joined them at the party. Other respondents argued that only religious families organize a religious gathering.

According to my Moroccan respondents, a *ṣadaqa* (i.e. charitable gift) invokes blessings (*baraka*) on the future couple and consists of a Koran recitation in the presence of men only. The guests and the *ṭalba*, who offer their services for a small monetary recompense, are served a meal. Even though the term *ṣadaqa* may suggest otherwise, it is unusual to distribute a part of this meal specified under Islamic law among the poor and needy. Some respondents explained this behaviour by reference to the relative prosperity of the Netherlands. Even in Morocco, it is unusual to distribute a part of the food of the *ṣadaqa* among the poor. One Moroccan respondent drew a distinction between a *ṣadaqa* as a gathering with a religious character in the course of which a meal is served to the guests on the one hand, and a *ṣadaqa* as a gift to the poor and the needy consisting of food on the other hand. He further said that in Morocco in the past the door was always open: a stranger was never turned out of a house. Nowadays by contrast one attends a *ṣadaqa* only by invitation.

The tradition of organizing a religious gathering preceding the actual wedding party seems to be more easily maintained in the countries of origin than the Netherlands, if only because professional reciters are more commonly available there. Surinamese Hindustani Muslims in the Netherlands have been better able to preserve this ritual in a migrational context than Moroccan and Turkish Muslims. The main reason for this seems to be the presence among the Surinamese Hindustani Muslims of a religious infrastructure in the Netherlands that produces and maintains religious knowledge.

The Henna Party

The henna party was called *kına gecesi* by my Turkish respondents, *laylat al-henna* by Moroccan respondents, and *rajaga* by Surinamese Hindustani respondents. *Rajaga* is the name that used to be given to the evening on which preparations for the wedding party were made and the *mehndie* or henna was applied.

In the Netherlands the henna party takes place either at the bride's home or in a hall. People opt for the latter possibility especially if many guests are expected. One Turkish respondent for example celebrated her henna evening sumptuously in a hall with a large number of guests because—unusually—there was to be no wedding party. Another Turkish henna party was held in a hall because the bride and groom lived in towns some distance apart; many guests, finding it difficult to attend the wedding party at the groom's place because of the distance, decided to attend only the henna party at the bride's, which was therefore organized in a hall.

According to Moroccan and Turkish respondents, the henna party is intended for women only. It often occurred however that a small number of male family members attended the ceremony alongside a larger number of women. It also occurred that the future husband joined the party in the course of the evening, when the palm of his hand or little finger was painted with henna. Normally both men and women are invited to Surinamese Hindustani henna parties. One Surinamese Hindustani groom had his own henna party. At the end of the evening following the *kitaab* ceremony a paternal aunt applied *mehndie*.

A Turkish bride is dressed in red at the henna party, or at least a red veil is drawn over her face when the ceremony of applying the henna begins. The Turkish respondents whom I interviewed were mostly unable to explain the manifold use of the colour red on this occasion other than by appeal to custom.[104] A Moroccan bride is beautifully dressed at her henna party, though her clothes are modest compared to those that she wears on her wedding day. On her wedding day she changes clothes several times whereas at the henna party she changes clothes at most once. At a Surinamese Hindustani henna party that I attended the bride was dressed in a red *sari*.

According to Westermarck, the object of applying henna to the bride is to purify her and protect her from evil influences. Henna is considered to contain great blessing (*baraka*) and is therefore used as a means of purification or protection on occasions when people think that they are exposed to supernatural dangers.[105] Purification and protection were not mentioned by respondents in explanations of the custom. According to some respondents, painting the bride with henna brings good luck. Other

[104] Burkhart, "Der rote Schleier", 450, gives several explanations for the manifold use of the colour red at Turkish wedding parties: "Die beiden Komponenten des roten Schleiers—die Tuchverhüllung von Gesicht und Oberkörper der Braut sowie die Farbe Rot—spielen nach ihrer Semantik und Funktion eine wichtige Rolle in dem initiatorischen Übergangsritus des Hochzeitsgeschehens: Sie fungieren als Zeichen des Übergangs von der jugendlichen zur fertilitätsbestimmten Lebensphase (Mädchen-Frau), als Schutz vor schädlicher Einwirkung von außen (Dämonen, Magie, böser Blick, Neid), also apotropäisch, und als glückbringendes, fruchtbarkeitssicherndes Dingsymbol, also eueterisch." See also ibid., 452–453: "Rot als die Farbe des Blutes und des Feuers hat in vielen Kulturen Symbolwert: Rot steht für Leben, Fruchtbarkeit, Reichtum, Kraft, Jugend, Schönheit und Liebe. . . . Es zeigt sich, daß im 'Hochzeitsdrama' der Türken und Bulgaren Rot tatsächlich die Farbe ist, die das Geschehen dominiert, und zwar in ihrer doppelten magischen Bedeutung, das heißt: mit apotropäischer (Übles abwehrender) und eueterischer (Gutes herbeiführender) Wirkung. Der traditionelle Brautschleier ist aus diesem Grund rot. Er stellt indes nur *ein*—wenn auch zentrales—Element in einer ganzen Reihe roter Hochzeitsbrauchelemente dar. Dazu zählen im türkischen Hochzeitsritual das Henna, mit dem der Braut Hände und Füße gefärbt werden; das Feuer der dabei brennenden Kerzen und das rote Tuch, das man der Braut auf den Kopf legt; der rote Gürtel, das rote Kleid, die roten Blumen und Perlenbänder im Kopfschmuck; die rote Hochzeitsfahne und das Blutzeichen im Brauthemd nach der Defloration, das zum Hissen eines roten Fähnchens auf dem Dach Anlaß gibt."

[105] Westermarck, *Marriage Ceremonies in Morocco*, 118 and 160.

respondents stressed that the custom of applying henna bears no comparison to showering a bridal couple with rice. They regarded the custom of applying henna to the bride's hands and sometimes feet as a prophetical *sunna* and consequently as belonging to Islam: "Henna is *sünnet*; our Prophet loves henna. You will get *sevap*, that means you will be rewarded for doing this." It was explained also on the basis of the respondent's cultural background without any further explanation: "That's the way things go, it is a traditional custom. It belongs to being Moroccan, it belongs to marriage." Particularly Moroccan respondents emphasized that henna makes the bride beautiful.[106]

On the henna evening, the bride generally begins to realize that she will soon leave her family. This thought may make her cry, or her crying is ritually induced. At Turkish henna parties, for example, the henna is not applied before the bride has been seen crying. The guests positioned around her sing songs to make her cry while her face is covered with a red veil.

The persons who bring in the henna and paint the bride with it are chosen carefully. In the majority of cases respondents explained the choice of persons for this task on the basis of custom, without further elucidation. At Surinamese Hindustani henna parties, the *mehndie* is applied by a paternal aunt of the bride. I could trace no explanation of the choice of this relative to apply the henna. The Surinamese Hindustani henna party that I attended was given in a hall and consisted of painting the bride with henna, dancing to music performed by a band invited for the occasion, and eating. Men as well as women were invited. The bride's aunt, who was to apply the henna, entered bearing a reed basket on her head, filled with potatoes, onions, and dried maize. Before she started painting the bride with henna, the bride's father presented gifts to her and to two women who were closely related to the family to thank them officially for their assistance with the wedding preparations. While the paternal aunt was painting the bride's hands and feet with henna, the guests placed sums of money in the aunt's basket. They stood around the bride who had begun to cry.

At Moroccan parties the task of painting the bride with henna is performed in the majority of cases by a *neggafa*, or dresser. Some skill and accuracy is required to apply the henna in the desired pattern. It takes two or three hours to paint the bride's hands and feet. At a Moroccan

[106] See also the findings of Elaroussi, "Pratiques du mariage au Maroc", 127, concerning the marriage of youngsters in El Jadida (Morocco). Elaroussi explains the importance attached to the henna party by reference to the aesthetic value of henna and the festive character of the henna ceremony.

henna party that I attended, which was held at the bride's home, the bride came downstairs dressed in a white gown with a gold band around her head. Two young girls holding lighted candles preceded her. A small green velvet box containing henna and eggs was carried in on a silver tray together with candles and incense. Moroccan respondents said that eggs symbolize fertility.[107] The *neggafa* applied the paint on the bride's hands and feet with a kind of sprayer, starting with her hands, first the right and then the left. Meanwhile the guests danced to the music. This continued until the *neggafa* started to paint the bride's left foot. At that point the guests were served a sumptuous meal. The groom, who joined the party in the course of the evening, had his little finger painted with henna after this meal. At the end of the evening the unmarried girls danced to the music holding the silver tray above their head. It is believed that this ensures that they too will marry soon. At a henna party that I attended in Morocco, the guests ritually brought the bride to cry while holding a cloth above her head, but this did not happen at the henna party in the Netherlands that I witnessed.

A Moroccan groom mostly joins the bride's henna party in the course of the evening. However, one Moroccan groom held his own henna party with his family and friends on the day following the wedding party at the bride's home. This custom seems to be a relic of the time that separate wedding parties were held for each of the spouses' families.[108]

At Turkish henna parties, a young unmarried girl brings the henna in.[109] At a Turkish henna party that I attended, the henna, decorated with small lighted candles, was presented on a dish. The room was darkened. The bride sat in the middle of the room with a red veil drawn over her face. All guests were standing around her in silence. The dish with henna and candles was held above her head. Meanwhile a woman was singing songs about leaving the family. The henna was not applied until she had been seen to cry. Unlike in the case of the Moroccan brides, the

[107] Eggs, says Westermarck, *Marriage Ceremonies in Morocco*, 164, have a favourable influence on the bride's future: like silver and milk, they make the bride's life bright and happy.

[108] Evers-Rosander, "Some Wedding Customs in Qbila Anjra Now (1976–87) and Then (1900–1910)", 119, presents testimony that this custom is known in Morocco even today. According to her, the *lila d'el arûs*, or the evening of the groom, in the company of his male family members and friends starts when the groom has collected his bride. During the evening the little finger of his right hand is painted with henna. The bride remains in a bedroom to await the arrival of the groom.

[109] According to Yerden, *Trouwen op z'n Turks*, 93, the henna is carried into the room by the bride's best friend.

henna was not applied in a pattern. As a game the bride kept her fists clenched, making it impossible to apply henna to her palms. She opened her hands only when she had been given some money.

The henna party thus seems to remain important for Moroccan, Surinamese Hindustani, and Turkish brides in the Netherlands.[110] This does not hold to the same extent for the countries of origin, where practice varies locally. According to Nancy Tapper, a henna party is no longer common usage in Turkey.[111] Khalid Elaroussi found that some youngsters in El Jadida (South Morocco) attached importance to painting the bride's hands and feet with henna on the basis of the aesthetic value of henna and the festive character of the ceremony, whereas other respondents considered the bride's ceremonial trip to the bathhouse more important. In their view the custom of applying henna serves no purpose and is outmoded.[112] In dealing with Surinamese Hindustani marriages in Surinam, Speckmann does not mention a henna party at all.[113] In contrast, other ceremonies that take place shortly before the actual wedding party, such as the bride's visit to the *ḥammâm* and putting together the bride's trousseau, are mentioned more frequently in regard to the countries of origin than to the Netherlands. There are only a few *ḥammâm*s in the Netherlands, a fact that explains why the bride's ceremonial visit to the bathhouse has lost importance in the Dutch context. I know of a *ḥammâm* in The Hague where private parties centred on the bride and her friends are regularly held. However, I have never attended such a party and neither had my respondents.

In her description of traditional wedding rituals in Eğirdir (Turkey), Tapper presents testimony that women's dancing parties are held before the wedding party either in the afternoon (*gelin hamamı*) or in the evening (*kına gecesi*), "although these no longer include either the bride's ceremonial trip to the bathhouse or her solemn adornment with henna".[114] Similarly, one Turkish respondent said that at her *kına gecesi* in Izmir she was not painted with henna. Another Turkish respondent distinguished the *kına gecesi* from the actual painting with henna. She was invited to a wedding in Aksehir where a henna party was held

[110] Similarly Yerden, *Trouwen op z'n Turks*, 94, comes to the conclusion that in the Netherlands the *kına gecesi* is important for all the girls involved in his inquiry. They regard the henna party as belonging to their culture.

[111] Tapper, "'Traditional' and 'Modern' Wedding Rituals in a Turkish Town", 149.

[112] Elaroussi, "Pratiques du mariage au Maroc", 127: "En revanche, les opposantes à cette tradition [e.g. painting with henna] la trouvent inutile et dépassée, même si elles acceptent de se rendre au hammam."

[113] Speckmann, *Marriage and Kinship among the Indians in Surinam.*

[114] Tapper, "'Traditional' and 'Modern' Wedding Rituals in a Turkish Town", 149.

during the daytime, but the painting of the bride with henna was postponed and took place in the company of only a few friends. The practice seems however to vary locally, for yet another respondent said that her *kına gecesi* in Turkey included henna painting. In this case the groom too held a kind of henna party for his friends,[115] but between times he came to the bride's henna party to be introduced to her family and to present her officially with the bridal gift, consisting of gold.

The same couple referred also to another custom which may take place in Turkey shortly before the actual wedding day and seems to have disappeared in the Netherlands: the custom that bride and groom present each other with gifts. The bride buys her future husband such items as suits, shirts, ties, socks, underwear, pyjamas, slippers, and a shaver, while the groom gives his future wife her bridal dress, clothes, nightclothes, and underwear. Both families, including the bridal couple, their parents, sisters, brothers, uncles and aunts, go shopping for these items a week or two before the wedding. On this occasion, besides the clothes, they bought gold jewellery for the bride as part of her bridal gift and presents for both families, such as pieces of cloth, handkerchiefs, shoes, and a *tespih* or kind of rosary. Aunts and uncles went shopping with them for these items. In the first weeks following the wedding the newlyweds visited each family household and gave their family members these presents or items of needlework.[116]

It was usual in the past, and not unknown today, for a girl from around the age of thirteen to work on her trousseau (*çeyiz*), consisting mainly of needlework, such as crocheted tablecloths, a bedspread and decorative pieces of cloth that hang on cupboards, television sets, chairs and couches, towels, handkerchiefs and headscarves with crocheted borders, and embroidered pillowcases and sheets. Shortly before the wedding the bride may come to the groom's home with a few relatives to arrange for the display of the trousseau.[117]

[115] Perhaps this was a *samah*. "On Saturday evening", says Tapper, "'Traditional' and 'Modern' Wedding Rituals in a Turkish Town", 149, "the groom may hold a rowdy drinking and dancing party (*samah*) for his own friends."

[116] For similar findings concerning the purchase of goods before an engagement, see Gailly, *Een dorp in Turkije*, 138: "Voor hun officiële verloving hadden Necati en zijn meisje elkaar drie keer ontmoet om samen met hun (pleeg)ouders in Samsun het verlovingsgoud te gaan kopen." Gailly, ibid., 137, lists the following engagement gifts with which the groom presents his future bride: an engagement gown, underwear, soap, comb, stockings, deodorant, handcream, make-up, bedclothes, and headscarves.

[117] See also Tapper, "'Traditional' and 'Modern' Wedding Rituals in a Turkish Town", 149, and Gailly, *Een dorp in Turkije*, 145.

According to Elaroussi, a visit to the *ḥammâm* plays an important role in marriage ceremonies in Morocco. In El Jadida (Morocco) brides who decline to have their hands and feet painted with henna may nonetheless visit the *ḥammâm* with family and friends. On the basis of this, Elaroussi draws the conclusion that this tradition is least challenged by modernity.[118] My findings provide evidence for the opposite. At a wedding in Larache to which I was invited, the bride visited the *ḥammâm* with only a few female family members. The wedding appeared to have really begun with the slaughter of a calf on the terrace of the bride's house on the next morning. From then on guests came trickling in. They attended the henna party that started late in the afternoon after the bride's visit to the hairdresser. In this case the bride was brought to cry. A few women held a silk cloth above the bride's head, making a sort of canopy. This cloth is comparable to the red veil of a Turkish bride which covers her face shortly before and during the ceremony of henna painting.

In Morocco practice concerning the henna party seems to vary locally. Some respondents said that in Morocco the henna is usually applied by a *neggafa*.[119] Others said that this task is performed by a relative of the bride, preferably a woman who has been married only once.[120] Westermarck found likewise that in Tangier the henna is applied "by a married woman who must have been married to a bachelor and not been married more than once".[121] Some respondents, when asked about the painting of the groom's little finger, said that it should be done by his sister or his cousin, whereas others said that it should be done by his eldest aunt. Whether the henna is applied in a pattern also seems to depend on the locality. According to Cammaert the henna is not applied in a pattern in the neighbourhood of Nadur whereas in Marrakech and Fez it is.[122]

In his account of marriage ceremonies of Surinamese Hindustani Muslims in Surinam, Speckmann does not make mention of henna parties: "However, the wedding ceremony is much simpler among the Moslems [than among Hindus], and no rite of any sort is performed before the actual celebration of the marriage. The preparations for the wedding are confined to the practical sphere: distribution of invitations, provision of a covered space in the compound, the cooking of the meal,

118 Elaroussi, "Pratiques du mariage au Maroc", 127.

119 The age of *neggafa*s too may vary locally. One Moroccan respondent thought of the *neggafa*s from Fez as witches because of their advanced age compared to the usually young *neggafa*s in the north of Morocco.

120 Buskens, *Islamitisch recht en familiebetrekkingen in Marokko*, 434.

121 Westermarck, *Marriage Ceremonies in Morocco*, 141.

122 Cammaert, *Migranten en thuisblijvers*, 71.

etc."[123] The important role that henna parties play among Surinamese Hindustani Muslims in the Netherlands and the distinctive form of these parties, which differs from that of Moroccan and Turkish henna parties, constitute however sufficient reason to assume that in Surinam too henna parties feature largely in the ritual of marriage.

The Wedding Party

Wedding parties vary widely according to ethnic group. In spite of this variety, three features characterize wedding parties irrespective of ethnic group. Marriage firstly means the establishment of a new household. This of course involves considerable expense, if only because of the wedding party, the honeymoon trip, and the furnishing of the couple's home. Therefore making gifts of money and games of all kinds involving money usually play an important role in wedding parties. Secondly, wedding parties generally give the two families an opportunity to become better acquainted with one another and the bridal couple. Variations on rituals of welcome and several ways of presenting the bride and groom to the each other's families therefore feature largely in wedding parties. Thirdly, whether the wedding party is celebrated at home, in a hall or on the premises of a mosque, it is common practice to entertain the wedding guests to a sumptuous meal (*walîma*).

Wedding parties differ also within ethnic groups. In the Netherlands the latter diversity shows itself most clearly in the choice of the venue for the wedding party, i.e. a hall rented for the occasion, (the premises of) a mosque or the home. The choice among these options may provide us with some indication of the degree of identification with Islam.

Surinamese Hindustani respondents who took their religion very seriously opted for a wedding party with no dancing to music. They therefore organized a party on the premises of a mosque with no music or in a hall where they entertain their guests with music but offer no opportunities for dancing. Other Surinamese Hindustani respondents had no objections to dancing. They held a party in a hall with a band to which their guests could dance if they wished.

Turkish respondents who identified to a high degree with Islam often held a stricter view concerning sexual segregation. They opted to organize a wedding party in the local mosque where they could accommodate their male and female guests in separate rooms. Contrarily, a Turkish wedding party in a hall generally implies dancing to music and no separate reception of male and female guests.

[123] Speckmann, *Marriage and Kinship among the Indians in Surinam*, 147.

Moroccan respondents opted for a wedding party either at home or in a hall. The choice depends in the first place on the family's financial means. However, religious arguments inducing people to modesty also seem to affect the choice. A party at home mostly has a modest character if only because of lack of space, and implies the separate reception of male and female guests. A party in a hall often involves hiring a popular band, a well-equipped *neggafa*, and no separation of male and female guests.

In the past wedding parties in the countries of origin involved the separate reception of men and women and also separate parties for both families: the bride celebrated the marriage at home with her family and friends before the groom collected her, while the wedding party of the groom's family started upon the arrival of the bridal couple at the groom's parental home. In recent years this practice has undergone change. Increasingly, particularly in the Netherlands but also in the countries of origin, the festivities take place at a venue where the guests of both families are received together. Once in my sample it occurred however that there were separate parties for the two families. The family of a Turkish bride held a henna party in a hall. The next day the bride was collected by the groom and brought to his family's home. The families initially had planned to organize a wedding party in a hall. However, things turned out differently due to a death in the groom's family. Moreover, relations between the two families were not good. Eventually the wedding took a form in many respects similar to that of traditional wedding in Turkey as described by Tapper.[124]

The next part of this chapter contains a more comprehensive treatment of Surinamese Hindustani, Turkish, and Moroccan wedding parties in the Netherlands and a somewhat briefer account of this ritual as it is performed in the countries of origin.

Wedding Parties in the Netherlands

If only on the basis of the information that the invitation provides concerning the venue and the band, if any, that will be playing, Surinamese Hindustani guests know what to expect at a wedding party. Some respondents, who disapproved of parties in a hall for religious reasons, did not accept an invitation to such a wedding party. They preferred to attend only the *kitaab* at the groom's home and the *nikah* ceremony, if this took place at the bride's home before the wedding party in a hall.

[124] Tapper, "'Traditional' and 'Modern' Wedding Rituals in a Turkish Town", 149–150.

If a Surinamese Hindustani wedding party takes place in a hall, the bride and her family are the first to arrive at the venue. The procession (*baraat*) of the groom and his family announces its arrival at a later time by sounding car horns and letting off fireworks in the street outside the hall. On hearing this, a male delegation of the bride's family walks out towards the groom and his party to welcome them. Female family members of the bride subsequently bid the groom a hearty welcome when he enters by offering him a drink, called *sharbat* or *paan*.

If the *nikah* has not already taken place at the bride's home, the wedding party begins with the religious ceremony of marriage. The majority of the Surinamese Hindustani parties in a hall that I attended started with the *nikah*. At the end of this ceremony the groom collects his bride, who has remained in a separate room during the religious ceremony and changed her *silwar* or *sari* for a white bridal gown afterwards, and brings her into the hall. The guests are served sweets and offer their congratulations to the bridal couple and their parents.

There is music throughout the evening. The guests, mostly sitting at tables in family groups, watch the musicians. Whether they also dance to the music depends among other things on the kind of band that has been hired to play.[125] In a separate area of the party room male family members serve a meal to the wedding guests. The wedding guests, often several hundred in number, dine not all together but in sittings of forty or so at a time; when one family rises from the table, another takes their seats.

In the course of the evening, before the wedding cake is cut, some bridal couples exchanged wedding rings. Once it also occurred that following this ritual the bride and groom drank a glass of champagne with their arms entwined. Alternatively, they may spray the air with champagne after having cut the wedding cake.

The groom and the men of his family are the last to be served. Playfully they refuse to eat until the bride's family has given them a sum of money, varying from *f*2,000 to *f*4,500.[126] Another playful touch is for a

[125] Silvie Karim and her band played at many parties that I attended. Their songs were not suitable for dancing. Many had a narrative character and the guests watched the band play as if watching a theatrical performance.

[126] This corresponds with the findings of Speckmann, *Marriage and Kinship among the Indians in Surinam*, 148. According to him, however, this game takes place the next morning: "Just as among the Hindus, next morning the bridegroom refuses to eat. The bride's father and his family now give the young man money. Only when his demands have been satisfied does he sit down to breakfast." From this one may conclude that in Surinam the couple passes the wedding night at the bride's home. It is only after breakfast that the bridal couple goes to the groom's house where the game of lifting the veil takes place. In the Netherlands most couples spend the wedding night at the groom's home.

young sister or niece of the bride to take away the groom's shoes, while the groom and his male party partake of their meal. The groom will not get his shoes back until he has given the girl some money.[127] These games take place either during the *nikah* at the bride's home or at the end of the wedding party.[128]

Other Surinamese Hindustani respondents said that they preferred to hold the wedding party on the premises of a mosque. By means of this choice they explicitly dissociate themselves from the music and dancing that normally go with a party in a hall. In other respects such a party proceeds just like a party in a hall, including the welcoming of the groom, the *nikah* ceremony, and a meal for all the guests. The importance that these respondents attach to religion once showed itself in a small display of aniconism. The groom's father removed the small statuette of a bridal couple at the top of the wedding cake, to the disappointment of the bride and groom.

The difference in preferences regarding the wedding party venue is found among Turks too. The majority of the Turkish wedding parties took place in a hall. However, some respondents, particularly members of the *Milli Görüş*, preferred to hold their wedding party in a mosque or on the premises of a community centre.

A Turkish bride is dressed in a white bridal dress with a red or sometimes a green sash round her waist, considered a symbol of virginity. Her father or brother ties this sash round her waist before she leaves her parental home. At the Turkish parties that I attended in the Netherlands the bride invariably wore a red sash round her waist, even if she was not a virgin.[129] As a game, the bride's family makes it difficult for the groom to collect his bride. They may for example prevent him from reaching the bride's room or block the departing procession until he has given them some money.

[127] Speckmann, ibid., 148, relates this game to the moment at which the groom is brought to the bride: "Towards four o'clock in the morning it is suggested that the bridegroom should make the acquaintance of the bride. The girl, heavily veiled, is alone in another room in the house. Before the bridegroom enters it he has to take off his shoes. . . . When he leaves the room he finds that a sister of the bride has taken his shoes away and he does not get them back until he has paid her a little money."

[128] The game of stealing the groom's shoes fits more naturally within the former situation, since the groom will have removed his shoes on arrival at the bride's place whereas he will keep on his shoes during a wedding party in a hall.

[129] Tapper, "'Traditional' and 'Modern' Wedding Rituals in a Turkish Town", 153, concluded that "the most modern couples (often those where the bride is trained for a high-status profession) may reject even vestigial gender symbols from the past, such as the red sash all brides normally wear around their waists".

Turkish wedding parties in a hall proceed as follows. On arrival the guests are offered some sweets and their hands are sprinkled with perfume. The bridal couple makes its entry into the hall after the guests, through an arch formed by girls holding each other's hands or through a candlelit archway.[130] The guests sit in family groups or men gather on one side of the room, in the passageway or at the bar. The entertainment consists mainly of dancing to music in couples or in lines of ten to twenty people, with the person at the head of the line flapping a brightly coloured handkerchief. In the course of the evening there follows a meal consisting of Turkish pizza or rice with chicken. The wedding cake, which the bridal couple cuts, concludes the meal.

A fixed item on the programme which often marks the end of the wedding party is the present-giving or *takı*. The wedding guests congratulate the bride and groom, who stand in a reception line with their parents and attendants. The guests present the bridal couple with gifts consisting mainly of money and gold jewellery. The amount of money or details of the jewellery, such as the length of a necklace or number of bracelets, and the name of the giver are announced to the company on a public-address system. Bridal attendants pin banknotes and gold medallions on the bride's and groom's clothes and the bride dons the gold necklaces, bracelets, and rings.

At Turkish mosque wedding parties men and women are received in separate rooms.[131] The stricter view concerning sexual segregation also shows itself in style of dress. The bride may have completely covered her hair and neck. Under a see-through bridal veil she may wear an opaque white veil. Another characteristic of these parties is that there is no music. Moreover, unlike wedding parties in a hall, which mostly take place in the evening, these parties are mostly organized in the afternoon.

[130] Ibid., 153, mentions the candlelit archway as an example of innovation: "Both wedding forms, but particularly the modern one (and especially its *balo*), the elements of which are less specific or predetermined, offer couples opportunities for innovation: the candlelit archway is but one example. The possibility of such innovation fosters a sense of independence and personal control over the ritual forms and enhances their meaning." One Turkish couple whom I interviewed referred to this and similar examples to illustrate their originality. They felt for example that they were the only couple to have an archway made by girls holding arches, and the first to have a particular kind of wedding cake. They were also convinced that their wedding party, unlike most other Turkish wedding parties, was well organized, as for example it was arranged that they should dance the opening dance alone—something which rarely happens since mostly many guests are on the dance floor then.

[131] A party in a mosque seems to be typical of the Dutch situation. Tapper, "'Traditional' and 'Modern' Wedding Rituals in a Turkish Town", 150, does not mention this possibility and presents evidence only for the fact that a more traditional family may prefer a wedding party at the groom's home to a wedding salon.

As in the case of Surinamese Hindustani parties on the premises of a mosque, the choice of a mosque for Turkish wedding parties expresses a rejection of particular features typical of parties in a hall. If the invitation mentions a mosque as the venue of the wedding party, the recipients understand that there will be no music or dancing. Some respondents stressed that a party in a mosque is more economical than a party in a hall, because these respondents would have been obliged to rent two party rooms for the separate reception of men and women.

A wedding party that I attended in a *Milli Görüş* mosque consisted of Koran recitation followed by the singing of religious songs (*ilahi*) and a play staged by friends of the bride dealing with life according to Islam and the wearing of headscarves. After the present-giving (*takı*), paper strips were spread out on the ground and a meal was served to the women seated on both sides of these strips. The men's party reportedly passed off in a similar way.

Whether Moroccan wedding parties are celebrated at home or in a hall depends above all on the family's financial means. A party at home resembles a party in a hall in many respects, but the scale of the former is necessarily smaller. If only because of space limitations, some customs, such as carrying the bride in a litter, cannot take place at home. The religious sentiment in favour of modesty and the avoidance of unnecessary luxury may therefore induce some Moroccans to prefer a party at home. An argument that counts against a party at home is that it quickly becomes poky.

Some respondents also suggested that Moroccans from the northern part of Morocco prefer to give a party at home whereas Moroccans from other regions prefer a hall. Similarly, they believed that Moroccans from the north make their own music whereas Moroccans from other parts prefer to hire a professional band.

A preference for receiving men and women separately and attitudes towards dancing to music do not greatly determine the choice of wedding party venue. A wedding party at home normally implies that men and women will be received separately, whereas this is mostly not the case at parties in a hall. At Moroccan wedding parties in a hall, female guests, dressed festively in *tekshiṭa* or *kandura*, sit together towards the front of the room and men further back, or men and women sit together in family groups. At Moroccan parties, both at home and in a hall, dancing is mainly a women's activity.

Whether a Moroccan wedding party is celebrated in a hall or at home, what mostly characterizes such a wedding is that the bride changes her clothes several times and is presented to the guests in each new attire.

The dresser (*neggafa*) brings bridal dresses and other accessories, such as litters called *al-amarya* or *ad-dura*, with her.[132] The first is a rectangular box with a roof that once served to carry the bride from her parental home to the groom's place. The second has an octagonal base and no roof. The *neggafa* sees to the bride's make-up and assists the bride in changing her clothes. According to some respondents Belgian *neggafa*s have a much wider assortment than *neggafa*s in the Netherlands. They also believed that Belgium has a larger number of Moroccan women bands than the Netherlands.

At a Moroccan wedding party in a hall that I attended, the bride changed her clothes four times. The first outfit was the green velvet gown with gold stitching typical of Fez.[133] She was carried round through the hall in *al-amarya*. Female guests walked behind the litter, singing the words, "*Ṣalât wa as-salâm ᶜalâ rasûl llah, lâ jâh ilâ jâh sayyidnâ Muḥammad, Allah, maᶜahu al-jâh al-ᶜâlî*",[134] followed by ululations (*t'zeghrita*). These words were sung and the *t'zeghrita* uttered each time the bride appeared in a new dress and made a circuit through the room with or without the groom. Each time the bridal couple subsequently sat for a while on an elevated seat, specially decorated for the occasion. When the bride donned her fourth outfit, the

[132] For more information on the use of *al-amarya* and *ad-dura* in Morocco in the early part of the twentieth century, see Westermarck, *Marriage Ceremonies in Morocco*, 137–138 and 167–168. In the exhibition catalogue *De buren vieren feest: Geboorte, overgang en huwelijk bij Antwerpse bevolkingsgroepen* (The neighbours are celebrating: Birth, transition, and marriage in Antwerp population groups), 109 and 114, these litters are called *ammaria* and *taïfour* respectively. Evers-Rosander, "Some Wedding Customs in Qbila Anjra Now (1976–87) and Then (1900–1910)", 116–119, also deals with the *buja* or *ᶜammariyya* custom, i.e. the bride's transport by *buja* to the groom's house.

[133] The bride may also be dressed in the manner of a Berber girl, in the traditional head-dress bearing coins or like an Indian princess. Photographs of several of these dresses are in *De buren vieren feest*, 72, 110, and 114. According to these findings, a bride especially in the North of Morocco makes her first appearance in an attire called *cheddah* with its characteristic collar of pearls, or else she would not be considered a virgin. Her second dress is the *taghlila*, the velvet gown of Fez.

[134] This can be translated as follows: "Prayer and peace be with the Messenger of God; there is no glory but the glory of our Lord Mohammed; Allah, with him is the highest glory". Errazki-van Beek, "Een vrouwenmuziekgroep uit Marrakech", 34–35, gives a different wording: "*ṣ-Ṣla u-s-salam ᶜli-k a ṛasul ḷḷah, lhaaa žah ila žah sid-na Muḥammed, Aḷḷah muṣalli ᶜli-k a ṛasul ḷḷah*", which is translated as follows: "Bless you and mercy be with you, o Messenger of God; O, there is no way but the way of our Lord Mohammed; God bless you, o Messenger of God". Contrarily, *jâh*, being considered as a corruption of the Arabic word *ittijâh*, is here understood to mean "direction, way". Errazki-van Beek considers this interpretation to be preferable to the interpretation "esteem, prestige".

groom changed his suit for a white *jellâba*. In turns the bride and groom were lifted up on *ad-dura* and the guests tossed flower-petals over them. Finally, the bride put on a white bridal dress. This was her own property, not from the collection of the *neggafa*. The bride in her white bridal dress and the groom, who had put his suit on again, walked through the hall once more, while the guests sang the above words followed by ululations. The sequence took up the whole evening. Meanwhile some guests, mostly women, but sometimes also a few young males, danced to the music played by a band consisting of eight men. In the course of the evening the guests were served a meal and presented with biscuits.

Another Moroccan wedding party that I attended was held at the bride's home. There was no changing of clothes by the bride and there was no *neggafa*. According to the family, these customs are not followed in Wajazza, in southern Morocco, from where they originated. The wedding party consisted mainly of dancing to music played on a tape-recorder. In the course of the evening Moroccan tea was served together with home-made biscuits. The latter were wrapped in cellophane, so that the guests could take them home if they wished. At the end of the evening the guests were served a meal. Around fifty female guests attended, sitting on the floor. The bride sat on an elevated, decorated seat. The male guests had gathered in a neighbouring house.

One Moroccan groom held his own party with his family and friends on the day after the wedding party, which had been held at the bride's home. He wore a white *jellâba* with the hood pulled down over his eyes. On this occasion his sister painted his little finger with henna. This reflects the custom, which once was common in Morocco, of holding separate parties for the families and friends of the spouses. Similarly, Eva Evers-Rosander describes the *lila d'el arûs*, or evening of the groom, in Morocco where she describes the festivities at the groom's home upon arrival of the bride there. She also describes the groom's outfit, which is typical of the occasion.[135]

Wedding Parties in the Countries of Origin

In her article on wedding ceremonies in Turkey, Nancy Tapper describes two ideal types of weddings: traditional (*eski*, *eski âdet*, *ananevi*) and modern (*yeni*, *modern*), also referred to as *yemekli* and *yemeksiz*, i.e.

[135] Evers-Rosander, "Some Wedding Customs in Qbila Anjra Now (1976–87) and Then (1900–1910)", 119.

with and without food respectively.[136] The picture that she gives of an ideal traditional wedding is as follows:

> At mid-morning on Sunday, a *mevlûd* recital of the well known poem commemorating the life of the Prophet Muhammad is given at the groom's home. Following this, the men's feasting begins. When most of the men guests have been fed, the groom leaves with an escort of friends for the bride's house, where they claim the bride from her family (*gelin çıkışı*) and tour the town in a noisy motorcade. The bride is then taken to her husband's house; she often steps over a newly sacrificed goat before she enters.
>
> From the time of the *mevlûd* onwards, guests, often several hundred of them, arrive for the traditional wedding meal. Throughout the morning the men are fed in groups of twelve to fifteen around circular tables (*sofra*) set up in the house or in the yard or alleyways near the groom's home. Early in the afternoon, when all the men have eaten, women guests begin to arrive, singly or in family or neighborhood groups, and they are served the same three-course meal. After the meal one of the guests offers a short table-grace, and the women rise, inspect the bride and her trousseau, and then return to their own homes. The bride is likely to remain seated and on view to the wedding guests until late evening, when, after the religious marriage ceremony, the groom joins her to consummate the marriage.[137]

One Turkish respondent resident in the Netherlands who brought her husband from Turkey gave a description of her marriage in Turkey, which was similar in many respects. In the morning she removed the henna that had been applied the previous evening, showered, and dressed. Her youngest brother tied a red sash round her waist, uttering the words *Bismillahi ar-rahmân ar-rahîm* (In the name of God, the Merciful, the Compassionate). When the groom came to take her to his house, where the festivities would take place, she bade her family farewell by kissing their hands. They stayed behind. Upon her departure from her parental home, the bride wore an *allık*, a red veil covering her face, and a red bag containing the Koran. As she got in and out of the car, an imam said a *duʿâ'*.

On arrival at the groom's home, the bridal couple were seated in a room where the bride's trousseau (*çeyiz*) was displayed. The guests came to congratulate them. The women gathered in the living room and men in the garden. The early afternoon comprised a visit to the mosque

[136] Tapper, "'Traditional' and 'Modern' Wedding Rituals in a Turkish Town", 140. This dichotomy, says Tapper, constitutes a primary contrast set. Of course, most wedding ceremonies exhibit a combination of elements which ensures that they do not conform exactly to either of the categories.

[137] Ibid., 149–150.

where a sermon on the rights and duties of the husband and wife was delivered. This religious proceedings at the mosque also included the recitation of sura *YaSin* and a *du^{c}â'*. In the afternoon the guests were entertained with a meal and women danced to the music. Later, a *hoca* recited the *mevlüt* and said a *du^{c}â'*, using a public-address system to reach both the garden and the room in which the women were. At seven o'clock in the evening the guests left and the *imam nikâhı* took place for a third time. The groom then went outside; he was driven back into the house by his friends who, patting his back, encouraged him to join his wife to consummate the marriage.

The father of the bride explicitly rejected the idea of holding the wedding party in a wedding salon: "That is not how it is done here. It [i.e. a wedding party in a wedding salon] is something for more modern people." Holding a wedding party in a salon is thus associated with a modern attitude. This fits in with Tapper's description of a modern wedding:

> The next day, that of the wedding, the groom, accompanied by his friends, close family, and some professional musicians, is driven in a limousine to the bride's house. There the groom collects his bride (*gelin çıkışı*), who leaves her parents' home wearing a white gown. Together the bride and groom drive around the town, followed by members of the groom's party in cars with horns blowing. The motorcade may drive to the town hall, where the civil marriage ceremony (*resmî nikâh*) may be performed before an audience of up to a hundred guests, mostly women. After the ceremony the bride and groom and their parents form a reception line to receive their guests, who offer their best wishes to the young people; the guests' hands are then sprinkled with perfume, and they are asked to take some sweets or cigarettes before they depart. Alternatively the motorcade may drive straight to the couple's new home, where the groom will relax with close relatives and friends before the *balo* celebration in the evening. The bride may go to a beauty parlor to have her hair elaborately coiffed. If the groom expects to drink alcohol at the *balo*, the religious marriage ceremony (*dinî nikâh*) may be performed at this point.
>
> The balo is held in a hired wedding salon, in Eğirdir or Isparta. On arrival, the guests, sometimes numbering more than a thousand, find their way to tables where they sit in family groups. The couple then arrives, perhaps through an archway formed by young people holding lighted candles. The bride (still dressed in white) and the groom sit at a decorated table in the center of the room. The evening begins with the short civil marriage ceremony, if this has not taken place already, after which the couple respectfully kiss their parents and then dance alone to the music of a rock band. Other couples and young girls together then begin to dance; later young men join in lively traditional folkdances. In the intervals, the bride and groom circulate through the room to greet the guests, who may pin bank notes on the bride. The end of the gathering, which may last until

> midnight, may be a reception line, if this was not done earlier. Finally, the bride and groom may be escorted to their car by a rowdy group of young men, while other guests find their own way home.[138]

The modern-style wedding has much in common with Turkish wedding parties in a hall in the Netherlands. Tapper relates the choice of a particular form of wedding to the degree of identification with and involvement in the social life of the town and the degree of identification with Islam; these are greater in the case of traditional weddings than for modern weddings.[139] Tapper does not discuss the degree of identification with Islam in much detail. In the Dutch situation the extent to which families identify with Islam seems decisive for the form of wedding party that they choose.

Tapper says that in the twentieth century "the once quite varied local customs have become remarkably standardized", due among other things to the considerable Republican propaganda effort in favour of western-style wedding ceremonies that followed the adoption of the new legal code.[140] In spite of this development, local varieties in wedding customs remain. The custom by which the bride steps over a goat on her arrival at the groom's home seems for example not to occur throughout Turkey; one of my Turkish respondents said that this custom occurs in Central Anatolia but not on the Black Sea coast, from where she originally came. Similarly, I found from my respondents that the custom of throwing money onto a cloth placed on the ground before the door when the bride leaves her parental home for the groom's house is known only in Eastern Turkey.

Buskens draws a distinction similar to Tapper's between traditional weddings and new wedding forms in Morocco.[141] Traditional weddings take place at home and involve separate receptions for male and female guests and also separate parties for the groom's and bride's families. The festivities for the bride's family and friends consist of a henna party and a wedding party at the bride's parental home. The festivities at the groom's house for his family and friends follow upon the bride's arrival there.

In Morocco, as in the Netherlands, the extent to which a marriage is celebrated depends primarily on the family's financial means. Buskens considers the choice to give a party as a choice for conspicuous consumption, aiming at strengthening the ties with family,

[138] Tapper, "'Traditional' and 'Modern' Wedding Rituals in a Turkish Town", 147–148.
[139] Ibid., 140 and 143.
[140] Ibid., 138.
[141] Buskens, *Islamitisch recht en familiebetrekkingen in Marokko*, 433–453.

friends, and neighbours.[142] In towns, however, middle-class couples increasingly opt not to organize any further festivities for family and friends after the marriage conclusion before the *ᶜudûl*.[143] For example, one Moroccan respondent, resident in the Netherlands, married before the *ᶜudûl* in Morocco, but did not feel inclined to organize a wedding party. She thought that in Morocco only rich people and have-nots organize a wedding party, and regarded investing money in the furnishing of their future home as preferable to wasting it on a wedding party.

This tendency towards frugality, which shows itself clearly in weddings not accompanied by any further festivities, and which Tapper has found also in western-style weddings in Turkey, has affected traditional weddings in Morocco too.[144] The average duration of wedding festivities in Morocco for example has fallen from seven days to between one and three days. Other changes concern the separate reception of men and women and the choice of the wedding party venue: in Morocco wedding parties increasingly take place not at home but in a hall, where male and female guests from both the groom's and the bride's side come together, leaving their children behind.[145]

The majority of my Moroccan respondents who married in Morocco preferred to organize a wedding party at home. This may work out as in the following example of a wedding party in Larache (Morocco) that I attended. The guests, mostly women wearing festive clothes (*tekshiṭa* or *kandura*) and gold jewellery, trickled into the bride's home during the afternoon. At that time the bride was still at the hairdressing salon: she, like most of the women who attended the wedding party, had her hair elaborately coiffed for the occasion.

[142] Ibid., 450 and 452.

[143] Ibid., 450–453. Elaroussi, "Pratiques du mariage au Maroc", 127, also presents evidence for both wedding forms and relates the choice between them to the families' financial means: "On ne peut évoquer le cérémonial nuptial sans aborder la présentation des mariés au public. A ce sujet, les opinions divergent. Les partisans de la présentation des deux conjoints aux invités, considèrent que le mariage est un grand événement et qu'il est nécessaire d'associer famille, amis, voisins . . . à la joie ambiante. Le mariage revêt un caractère publicitaire, que les fiancés apprécient ou n'osent pas réfuter. . . . En revanche, un nouveau courant d'idées s'amorce, affirmant qu'il n'est pas nécessaire d'inviter la famille ou autres. . . . On peut penser que des raisons économiques sont sous-jacentes."

[144] Tapper, "'Traditional' and 'Modern' Wedding Rituals in a Turkish Town", 138.

[145] Cf. Buskens, *Islamitisch recht en familiebetrekkingen in Marokko*, 436–437 and 452–453.

The bride changed her clothes several times during the party.[146] Each time the bride, with or without the groom, appeared in a new dress, the guests walked behind her singing the words *Ṣalât wa as-salâm* . . . followed by ululations. In each new attire, the bride, with or without the groom, sat for a while on an elevated, decorated seat and the guests joined her in turns for photographs. Moroccans expect the bride not to laugh during the wedding party, since by laughing she would express her longing to be joined with her husband, whereas she ought to appear sad at leaving her family. The entertainment on this occasion further consisted of dancing to music played by a women's band, pouring out tea and the distribution of home-made biscuits among the guests, and a sumptuous meal served at the end of the evening.

Berbers from the northern part of Morocco, some respondents claimed, are especially likely to make their own music. In Morocco it may also occur that a music and dance band consisting of women, named *shikhât*, play music and perform dances. The performances of the *shikhât* are rewarded with money in the form of banknotes tucked into their belt or along their neckline. In the north of Morocco *shikhât* have a poor reputation among some people.[147] This made respondents from Fez and Ksar el-Kebir prefer modern bands consisting of professional musicians playing on modern instruments, such as violin and guitar, or local women's bands playing traditional instruments. These women have a better reputation than the *shikhât*, if only because they finish work at a decent time.

In Morocco, like the Netherlands, the presentation of home-made biscuits wrapped in cellophane—to take home if one wishes—and a rich meal normally form part of a wedding party. For this, in Fez and also in other Moroccan towns, one Moroccan respondent said, people increasingly make use of the services of professionals, named *sabayât* and *hajama*s, women and men who attend to the wedding party. These professionals provide the wedding party room and tableware,

[146] Wiersma, "De bruid in veranderende huwelijksrituelen in Ben Smim", deals with present-day wedding rituals in Ben Smim (Middle Atlas, Morocco), but does refer to the custom of the bride's changing her clothes. Westermarck, *Marriage Ceremonies in Morocco*, 137–138, mentions this custom in his description of ceremonies in the bride's home in Fez only.

[147] Unlike a *mughanniyya*, such as the famous Egyptian singer Oum Khaltoum, a *shikha* may be considered socially marginal because of the sexual and other liberties that she allows herself in her performance, such as in her provocative dance movements and the content of her songs, as well as in her private life, says Kapchan, "Moroccan Female Performers Defining the Social Body", 102.

take care of the cooking, and serve drinks and food at the wedding party.

In Morocco the wedding party takes place mostly at the bride's home but sometimes in a hall. At the end of the evening, or on the next day, the groom collects the bride by car to take her to his home. Once, the bride was carried to the groom's home in a litter called *al-amarya*. This litter still features in Moroccan wedding parties but plays a different role. One Moroccan respondent, for example, whose prospective husband lived at some distance in another town, gave this ceremony of carrying the bride in a litter to the groom's home a different turn: she was carried in *al-amarya* from her cousin's house to the room where the wedding party took place. Correspondingly, as we saw, at a wedding party in a hall in the Netherlands, the bride was carried round the hall in *al-amarya*, wearing her first attire of the evening, the green velvet gown typical of Fez.

The Reception of the Bride at the Groom's Home

As we have seen, in Morocco the wedding party mostly takes place at the bride's home. The same evening or the next day the groom collects the bride to bring her to his parental home or to their future home where the festivities continue. In Turkey the henna party is held at the bride's home and in the case of traditional wedding parties the subsequent festivities take place at the groom's home. In Surinam, says Speckmann, the wedding party takes place at the bride's home, where the wedding night is also spent. The bride stays for several days thereafter at the groom's home.[148] Welcoming rituals—such as the *moe dighauni* among the Surinamese Hindustani Muslims—accompany the reception of the bride, and family representatives—such as the *sağdıç* among Turks—may protect the bride's interests at the groom's home.

At the end of a Turkish wedding party the bridal couple leaves for their future home accompanied by their *sağdıç*s. These attendants, usually two married couples, assist the bridal couple at the wedding party and inform the bridal couple about the wedding night. Since many bridal couples have had sex education, the main task of the *sağdıç*s is to accompany the bridal couple. However, at Turkish traditional-style wedding parties,[149] they also look after the bride's interests at the groom's home, because she is received there without any family member to

[148] Speckmann, *Marriage and Kinship among the Indians in Surinam*, 148.

[149] For a description of this wedding party style, see Tapper, "'Traditional' and 'Modern' Wedding Rituals in a Turkish Town", 149–150.

accompany her. In such a case it is important that one of the couples appointed to fulfil the task of *sağdıç* belong to the groom's family because they are familiar with the family's life.

On their arrival at the couple's future home[150] the groom again leaves for the mosque to perform the *ṣalât*, or simply leaves the house for a few minutes. The bride remains at home with the two female *sağdıç*s, who inform her about the wedding night. The bride awaits the groom's arrival with her face veiled. On the return of the groom, a prayer (*duᶜâ'*) is recited at the front door. Thereupon, friends who have accompanied him push him into the house, striking him lightly on the back, thus encouraging him to join his wife for the marriage consummation. The groom welcomes the bride into their new home. As a game, the bride remains silent and does not allow her husband to unveil her until he has presented her with some money or a gift. Thereupon, the *sağdıç*s leave the bridal couple alone. They may say a few words upon leaving, as one *Milli Görüş* respondent did, who laid the hands of the bridal couple on one another and said: "I brought a rose from paradise. I give the rose to you. I give you to the rose. I give you both to God." According to some Turkish respondents the bridal couple must perform a supplementary *ṣalât* before consummating the marriage.

Among Surinamese Hindustani Muslims, women of the groom's family officially receive the bride with a ceremony called *moe dighauni*.[151] During this ceremony the bride shows her face to the groom's female family members. The *moe dighauni* was once the first occasion on which the bride and the groom's female family members met, since only a male delegation from the groom's side took part in the religious wedding ceremony at the bride's home.

In the Netherlands the ceremony of *moe dighauni* takes place at the groom's home following the religious and civil marriage ceremony or following the wedding party. For example, one Surinamese Hindustani bride, whose *nikah* took place in the morning at her parental home in the presence of only male family members from both sides, and whose civil

[150] Today most newlyweds start living on their own and not with the groom's parents, according to Yerden, *Trouwen op z'n Turks*, 105. The following account of the wedding night corresponds to a large extent to the findings of Yerden concerning Turkey, ibid., 98–99.

[151] In his description of a similar ritual among Hindus in Surinam, Speckmann, *Marriage and Kinship among the Indians in Surinam*, 146, uses the word *munhdekhi*. He gives a short description of a similar ritual among Muslims as well but does not use the word *moe dighauni* or its Hindu equivalent.

wedding at the town hall in the presence of both male and female family members took place in the afternoon, went through the ceremony of *moe dighauni* in the evening. She sat in the middle of the living room with her face veiled. In turns the groom's female family members approached her and lifted her veil to see her face, kissed her, and presented her with gifts. In this case, the bride returned to her parental home afterwards, because the wedding party would take place on the next day.

After the wedding party, Surinamese Hindustani couples normally stay at the groom's parental home or their future home for a few days. The bride then returns to her parental home. She stays there for a few more days to pack and to prepare for taking up residence permanently with her husband. Speckmann gives a similar account for Surinam of the bride's temporary return to her parental home: "The bride remains with her husband's family for three or four days, during which period she has no contact with her husband. Thereafter she returns to her parents for fourteen days, and subsequently moves to her husband's house for good."[152] Speckmann does not explain why the bride has no contact with her husband when she stays with her husband's family.

At wedding party in Larache (Morocco) that I attended, the groom fetched the bride by car. It also occurs that the bride is carried to the groom's house in the litter (*al-amarya*), or by car and *al-amarya*.[153] In the Netherlands this litter features in wedding parties in a hall, but is not used for the bride's transport to the groom.

The bride may be accompanied by many young women when she is taken to the groom's home. On arrival at the groom's house, the bride and groom exchange milk and dates and the youngsters who accompany the bride are entertained with dancing to music and a meal. Generally the bride's parents do not come with the bride.[154] One Moroccan respondent celebrated her marriage in Fez, from where she originally came, and two days later in Berkane, the groom's home town. Her mother, brothers, and sisters accompanied her to Berkane, but her father stayed in Fez. In both Berkane and Fez she changed her clothes several times, which is unusual: the bride normally

[152] Ibid., 148–149.

[153] Evers-Rosander, "Some Wedding Customs in Qbila Anjra Now (1976–87) and Then (1900–1910)", 116, presents evidence on the basis of her fieldwork in Anjra of a combination of car and litter: "If the girl got married far from her home, she was therefore taken for just a short ride in the cage around her home village and then went by car to near the groom's home. From there another cage transported her to the doorstep of the groom's house."

[154] Ibid., 117.

changes her clothes at the wedding party before she leaves her parental home, but not when she is received at the groom's home.

A Moroccan bride subsequently stays with her husband for seven days without seeing her parents. The bride's mother may have prepared the bridal couple's first breakfast, but she pays no visit to the bridal couple on the morning after the wedding night: only a few young females do this. During this period of seven days the bride wears no girdle. Thereupon life resumes its normal course, the bride starts wearing her girdle again and her mother pays her a visit.[155]

Moroccan and Turkish Muslims, apparently more than Surinamese Muslims, highly value the bride's virginity at her first marriage.[156] In Morocco it may occur that the *sirwâl* (trousers) or sheet stained with virginal blood is shown to the wedding guests.[157] Like the *sağdıçs* in Turkey, the *luzir* and *luzira* in Morocco may assist the bridal couple in case of problems in producing this evidence.[158] In towns in Morocco, middle-class families increasingly shrink from displaying the blood-stained cloth.[159] At the marriage in Larache that I attended, young female family members visited the bridal couple at the groom's home on the morning following the wedding night. However, they asked the bride only whether everything was all right with her. Some Moroccan respondents, like most of the Surinamese respondents, emphasized that whether the bride is a virgin is a matter for bride and groom only.

The bride's virginity is generally highly valued among Turkish Muslims in the Netherlands too.[160] "The most modern couples (often those

[155] Westermarck, *Marriage Ceremonies in Morocco*, 291–295, gives a detailed account of the girdling of the bride. The day of the girdle, as it sometimes called, is often the seventh day, but sometimes the sixth day.

[156] The terms used for virgin are *bikr* and *ᶜadhrâ'*. *Bikr* means that a girl has not married before, which makes her virginity probable; *ᶜadhra'* explicitly refers to her physical integrity. See Buskens, *Islamitisch recht en familiebetrekkkingen in Marokko*, 470.

[157] Concerning wedding rituals in Ben Smim (Middle Atlas, Morocco), Wiersma, "De bruid in veranderende huwelijksrituelen in Ben Smim", 83, reports that nowadays the *sirwâl* is publicly displayed to women and men whereas in the past it was shown only to her parents and female family members.

[158] Ibid., 71.

[159] Cf. Buskens, *Islamitisch recht en familiebetrekkingen in Marokko*, 443–446. According to Elaroussi, "Pratiques du mariage au Maroc", 129, youngsters may consider this practice of showing the *serwal* with blood outmoded, but: "Les mentalités changent, les pratiques évoluent, mais lentement. A l'heure actuelle, on ne peut pas affirmer que la coutume du *serwal* porté sur un plateau soit tombée en désuétude."

[160] Cf. Yerden, *Trouwen op z'n Turks*, 46. De Vries, *Ogen in je rug*, 151–152, explains the importance of the bride's virginity by reference to fear of gossip and to the harmful consequences that an unmarried girl may experience if she is not a virgin: the

where the bride is trained for a high-status profession)", says Tapper, "may reject even vestigial gender symbols from the past, such as the red sash all brides normally wear around their waists."[161] According to Santing, the blood-stained sheet will hardly ever be shown to a female gathering. In most cases the bride's parents will not go to bed on the wedding night until they have been informed by the bride's mother-in-law.[162] One Turkish respondent said: "When the girl is deflowered, something must be put outside the room, indicating that everything is all right. Everyone then goes to bed. We have put a slipper outside the room. The next morning the sister of . . . [name of the groom] came to see the cloth. She is the only one to have seen it. She immediately washed the cloth." The bride's parents were told by telephone that everything was all right.

In Turkey the newlyweds may visit the groom's family on the days following the wedding night. The bride may present them with gifts from her *çeyiz* (trousseau), such as needlework or presents bought on the day on which the families went shopping together. One Turkish respondent paid three visits a day in the week following the wedding. In her account of traditional weddings, Tapper presents evidence for a similar custom: "All being well, the families of the couple dine together at each others' houses on successive evenings."[163]

4.4. Conclusions

The ritual of marriage has changed in many respects due to migration to the Netherlands. The changes are particularly salient in two areas. The change of juridical context has strongly influenced the marriage practice of Muslims in the Netherlands, particularly among Surinamese Muslims since they, unlike Moroccans and Turks, have mostly taken Dutch nationality. Moreover, migration to the Netherlands has affected the character of the wedding celebrations.

The Moroccan and Turkish respondents in my sample mostly had not taken Dutch nationality. In the majority of cases they contracted marriages at their country's consulate in the Netherlands or in the country of origin. In these cases the marriage legislation of their country applied to them and migration consequently did not involve a

prospective husband may fail to show respect to her and look for another partner. Her respondents regarded virginity also as a matter of self-respect.

[161] Tapper, "'Traditional' and 'Modern' Wedding Rituals in a Turkish Town", 153.

[162] Santing, *Die vrouw, dat ben ik*, 34.

[163] Tapper, "'Traditional' and 'Modern' Wedding Rituals in a Turkish Town", 149.

change of legal system. Nevertheless, moving the scene to the consulate has somewhat changed the character of the civil wedding ceremony.

Many Moroccan and Turkish respondents said that they found the consular ceremony disappointing. They experienced the routine at the consulate as unofficial, complaining for example about the short duration of the ceremony and the carelessness in the design of the wedding room. The fact that it is unusual for the bride to wear a bridal gown at a consular wedding and the small number of guests normally attending the ceremony in the Netherlands added to this feeling. At the Moroccan consulate the stipulations of the *Mudawwana* were moreover not always followed strictly: the marriage conclusion of one couple in my sample took place without the two professional witnesses (*ᶜudûl*) required under Moroccan marriage law, something which is inconceivable in Morocco.

In Turkey and Morocco, by contrast, the civil ceremony exhibits its festive character in various ways. For example, in Turkey most brides wear a bridal gown at the *resmî nikâh*, many guests attend the ceremony, and to add to its festivity they customarily receive sweets afterwards. In Morocco the civil wedding ceremony may take place at home in a small circle and be followed by a religious ceremony which marks in yet another way the festive character of the event.

The change of juridical context has affected marriages of Surinamese Muslims in the Netherlands even more. In Surinam marriages contracted in accordance with the teachings of Islam are accepted as legally valid under certain conditions. Surinamese Muslims in the Netherlands have mostly taken Dutch nationality and consequently Dutch marriage law, which does not recognize marriages concluded before a religious leader, applies to them. This means that as well as a marriage in an Islamic manner, which is recognized as legally valid in Surinam but not in the Netherlands, they must conclude a civil marriage before a Dutch registrar at a town hall for legal validation. In the Netherlands the conclusion of Surinamese Hindustani marriages consequently took place mostly twice. However, some couples held only a religious ceremony to legalize their relations on a religious basis thus making cohabitation possible, but postponed the civil ceremony for financial reasons.

In some respects Islam seems to play a more prominent role in the marriage practice of Muslims in the Netherlands than in the countries of origin. The religious wedding ceremony has for example evidently gained importance. The development visible among certain strata of the population of Surinam and Turkey, that they conclude a civil marriage and no religious marriage,[164] is not found in the Netherlands. On the contrary, none of my Surinamese and Turkish respondents omitted to hold a religious marriage ceremony. Even respondents who did not practice their religious obligations may attach importance to the religious wedding ceremony. Similarly, the migrational situation provides room for stricter religious viewpoints for which there is no room in the countries of origin. For example, Turkish respondents associated with the *Milli Görüş* said that in Turkey it is unusual to conclude an *imam nikâhı* as early as on the acceptance of the marriage proposal or at the engagement whereas this is common in their circles in the Netherlands.

The character of the wedding celebrations has also changed in the Netherlands. Two factors that have caused changes in the ritual of circumcision in the Netherlands appear to have influenced the marriage ritual too: the difference in the housing and the fact that certain services, which are commonly available in the countries of origin, are less easy to come by in the Netherlands. Both have had an impact particularly on Moroccan wedding parties because Moroccans in the Netherlands sometimes hold their parties at home and not in a hall or on the premises of the mosque, as is typical of Surinamese and Turkish wedding parties. Unlike houses in Morocco, Dutch houses do not provide for rooms for the separate reception of men and women. Moreover, dressers (*neggafa*s) in Morocco have a much wider assortment than dressers in the Netherlands, and the wide selection of professional Moroccan bands available at home is absent in the Netherlands.

Certain developments are typical not only of the Dutch situation, but also of urban contexts in the countries of origin. For example, the length of the wedding festivities has decreased in both the Netherlands and cities in the countries of origin. Similarly, in both settings wedding parties are to an increasing extent held in a hall rented for the occasion. One also finds an increasing professionalization.

Other developments that are observable in the home countries seemed to have gained momentum in the Dutch context. For example, whereas

[164] This development cannot be observed in Morocco because the Moroccan legal system makes no distinction between a religious and a civil ceremony. The Moroccan civil wedding ceremony has an Islamic character which obviates the need of a religious wedding form alongside the civil wedding ceremony. Turkish marriage law expressly distinguish between the two wedding forms; only the *resmî nikâh* has legal force, whereas the *imam nikâhı* is considered a private matter. Surinamese marriage law recognizes Islamic marriages but also offers their citizens the opportunity to follow the nonreligious route.

the separate wedding parties for both families still occur in the countries of origin, in the Netherlands this phenomenon seems to have disappeared: the wedding parties are increasingly held in a venue where the male and female guests of both families gather together.

5
DEATH

> From it [the earth] did We create you, and into it shall We return you, and from it shall We make you appear once again.
>
> —Koran 20:55

The ritual of death shows how strong the ties of Muslims in the Netherlands with the countries of origin are. Mainly because of their strong relationship with them, Moroccan and Turkish Muslims in the Netherlands generally opt for a burial in their countries of origin. Small children of these communities are mostly buried in the Netherlands. Surinamese Muslims on the contrary mostly opt for a burial in the Netherlands.

In dealing with the ritual of circumcision, we saw how an infrastructure for the performance of this operation has gradually unfolded in the Netherlands. Similar developments in the field of burial seem to have begun only recently. The new Dutch Corpse Disposal Act (Herziene Wet op de lijkbezorging), passed in 1991, has allowed the option, designed specifically for Muslims, of burying the dead without a coffin and within twenty-four hours of the death, in line with Islamic prescriptions. However, Surinamese Muslims in the Netherlands, who generally opt for a burial in the Netherlands, have not made use of this regulation up to now. This might change with future generations, as an increasing number of Muslims are buried in the Netherlands. The differences between burial practices of the several ethnic groups, which may then become apparent, will probably cause them to adapt their burial practice.

In this chapter we examine every phase of the ritual of death, beginning with the process of dying itself and the subsequent burial preparations, consisting of the ritual purification and shrouding of the deceased and the performance of the funeral prayer. Section 5.2 focuses on the burial and section 5.3 deals with the condolence visits and the mourning period.[1]

5.1. Death and Burial Preparations

When it becomes clear that a person will soon die, he or she is to be laid in the direction of the *qibla*, towards Mecca. According to Islamic law,

[1] An introduction to the funeral and mourning practices of Muslims in the Netherlands can be found in Dessing, "Uitvaart- en rouwrituelen bij moslims in Nederland".

there are two ways of doing this. Turning a dying person onto his or her right flank with the face turned in the direction of the *qibla* is the best way. Alternatively, one can also leave the person lying on his or her back with the feet pointing in the direction of the *qibla* and with the head lifted a little so that the face is also oriented in that direction.[2]

Death is considered to be a difficult and painful experience, as the following reference by Smith and Haddad to prophetical traditions makes clear:

> One very famous report relates a conversation taking place between the Prophet and his wife ᶜĀ'isha after she realizes that someday he, too, will have to depart this life. The Prophet describes for her the extreme difficulties encountered by the dying person in the process of leaving his home with his children crying for him, being put into the grave and covered with dirt, watching in the form of a disembodied spirit the washers preparing him for burial—"O washer, by God I swear to you, take off my clothes gently, for I have gone out from the devastating power of the angel of death"—having his body, which is suffering from the removal of the spirit, washed with water too hot or too cold, and in general agonizing over separation from his loved ones: "By God, O washer, do not make the winding around me tight, so that I can yet see the faces of my people and my children and my relatives; this is the last time I can look at them, for today I will be separated from them and will not see them until the Day of Resurrection. . . ."[3]

It is believed that at the moment of death the angel ᶜIzrâ'îl appears to the dying person to remove his or her soul. ᶜIzrâ'îl's appearance is described as a devastating experience. Moreover, the dying person will already have endured hardship during the process of dying itself because of the appearance of the devil (*shaiṭân*) at his deathbed. Persons close to death are believed to suffer a burning thirst and *shaiṭân* attempts to induce them to give up their faith in exchange for a sip of water.[4]

In the face of this suffering, a Muslim is encouraged to support his or her dying fellow believer, for instance by offering him or her some water to drink. Furthermore, he or she may offer support by uttering the *shahâda* quietly and by reciting sura *YaSin* (36) or *duᶜâ's*.[5] It is *sunna* to prompt the dying person to repeat the *shahâda*, so that these will be his or her last words. However, one should not be excessively insistent.[6]

[2] Shadid & Van Koningsveld, "Stervensbegeleiding en begrafenisriten in de islam", 18–19.

[3] Smith & Haddad, *The Islamic Understanding of Death and Resurrection*, 37.

[4] Ibid., 35–38.

[5] Shadid & Van Koningsveld, "Stervensbegeleiding en begrafenisriten in de islam", 19, and Van Bommel, "Rouwgebruiken bij moslims", 105.

[6] Van Bommel, "Rouwgebruiken bij moslims", 105.

Furthermore, according to Islamic law it is preferable that in the final phase only those who contribute to the inner calm of the dying person be present.[7] In order to remind the dying person of God, the repentance of his or her sins and his or her last will, only the most beloved, considerate, and pious family members should be present.[8]

A Turkish respondent related that her family had prepared a special room for her father's deathbed. This room had recently been painted, so that he could breathe his last in clean surroundings. Her family allowed only the closer relatives and acquaintances to sit for a moment at the deathbed to take leave of her father. This farewell consisted of the recital of *Hakkı helal olsun* by both the dying person and the visitor. With this phrase, they absolve each other from every known or unknown sin that they have committed against one another. We will see that for Turkish Muslims this acquittal of the deceased forms an integral part of the funeral prayer (*ṣalât al-janâza*) as well.

My respondents generally emphasized the importance of reciting the *shahâda* at a person's deathbed in the final phase, so that the dying person will repeat these words. A Moroccan respondent indicated that, even though one should not be too insistent, one should do one's very best to ensure that the person repeats these words. A Turkish respondent did not admit acquaintances of her father to sit at his deathbed, since they were not really close to the family. Moreover, these visitors emphasized all too obviously the importance of Koran recitation and the presence of an imam, which made their presence annoying for the family.

In his description of changes in the death rituals among Turkish migrants in Germany, Dursun Tan points out that in Germany in general nowadays death occurs in a hospital and not at home, as was usually the case in Turkey. This has, according to Tan, important consequences for the further course of events because the hospital acquires a mediating role, drawing apart the dying person and the living.[9] This development fits into the overall picture of professionalization and institutionalization, which is characteristic not only of the migrant situation but also of urban contexts in the countries of origin. The growth in the number of Muslim undertakers in both the Netherlands and Turkey is an example of this development.

Another development is however typical of the migrational situation only. In Turkey, death usually occurs at home in the midst of family

[7] Ibid., 106.
[8] Shadid & Van Koningsveld, "Stervensbegeleiding en begrafenisriten in de islam", 19.
[9] Tan, "Wandlungen des Sterbens und der Trauerrituale in der Migration", 117–118.

members. During the short time between death and burial, everyone around became involved in the preparations for the burial and in the burial itself.[10] This involvement necessarily changes in the migrant situation, among other things because the preparations and the burial itself are split up, spatially and in time.[11]

Even if death occurs at home, and even though Turkish and Moroccan Muslims in the Netherlands will be unable to bury the deceased on the day of the death if they opt for burial in the country of origin, the body of the deceased is normally nonetheless taken out of his familiar surroundings to a mortuary shortly after the death to be prepared for burial.

The sequence of events takes for instance the following form. Upon the death of a Turkish man, his eyes were promptly closed. A cloth was fastened around his head to tie up his jaw. He was undressed and covered with white towels. His arms were made to lie straight along his body. Once the death had occurred, the deceased's wife no longer entered the room where her husband lay.[12] Within a few hours, he was taken for the ritual ablution, shrouding, and coffining for transport. His wife and children remained at home. Immediately, visitors arrived to offer their condolences to the bereaved. In Turkey, these visits of condolence take place only after the burial and not beforehand, whereas in the Netherlands this order has changed because of the comparatively long interval between death and burial.

The ritual purification and shrouding of the corpse as well as the performance of the *ṣalât al-janâza* belong to the collective duties (*farḍ kifâya*) of the Muslim community. This means that if these duties are fulfilled by a sufficiently large number of individuals, other individuals are excused from fulfilling them. In the following we will elaborate on these three tasks of the Muslim community. The washing and shrouding of the corpse as well as the performance of the *ṣalât al-janâza* take place preferably on the day of burial, if the burial will occur in the Netherlands,[13] and shortly before the transport to the country of origin otherwise.

[10] Ibid., 119.

[11] Ibid., 121–122. Tan points out that this has strong emotional consequences for the bereaved: "Innerhalb kürzester Zeit befinden sich die Trauernden in einer völlig anderen Welt, unter anderen Menschen und an einem Ort, der nicht mehr ihr gewohnter Intimbereich ist."

[12] According to the Hanafites, as e.g. Al-Jazîrî, *Al-fiqh ᶜalâ al-madhâhib al-arbaᶜa*, vol. 2, 504 n. 1, reports, a marriage ceases to exist on the death of one of the partners, although upon the death of a man, the widow must observe the legally prescribed waiting period (*ᶜidda*) of four months and ten days, during which the marriage is considered to be still in existence. Thus, a widow may see her husband's body upon his death if she wishes and perform the ritual washing, whereas this is not permitted to a man after his wife's death. The refusal of the Turkish woman mentioned above to enter the room where her husband's body lay is to be explained as a rather widespread misinterpretation of this Hanafite point of view.

[13] In Morocco and Turkey the burial takes place generally on the day of death. Consequently the preparatory tasks are also performed on that day. See for Morocco

Ritual Purification

Islamic law treats the ritual purification of the deceased, shrouding, and the *ṣalât al-janâza* either as part of the chapter on the *ṣalât* or as a separate chapter after the chapter on the *ṣalât*, and describes in detail how those who perform these tasks should proceed. The ritual washing enables the deceased to meet God in a state of purity, and thus bears comparison with the washing that is performed in preparation for the daily *ṣalât*.

The ritual purification of the deceased must be performed by a Muslim who knows how to proceed. If the deceased is a man, the persons best qualified to administer the ritual bath are those thus designated in his will. Next in order are his father, grandfather, and lastly certain other male family members. If a woman has died, those best qualified to wash her body are her mother, grandmother, and certain other female family members.[14] In principle, a dead man's body is to be washed only by men and that of a woman only by women. The Malikites and the Shafiᶜites take the view that the spouse of the deceased is also permitted to perform the ritual washing of body. By contrast, the Hanafites take the view that a man may not wash his wife because their marriage has come to an end with her death, and consequently he has become a stranger to her. However, a woman is allowed to wash her husband, because the marital bond between them ceases to exist only when her waiting period (*ᶜidda*) has come to an end.[15] It is permissible for a child to be washed by an adult of the opposite sex.

Numerous traditions call on the washer to handle the corpse with respect. It is for example not allowed for washers to turn the deceased onto his or her face and it is recommended that they use lukewarm water. Those who wash a body are held not to divulge any physical imperfections of the deceased that they may have noticed during the washing. According to Islam, it is strongly reprehensible to accept payment for washing a body.[16]

e.g. Renaerts, *La Mort, rites et valeurs dans l'islam maghrébin*, 44: "Les ablutions doivent de préférence être effectuées le jour de l'enterrement. Au cas où le corps est sale on peut faire un petit lavage (*ghasl lᶜarâq d-l-miyyit*) avant les ablutions rituelles afin de le nettoyer des impuretés sexuelles ou des excréments." See also Westermarck, *Ritual and Belief in Morocco*, vol. 2, 446. Similarly, a Surinamese Hindustani respondent stressed that the *istinjâ'* and the *wuḍû'* will take place immediately upon death in the hospital or at home, since otherwise, he argued, it would not be possible to recite the Koran in the room where the deceased lies. The ritual washing will take place later on the premises of the mosque.

[14] Shadid & Van Koningsveld, "Stervensbegeleiding en begrafenisriten in de islam", 20.

[15] Al-Jazîrî, *Al-fiqh ᶜalâ al-madhâhib al-arbaᶜa*, vol. 2, 504.

[16] See Van Bommel, "Rouwgebruiken bij moslims", 111.

Before undertaking the washing, according to the Hanbalites, it is obligatory to express the intention (*niyya*). The Malikites take the view that the *niyya* for the washing is not laid down in law, whereas according to the Shafiᶜites the expression of the *niyya* is *sunna*. The Hanafites hold the view that the expression of the *niyya* is a prerequisite for gaining merit for the performance of this task. However, the *niyya* is in their view not a necessary condition for the validity of the act.[17]

The ritual washing of the deceased (*ghusl al-mayyit*) is according to Islamic law generally understood to proceed as follows. The washing must take place in a room that is screened off. It is obligatory to cover the corpse from the navel to the knees during the washing. First, any impurities should be removed from the corpse. The washer then gently presses the belly, to empty the intestines. According to most law schools, it is recommended to burn incense during this process to mask any unpleasant odour.[18] It is recommended to perform the *wuḍû'*, consisting of washing the hands and arms up to the elbows, feet, face, neck, and ears, and rinsing the nose and mouth with water, before performing the *ghusl*, the full washing of the body.[19] The entire body must be washed an odd number of times, three or if necessary five or seven. Each washing must begin with the right side from the front to the back and from head to toe, followed by the left side.[20] The washing is to be

[17] Al-Jazîrî, *Al-fiqh ᶜalâ al-madhâhib al-arbaᶜa*, vol. 2, 510–513.

[18] Only the Malikites differ, for according to them it is not recommended to burn incense, as Al-Jazîrî, *Al-fiqh ᶜalâ al-madhâhib al-arbaᶜa*, vol. 2, 508, reports.

[19] Ibid., 508. Instead of rinsing the nose and mouth with water, the washer should clean the teeth and nostrils of the dead person with a piece of cloth, according to the Hanafites and the Hanbalites. According to the Malikites and the Shafiᶜites, it is recommendable to clean the nostrils and teeth with a piece of cloth. However, according to them, the *wuḍû'* also includes the rinsing of the nose and mouth with water.

[20] Ibid., 510–512. According to the Hanafites, the *ghusl* consists of (1) the *istinjâ'*, the washing of genitals and anus, (2) the *wuḍû'*, omitting the washing of the hands and the rinsing of the nose and mouth, and (3) turning the deceased on to his or her left side and washing the right side three times from head to foot. The Muslim community thereby fulfils its collective duty (*farḍ kifâya*). However, according to the Hanafites, it is *sunna* to add two washings, consisting of turning the body onto his or her right side while the same procedure is followed, then of propping the body up in a sitting position while the belly is pressed and any released fluids are washed away, and finally of turning the deceased onto his or her left side and washing the right side from head to foot three times. According to the Malikites, the *ghusl* consists of (1) washing the hands of the deceased, (2) gently pressing the belly, (3) the *wuḍû'*, including rinsing nose and mouth with water, and (4) washing the right and left side of the deceased with pure water. It is recommended that this procedure be performed twice more, using water and soap, and water and camphor. According to the Shafiᶜites, the *ghusl* consists of (1) gently pressing the belly, (2) cleaning nostrils and teeth with a piece of cloth, (3) the *wuḍû'* including rinsing nose and mouth, (4) washing head and beard, and (5) washing the right and left side of the deceased three times. It is considered to be *sunna* to repeat the *ghusl* twice.

performed with water and soap or a similar substance. Camphor or another odorous substance is added to the water for the last washing. Then, the corpse is dried, to prevent the shrouds from becoming wet.[21]

In the Netherlands the ritual purification of the dead is mostly performed as described above either at a funeral parlour, in the hospital or on the premises of a mosque. Some people favour a funeral parlour because its washing room is provided with various facilities, such as a special washtable for the corpse and a hand shower. This preference for the funeral parlour exists in particular among the Surinamese Javanese Muslims in the Netherlands, who may perform all three *farḍ al-kifâya* tasks consecutively at the funeral parlour, shortly before the burial.

Some Surinamese Hindustani respondents expressed a preference for performing the washing on the premises of their mosque either in a screened-off area of the washplace or in a special room for the washing of the dead. This preference for the mosque is motivated by the fact that the family will be able to keep watch over the corpse overnight only if it lies on the premises of a mosque. This would not be possible if the deceased lay at a mortuary, which normally closes at night.

Special washplaces for the dead are available on the premises of some Moroccan and Turkish mosques too. However, in most cases the ritual purification takes place in a hospital or funeral parlour. Even though the burial of Moroccan and Turkish Muslims is postponed for at least one or two days, if only because of the transport to the country of origin, it has not become common usage among these groups to keep watch over the dead until burial. To the contrary, the body is often taken away from its home surroundings shortly after death.

In practice the next of kin prefer in many cases not to undertake the ritual washing themselves, but to leave it to outsiders.[22] Some argue that

[21] Shadid & Van Koningsveld, "Stervensbegeleiding en begrafenisriten in de islam", 20–21, and Van Bommel, "Rouwgebruiken bij moslims", 111.

[22] From Westermarck, *Ritual and Belief in Morocco*, vol. 2, 443, one may conclude that in Morocco it was already common practice in earlier times to leave the ritual washing to outsiders, since: "In towns there are professional male and female washers. . . . At Fez the male washers, as well as the washing board . . . and the bier . . . are fetched from … a holy place with a small mosque and a madhouse with a prison for women above it. Well-to-do towns-people, however, may prefer not to make use of public washers, since it is considered important that the dead body should be washed by a person possessed of some *baraka*—a shereef or shereefa, a scribe, or a good and pious man or woman. In country places the body of a man is washed by the *fqî*, or schoolmaster, of the village or, if there is no *fqî*, by some other good and religious man, with the assistance of one or two other men; and the body of a woman is washed by the midwife of the village or some other woman of good reputation, by preference one who is in the habit of praying, with the asistance of one or two other women."

they do not know exactly how to proceed. The fact that they do not feel emotionally able to perform this task may also play a role. A Turkish respondent further attributed the reserve on the part of family members to shame, since a daughter does not want to see her mother's body naked. Some respondents stressed also that those performing the purification must meet certain requirements. They must know how to proceed and they must remain silent about any physical imperfections of the deceased that they may notice.

Surinamese Hindustani and Javanese mosque organizations in the Netherlands periodically organize courses on how to perform the washing of the dead. This ensures that a sufficient number of their members know the procedure. Moreover, since the washing of a corpse is attended by about five persons, a number of them gains experience in the procedure on each occasion. However, among Surinamese Javanese Muslims, it occasionally also occurs that an imam is present in the washplace when a dead woman is washed, to give the women instructions if they do not know the procedure exactly.[23] In Moroccan and Turkish mosques in the Netherlands, there are always a number of people who know how to perform the washing. My Turkish respondents indicated that the imam performs this task together with one or two helpers.[24] If the deceased is a woman, the imam's wife plays a central role in some instances. According to the findings of Marrie Bot, Turks in Amsterdam and Utrecht make use in such cases of female professional washers, who receive payment for the performance of this task, even though this is regarded under Islamic law as reprehensible.[25]

My respondents indicated that in practice the ritual purification consists of the removal of impurities, the *istinjâ'* (washing of anus and genitals), the *wuḍû'*, and the *ghusl* (washing of the whole corpse). The removal of impurities from the corpse, the *istinjâ'*, and the *wuḍû'* are performed with water only. The *ghusl* is performed with water and soap and sometimes also with olive leaves, each time proceeding from the ventral side to the back and from head to toe. The *ghusl* is performed an odd number of times, in the majority of cases three times, but if necessary up to seven times. Meanwhile the belly is gently pressed and the

[23] Bot, *Een laatste groet*, 132 and 134, including a photograph of a male Surinamese Javanese religious leader assisting women with the washing of a dead woman.

[24] One often encounters a division of tasks, which is also described by Renaerts, *La Mort, rites et valeurs dans l'islam maghrébin*, 41, as regards Morocco: "Les personnes présentes au lavage du mort sont généralement au nombre de trois: celui qui apporte l'eau, celui qui verse l'eau sur le corps et le troisième qui effectue le lavage."

[25] Bot, *Een laatste groet*, 132.

istinjâ' is performed. Camphor may be added to the water for the last wash.

Before beginning the washing, the washers may burn incense and perhaps walk round the corpse while holding the burning incense to mask any unpleasant smell. Some Surinamese Javanese respondents, however, viewed this as reprehensible as they associated this practice with the making of *sadjèn* offerings.[26] They preferred instead to add camphor to the water for the first wash, which has the same effect as incense.

Among Turkish Muslims one sometimes also encounters the custom of pouring water over the deceased. As soon as the washers have completed their task, fellow believers enter the washplace in turns to pour water over the deceased. The community thus becomes closely involved in the performance of this collective duty. Some Turkish Muslims in the Netherlands, however, reject this practice.

In the countries of origin the ritual washing often takes place at home, either indoors or in the open.[27] Mosque organizations may provide various appliances needed for the ritual purification, such as a special washtable, a screen,[28] and pans to warm the washwater.[29] A Surinamese Javanese respondent indicated that in Surinam, even if one has died in hospital, one is brought home to be buried from there. A Turkish respondent said that one finds an increasing professionalization of the ritual in towns in Turkey. There may be special rooms for the washing of the dead, and special packages of services and goods may be offered for various fees, consisting for instance of soap for the ritual purification, bleached or unbleached cotton for the shrouding of the corpse (*takfîn*), and hearses. However, she said also that this kind of professionalization has not yet occurred in the countryside.

Shrouding

The shrouding of the deceased is another collective duty of the Muslim community (*farḍ kifâya*). The entire corpse, including the head, is to be

[26] The westward-prayers among the Surinamese Javanese Muslims attach great interest to making *sadjèn* offerings to the spirits, whereas the eastward-prayers disagree with this and prefer to give a *slametan* or, as they prefer to call it, a *ṣadaqa*. Burning incense at *sadjèn* offerings is meant to make contact with the spirits and for this reason the eastward-prayers reject coal, which is used by the westward-prayers, even more strongly than sticks.

[27] For similar findings, see e.g. Westermarck, *Ritual and Belief in Morocco*, vol. 2, 444.

[28] A Surinamese Javanese respondent, as well as De Waal Malefijt, *The Javanese of Surinam*, 167, presented evidence for the fact that in Surinam the corpse is screened off by people holding up four large sheets, thus forming a roofless tent.

[29] See for instance Gailly, *Een dorp in Turkije*, 149, for Turkey, and Renaerts, *La Mort, rites et valeurs dans l'islam maghrébin*, 36, for Morocco.

covered with cloth before being put into the grave. During the lifetime of the Prophet, clothes that the deceased had worn during his or her life were used for this end. Nowadays, the shroud (*kafan*) consists of lengths of new cloth rather than items of clothing.[30] In most cases, plain white cotton cloths are used, for women as well as men.[31] This preference for simple material irrespective of the person's status symbolizes the equality of all before God. The same meaning is attached to the unsewn white clothes worn in Mecca during the pilgrimage.[32]

One finds a preference for an odd number of wrappings, usually three cloths for men and five for women.[33] It is argued, particularly among the Hanbalites and the Shafiᶜites, that the *kafan* of a man should not include a *qamîṣ* (long shirt-like garment) or a turban.[34] The basis of this is a *ḥadîth* of Aisha: "The Prophet of God—God bless him and grant him peace—was wrapped into three Yemenite, white *Suḥûliyya* cloths made of cotton, but not into a *qamîṣ* or a turban".[35] The Hanafite scholars hold the opinion that a *qamîṣ* is *sunna*, for which they cite a *ḥadîth* of Ibn ᶜAbbâs:

> The Prophet—God bless him and grant him peace—was shrouded into three clothes, including his *qamîṣ*. The clothes [that he wore] after his death were based on the clothes [that he wore] during his lifetime except for the fact that during his lifetime he wore *sarâwîl* [plural of *sirwâl*, a kind of trousers] so that, when he walked, his *ᶜawra* was not uncovered. However, there was no need for this after his death. Then the *izâr* substituted for the *sarâwîl*, whereas during his lifetime the *izâr* was under [shorter than] the *qamîṣ* to make walking easy for him. But after his death the *izâr* was

[30] Grütter, "Arabische Bestattungsbräuche in frühislamischer Zeit", part 2, 86–87. Grütter explains this change of preference from worn clothes to new cloths by reference to the greater ritual purity that is considered to go with new cloths rather than with worn clothes and from the greater wealth which came with the conquests.

[31] Van Bommel, "Rouwgebruiken bij moslims", 111.

[32] Shadid & Van Koningsveld, *Moslims in Nederland*, 105.

[33] For a description of the several articles of clothing that may be used for shrouding, see Grütter, "Arabische Bestattungsbräuche in frühislamischer Zeit", part 2, 82–85. She mentions among other items: *qamîṣ* (long shirt-like garment), *ᶜimâma* (turban as well as the cloth wrapped around the turban several times), *ridâ'* (loose outer garment, cloak), and *izâr* (large cloth wrapped around the lower part of the body). The *ᶜimâma*, that is in this case the cloth wrapped around the turban, may be used also to bind together the feet of the deceased.

[34] The Muslim World League's brochure on death and burial presents a similar point of view: see the translation of Shadid & Van Koningsveld, "Stervensbegeleiding en begrafenisriten in de islam", 22. See also Stichting Lalla Rookh, *Huwelijk, geboorte en overlijden bij moslims*, 23. According to the Hanafite scholar Al-Sarakhsî (d. 483/1090), *Kitâb al-mabsûṭ*, vol. 2, 60, the Shafiᶜites also take this position on the basis of the same *ḥadîth*. From Al-Jazîrî, *Al-fiqh ᶜalâ al-madhâhib al-arbaᶜa*, vol. 2, 513–516, one may conclude that the Hanbalites and the Shafiᶜites have taken this position.

[35] Al-Albânî, *Aḥkâm al-janâ'iz wa bidaᶜuhâ*, 63. *Suḥûl* is a town in Yemen noted for its white cotton cloth: see Grütter, "Arabische Bestattungsbräuche in frühislamischer Zeit", part 2, 85.

above [longer than] the *qamîṣ* from shoulder to foot because there was no need for walking.[36]

Disregarding nuances, we can summarize the view of the four law schools as follows. The *kafan* of a man consists of a long shirtlike garment (*qamîṣ*), a cloth that covers the corpse from head to foot (*izâr*), and an outer winding (*lifâfa*). The corpse is wrapped in the windings in the aforementioned order. In the case of a woman, a head covering (*khimâr*) and an extra *lifâfa* (Malikites, Shafiᶜites, and Hanbalites) or a breast cloth (Hanafites) are added to these three windings. The breast cloth, which covers her from the shoulder to the knee, may come before or after the *izâr*.[37]

The winding sheets are laid out over one another, the largest underneath, since the cloths are to be wrapped round the deceased according to size. The uppermost cloth, which is the smallest, is wrapped first round the right side of the corpse and then the left. The same procedure is followed with the other windings.[38] The *kafan* is thereafter fastened with a few strips of the cloths.

My Surinamese Hindustani respondents clearly reflected the Hanafite point of view concerning the *takfîn* in practice. According to them, the *kafan* of a man consists of three cloths (*tjadar*, *tahband*, and *kafnie*, in order of decreasing size) and of a woman of five (*tjadar*, *sienaband*, *tahband*, *kafnie*, and a veil). The *kafnie* is a kind of shirt that is put on over the head. The neck is cut widthwise for men and lengthwise for women. According to some respondents this usage is due to the fact that a woman will have breast-fed her children.[39]

The *kafnie* is the first shroud to be put on. Next, if the dead person is a woman, she is veiled: the veil is placed around her head and the ends are laid on either side of her shoulders. If a man used to wear a small white head-covering during his life, this may be put on his head when he is shrouded.

[36] Al-Sarakhsî, *Kitâb al-mabsûṭ*, vol. 2, 60.

[37] Al-Jazîrî, *Al-fiqh ᶜalâ al-madhâhib al-arbaᶜa*, vol. 2, 513–516. One finds the Hanafite point of view reflected also in Van Bommel, *Kom tot het gebed*, 71. Van Bommel gives the following names to the windings: for a man, a *lifafe* (a covering longer than the *izâr* so that both ends can be tied), an *izâr* (a covering longer than the body), and a *kamîs*; for a woman, a *dirî* (also a kind of shirt but with an opening for her breast, i.e. a lengthwise opening), a *hîmar* (wound around her head), a *chirqah* (covering her from her shoulders to under her knees), an *izâr*, and a *lifafe*.

[38] Shadid & Van Koningsveld, "Stervensbegeleiding en begrafenisriten in de islam", 22.

[39] This corresponds with the *dirî*, a kind of shirt with a lengthwise opening, mentioned by Van Bommel, *Kom tot het gebed*, 71. In his presentation of the Hanafite point of view, Al-Jazîrî, *Al-fiqh ᶜalâ al-madhâhib al-arbaᶜa*, vol. 2, 515, similarly calls the *qamîṣ* of a woman a *dirᶜ*.

The next covering, the *tahband*, covers a dead man from his chest to just below his knees. The *tahband* of a woman is longer, extending to her ankles. There follows a *sienaband*, which covers her from the chest to the knees. The final covering, the *tjadar*, is the same for men and women, and is longer than the body of the deceased, thus also covering his or her head and feet. Each covering is wound first from the left to the right side and then from the right to the left side.

One finds a variation on this among the Turkish respondents. They reported that the *kafan* of a man consists of a *qamîṣ* (or *kamis*, a kind of shirt), an *izâr* (which follows upon the *kamis* and is longer than the body of the deceased), and a *lifafe* (the outer winding, which is somewhat longer than the *izâr*). The *kafan* of a woman consists further of a *göğüs örtüsü* (which covers her breast, but which does not extend below her waist) and a *başörtüsü* (with which her face is covered).[40]

According to the *ḥadîth* of Ibn ᶜAbbâs (which is put forward in support of use of the *qamîṣ*), the clothes in which the Prophet was dressed after his death were similar to the clothes that he used to wear during his life except for the *sarâwil* (a garment similar to trousers). However, Moroccan respondents indicated that the *kafan* of a man also consists of trousers apart from an outer winding and a kind of shirt.

These accounts agree with the findings of Monique Renaerts concerning Morocco, according to which the *kafan* of a man consists of a *serwal* or trousers (which covers him from his navel to his knees or his ankles), a *tshamir* or shirt (which stretches from his neck to his knees), and the *udjah l-kfen* or shroud. Two other coverings may be added: an *ᶜamâma* or turban and a *fâfa* which covers the head and the body to the knees. As well as the trousers, the shirt, and the shroud, the *kafan* of a woman consists of an *izâr*, which covers her body, and a *litâm*, which covers the lower part of her face.[41] The findings of Renaerts agree to

[40] See also Karakaşoğlu, "Die Bestattung von Muslimen in der Bundesrepublik aus der Sicht türkisch-islamischer Organisationen", 85.

[41] Renaerts, *La Mort, rites et valeurs dans l'islam maghrébin*, 45–46. A Moroccan respondent reported that in Morocco, when a death has occurred, one may see a *fqih* sewing a *kafan*. As I expected the *kafan* to be unsewn, this observation surprised me. However, Renaerts, ibid., 46, referring to the study of Hart concerning the Aït Waryaghar, also presented evidence for this: "Chez les Aït Waryaghar le linceuil doit être cousu avec une longue aiguille spéciale. Les trous du linceuil par où l'aiguille doit passer sont faits à l'aide d'un couteau. Le fil doit être du fil qui provient du même tissu que le lincueil. Les Beni Snassen cousent le linceuil en faisant passer sans aiguille du fil provenant du même tissu par des trous obtenus à l'aide de ciseaux ou d'un couteau."

a great extent with the earlier observations of Westermarck concerning Morocco. However, according to Westermarck's findings, at Tangier, the grave clothes of a man usually consist of five pieces.[42]

In the Netherlands as well as in the countries of origin, a family member buys some lengths of simple white cotton cloth when a death occurs. Some people prepare a case containing a *kafan* and other items needed for the washing, such as soap, camphor, and incense, for their relatives to use after their death.

Ṣalât al-Janâza

The funeral prayer for the deceased (*ṣalât al-janâza*) is another collective duty of the Muslim community (*farḍ kifâya*). Unlike the daily *ṣalât*, which includes prostrations, the funeral *ṣalât* is performed standing. Its basic elements are the expression of the intention (*niyya*) for its performance, four *takbîr*s (e.g. the utterance *Allâhu akbar*, God is the greatest), a prayer (*du*ᶜ*â'*) for the deceased, and finally the *taslîm*. The *taslîm* also forms part of the daily *ṣalât* and consists of the utterance *Salâm alaykum wa raḥmatullâh* (Peace be upon you and the mercy of God). All participants in the *ṣalât al-janâza* direct these words firstly to their right and then to their left. This brings the *ṣalât al-janâza* to an end.[43]

According to the Malikites, Hanafites, and Hanbalites, one should raise one's hands only when saying the first *takbîr*. The Hanafite scholar As-Sarakhsî explains this from the fact that every *takbîr* substitutes for a *rak*ᶜ*a* (part of the daily *ṣalât* consisting of a bending of the torso from an upright position, followed by two prostrations) and because one does not raise one's hands at every *rak*ᶜ*a* performed in the other *ṣalât*s, one should no more do this in the *takbîr* in the *ṣalât al-janâza*.[44] By contrast, the Shafiᶜites take the view that it is *sunna* to raise one's hands at every *takbîr* and not only the first.[45]

The further contents of the *ṣalât al-janâza* vary from one law school to another. According to the Hanafites and the Malikites, after the first *takbîr*, one should recite the opening prayer (*du*ᶜ*â' al-istiftâḥ*),[46] whereas

[42] Westermarck, *Ritual and Belief in Morocco*, vol. 2, 447.

[43] Cf. Al-Jazîrî, *Al-fiqh* ᶜ*alâ al-madhâhib al-arba*ᶜ*a*, vol. 2, 518–521.

[44] Al-Sarakhsî, *Kitâb al-mabsûṭ*, vol. 2, 65.

[45] Al-Jazîrî, *Al-fiqh* ᶜ*alâ al-madhâhib al-arba*ᶜ*a*, vol. 2, 518 and 520.

[46] See Van Bommel, "Rouwgebruiken bij moslims", 72; Al-Sawwaf, *Waakt over uw gebeden!*, 81, and Surinaamse Moeslim Associatie Ahle Sunnat-Wal-Jamaat (Hanafi), *Tartiebus-Swalaat*, 19. The *du*ᶜ*â' al-istiftâḥ* runs as follows: "*Subḥânaka allâhumma wa bi-ḥamdika wa tabâraka ismuka wa ta*ᶜ*âlâ jadduka wa jalla sanâ'uka wa lâ illâh ghayruka*", which means "Praised be you, o Lord, praised be you highly, blessed be your name, your majesty is exalted, your splendor is great and there is no god than you".

the Hanbalites and the Shafi^c^ites argue that one should recite the *Fâtiḥa*.[47] The central point in dispute is whether or not the *ṣalât al-janâza* is really a kind of *ṣalât* or rather a *du^c^â'*. The view that the *ṣalât al-janâza* is a kind of *ṣalât* implies that the *Fâtiḥa* is to be recited after the first *takbîr*. After the second *takbîr* one may recite the Abraham prayer[48] and after the third *takbîr* one may ask God's forgiveness for the deceased with a *du^c^â'* which differs from one law school to another.[49] There then follow the fourth *takbîr* and finally the *taslîm*.

There are two answers to the question whether the *ṣalât al-janâza* may be performed twice. According to the Shafi^c^ites and the Hanbalites, it is permitted to hold a second *ṣalât al-janâza* for a dead person, but no one should attend more than one performance. According to the Hanafites and the Malikites it is reprehensible to perform the funeral prayer a second time, if the first performance took place collectively, in the presence of the community.[50]

The Hanafites and the Malikites hold the view that it is reprehensible to place the corpse inside the mosque and to perform the *ṣalât al-janâza* there. Contrarily, the Shafi^c^ites consider this to be recommendable.[51] Opinions concerning the position of the imam in relation to the corpse and the participants in the prayer vary as well. The Hanafites hold the view that the imam should stand opposite the corpse at breast height, regardless of the sex of the deceased. The Malikites, Shafi^c^ites, and

[47] For more information, see Al-Sarakhsî, *Kitâb al-mabsûṭ*, vol. 2, 64–65; Al-Jazîrî, *Al-fiqh ^c^alâ al-madhâhib al-arba^c^a*, vol. 2, 521; Al-Albânî, *Aḥkâm al-janâ'iz wa-bida^c^uhâ*, 119–120; and Shadid & Van Koningsveld, "Stervensbegeleiding en begrafenis-riten in de islam", 23.

[48] The Abraham prayer runs as follows: "*Allâhumma ṣalli ^c^alâ Muḥammadin wa ^c^alâ âli Muhammadin kamâ ṣallayta ^c^alâ Ibrâhîma wa ^c^alâ âli Ibrâhîma. Innaka ḥamîdun majîdun. Allâhumma bârik ^c^alâ Muḥammadin wa ^c^alâ âli Muḥammadin kamâ bârakta ^c^alâ Ibrâhîma wa ^c^alâ âli Ibrâhîma. Innaka ḥamîdun majîdun.*" This means: "O God, grant Muhammad and the family of Muhammad salvation like you have granted salvation to Abraham and the family of Abraham. You are praiseworthy and exalted. O God, bless Muhammad and the family of Muhammad like you have blessed Abraham and the family of Abraham. You are praiseworthy and exalted."

[49] A well-known *du^c^â'* runs for instance as follows: "*Allâhumma-ghfir li-hayyinâ wa mayyitinâ wa shahidinâ wa ghâ'ibinâ wa ṣaghîrinâ wa kabîrinâ wa dhakarinâ wa unthânâ. Allâhumma man aḥyaytahu (/hâ) minnâ fa-aḥyihi (/hâ) ^c^alâ-l-islâmi wa man tawaffaytahu (/hâ) minnâ fa-tawaffahu (/hâ) ^c^alâ-l-îmân. Allâhumma lâ taḥrimnâ ajrahu (/hâ) wa lâ taftînnâ ba^c^dahu (/hâ).*" This means: "O Lord, forgive the living and the dead, those of us who are present and those of us who are not, our younger and our old, our men and our women. O Lord, let him (or her) of us who you have endowed with life, live according to Islam and let him (or her) of us who is taken to you, be taken in faith. O Lord, do not deny his (or her) reward and please do not put us after him (or her) to the test."

[50] Al-Jazîrî, *Al-fiqh ^c^alâ al-madhâhib al-arba^c^a*, vol. 2, 527.

[51] Ibid., 527, and the Hanafite scholar Al-Sarakhsî, *Kitâb al-mabsûṭ*, vol. 2, 68.

Hanbalites draw a distinction according to sex. According to the Malikites, for instance, the imam should stand at waist height if the deceased is a male, and at shoulder height in the case of a woman.[52]

The *ṣalât al-janâza* is performed in silence, except for the *takbîr*s and the *taslîm*, which are spoken aloud by the imam. For this reason it was difficult to determine the exact wording of the funeral prayer as it is performed in practice. However, consistent with the Hanafite point of view, Surinamese Hindustani and Turkish respondents emphasized that one should not recite the *Fâtiḥa*. A Turkish respondent explained this from the fact that the *ṣalât al-janâza* is not a *ṣalât* in the strict sense (for there are no prostrations in it) but rather a *duᶜâ'*, and therefore it is not obligatory to recite the *Fâtiḥa*, as it is in the daily *ṣalât*. A Surinamese Javanese respondent, as a Shafiᶜite, expressed the view that it is only the *Fâtiḥa* that is to be recited after the first *takbîr*.

Likewise, one finds the Hanafite point of view, that it is reprehensible to perform the *ṣalât al-janâza* in the mosque, reflected among the Surinamese Hindustani and Turkish respondents. The majority of the Surinamese Hindustani respondents declared a preference for performing it in the open air in the graveyard or else in the funeral parlour. Many mosques and graveyards in Turkey have a stone table (called *muṣalla taşı*) in the open air on the *qibla* side of the building, on which the coffin will be placed and where the *ṣalât al-janâza* will be performed.[53] Prevailing practice in Turkey prompted them in the Netherlands to perform the funeral prayer outside the mosque, at its entrance, or alternatively on its premises but certainly not in the prayer room.

One would expect Surinamese Javanese Muslims, as Shafiᶜites, to perform the funeral prayer in the mosque. In practice, they too often perform it on the grounds of the graveyard shortly before the burial. In Surinam, by contrast, Javanese Muslims choose in most cases to perform the three *farḍ kifâya* tasks, including the *ṣalât al-janâza*, at home, even if the death occurred in a hospital. Contrary to what the Malikite viewpoint outlined above would lead us to expect, Moroccan respondents accepted that in the Netherlands the funeral prayer may take place in the mosque. However, they indicated too that in Morocco it may also take place in the open air in the graveyard.[54]

[52] Al-Jazîrî, *Al-fiqh ᶜalâ al-madhâhib al-arbaᶜa*, vol. 2, 517–518.

[53] See also Gailly, *Een dorp in Turkije*, 150.

[54] This agrees with the findings of Westermarck, *Ritual and Belief in Morocco*, vol. 2, 457: "On the arrival at the cemetery . . . the bier is placed at the side of the grave . . . and the prayer for the dead is said, unless it has been already done at a mosque".

My respondents did not distinguish according to the sex of the deceased in their remarks about where the imam should stand relative to the corpse. Most respondents reported that the imam stands opposite the deceased at breast height, the coffin being placed between the *qibla* and the imam. By contrast, Karakaşoğlu states explicitly that in Turkey the imam usually positions himself opposite the end of the coffin of a woman and at the head of the coffin of a man, contradicting the Hanafite point of view.[55]

The preference for a burial in the country of origin among the Moroccan and Turkish Muslims in the Netherlands has the result that in some cases the *ṣalât al-janâza* is performed in the Netherlands or in the country of origin, and that in other cases it is performed once in each country. Turkish respondents argued that if the *ṣalât al-janâza* is performed only once, most families prefer to hold it in the country where more people are able to take part: it is argued that if more people pray for the deceased, more prayers will possibly be accepted.[56] Thus, the Netherlands will be preferred if one expects more people to attend there than in Turkey. Some respondents argued, however, that even though fewer people may be present in Turkey, it is nonetheless better to perform the *ṣalât al-janâza* there because in the Netherlands there is no appropriate room, whereas in Turkey there will be a stone table of fixed height in the graveyard or near the mosque. In most cases, however, the *ṣalât al-janâza* is performed twice, both in the Netherlands and in the country of origin.

In most cases women do not take part in the *ṣalât al-janâza*.[57] Some people reason, as the case of the burial, that, being more emotional and tender-hearted than men, women are liable to break down. To prevent any excessive wailing, their participation in this *ṣalât* is therefore discouraged if not prohibited. Among Surinamese Javanese Muslims it sometimes occurs that women attend the ceremony, which is performed by men. They are thus present in the room without taking part in the *ṣalât al-janâza*. A Moroccan respondent said that if the *ṣalât al-janâza* takes place after the Friday prayer and many women are present to perform the *ṣalât*, they also participate in the *ṣalât al-janâza* on this occasion.

[55] Karakaşoğlu, "Die Bestattung von Muslimen in der Bundesrepublik aus der Sicht türkisch-islamischer Organisationen", 85. I expected Turkish Muslims as Hanafites to be the only ones not to differentiate according to gender in this respect.

[56] The same argument is put forward by Moroccan Muslims in the Netherlands.

[57] However, this seems to be subject to change. *NRC Handelsblad*, "Imam voor gemengd bidden", reports that a Turkish imam in Izmir (Turkey) invited women to participate in the funeral prayer at the graveyard.

Among the Surinamese Javanese Muslims, it also occurs that a number of men do not participate in the *ṣalât al-janâza*, even though they are present at it. In this case it is argued that, if one never performs the *ṣalât*, then one should not perform it even for a dead person. However, no-one will prevent these men from taking part, as the choice is considered their own responsibility.

In the view of Turkish Muslims, both in Turkey and in the Netherlands, an integral part of the ritual of death is the *tezkiye etmek* or *helal etmek*.[58] This is an absolution of the deceased by his fellow believers, and follows immediately upon the *ṣalât al-janâza*. In this ritual the imam asks those present three times how they know the deceased. With their reply "We know him [her] doing fine", they, on their own behalf and not in the name of God, clear the deceased of any possible harm that he or she may have done them. The questions together with the replies are called *tezkiye etmek*, whereas the act of answering such questions and thereby absolving the deceased is called *helal etmek*. It may occur that some of those present on this occasion are unwilling to give the expected answer. In that case the family of the deceased discusses the matter with them, so that in the end the dead person can be forgiven. The settlement of any monetary debts is not part of the *tezkiye etmek*; this would already have taken place before the *ṣalât al-janâza*.

5.2. Burial

According to Islam, a dead person must be buried and not cremated, the latter method of disposal being associated with the fires of hell.[59] Transporting the deceased to the graveyard and burying the corpse belong to the collective duties of the Muslim community (*farḍ kifâya*).[60]

Migration to the Netherlands has had a deep effect on the rituals and customs surrounding burial. The short interval between death and burial

[58] Karakaşoğlu, "Die Bestattung von Muslimen in der Bundesrepublik aus der Sicht türkisch-islamischer Organisationen", 85, gives a clear description of this usage: "Schließlich fragt der Imam die anwesende Gemeinde mit den Worten '*bu müslüman kardeşinizi nasıl bilirsiniz*?' (sinngemäß: Wie kennt Ihr diesen Euren muslimischen Bruder bzw. Eure muslimische Schwester?), ob sie den Verstorbenen als guten Muslim/gute Muslimin in Erinnerung habe, ob er/sie ein guter Freund, guter Nachbar gewesen sei. Die Gemeinde antwortet darauf mit einem '*iyi biliriz*' (sinngemäß: Wir kennen ihn als guten Muslim, Freund, Nachbarn). Damit ist vor allem gemeint, daß er/sie sich im Sinne des Islam und gegenüber der Gemeinde der Gläubigen nichts zuschulden kommen ließ. Der Vorgang die hiermit abgeschlossen wird, nennt sich auf Türkisch *hakkını helal etmek* (gemeint ist damit: jemanden von sämtlichen Verpflichtungen, die er gegenüber den einzelnen Mitgliedern der Familie und der Gemeinde hatte, zu befreien)."

[59] Grütter, "Arabische Bestattungsbräuche in frühislamischer Zeit", part 3, 168.

[60] Al-Jazîrî, *Al-fiqh ᶜalâ al-madhâhib al-arbaᶜa*, vol. 2, 530 and 534.

in the countries of origin has, with some exceptions, lengthened in the Netherlands. In the course of time a special grave design has become common usage among Muslims in the Netherlands. Moreover, the use of a coffin has become common practice among them, notwithstanding the 1991 Dutch Corpse Disposal Act, which permits the burial of a corpse without a coffin. Another characteristic of the Netherlands is the institution of funeral funds, which ensued from the wish of Turkish and Moroccan Muslims in the Netherlands to be buried in their countries of origin.

In other respects, the customs of Muslims who bury their dead in the Netherlands and the burial customs prevailing in the countries of origin show considerable similarities. These pertain for instance to the practice of carrying the corpse to the burial place by foot, the manner of placing the corpse into the grave, the participation of women in the funeral procession and their attendance at the burial, and lastly the practice of staying at the grave for a time after the interment.

Country of Burial

The discussions on the permissibility of burial in a non-Islamic country may arise within the larger framework of present-day Islamic discussions on the applicability of the religious qualifications *dâr al-Islâm* (territory of Islam), *dâr al-harb* (territory of war), and *dâr al-ᶜahd* (territory of treaty) to Western European countries.

The present-day Moroccan scholar Ibn al-Siddîq argues, for example, that the countries of Western Europe and the United States now show characteristics such that their citizens can be considered residents of an Islamic country in terms of Muslim legal scholarship.[61] Ibn al-Siddîq thus revives the old Shafiᶜite doctrine that states that *dâr al-Islâm* exists wherever a Muslim is able to practise the major religious rites and observances.[62]

Following Ibn al-Siddîq, Al-Ghannouchi, the main intellectual leader of the Tunisian Islamist Nahda movement, took the view that France had

[61] Shadid & Van Koningsveld, "Loyalty to a Non-Muslim Government", 98.

[62] Ibid., 98. In dealing with the historical case of individual Muslims, or of small numbers of Muslims, living—temporarily or for an indefinite period of time—in a country ruled by a non-Muslim government, Shadid & Van Koningsveld, ibid., 89 and 110, pointed out that in principle Islamic scholars accepted such a stay on condition that the Muslims concerned were able to perform openly the basic religious prescriptions of Islam and that their own safety as well as that of their family was safeguarded. The expression used in Islamic jurisprudence for the former condition is "to manifest the signs of Islam". The precise definition is a subject of further discussion among scholars.

become *dâr al-Islâm*. This view was endorsed in 1991 by the Committee for Reflection on Islam in France (CORIF) on the grounds that Muslims in France could be buried in sections of cemeteries reserved for Muslims.[63]

A reply to a reader's letter in the English-language Saudi Arabian daily *Arab News* on 6 September 1993 fits in with this line of thought. The letter describes the case of a Muslim who died in Hong Kong and whose burial in his home country took place only after ten days. The *muftî* answering the readers' letters takes the following position:

> It would have been more appropriate that the deceased person was buried in the place where he died. I realize that he died in a non-Muslim country, but most probably there is a graveyard for Muslims in that country, or at least a part of a graveyard. If it was possible to prepare him for burial in a Muslim way and bury him there in a Muslim area, that would have been more appropriate than bringing his body back to his home country.[64]

The meaning of "in a Muslim way" is not further explained. Thus, beginning from the present-day discussions about the position of Muslims in Western countries, one could argue that a burial in a non-Islamic country is permissible, provided certain conditions are met. Great importance is attached to a burial in (sections of) graveyards intended for Muslims only.[65] But what if a burial in a non-Islamic country cannot take place within twenty-four hours? And what about the use of a coffin?

In most cases Moroccan and Turkish Muslims in the Netherlands opt in practice for a burial in the country of origin, whereas Muslims with a Surinamese background mostly opt for burial in the Netherlands. An explanation for the preference of Moroccan and Turkish Muslims is that, owing to the historical background of their settlement in the Netherlands, the ties with their countries of origin have remained very strong. A significant statement in this respect came from a Turkish respondent, who said that he wants to sleep where his father sleeps his last sleep.[66]

[63] Ibid., 98.

[64] Heine, "Die Bestattung von Muslimen außerhalb der islamischen Welt als Problem des islamischen Rechts", 14.

[65] In the brochure of the Muslim World League, in the translation of Shadid & Van Koningsveld, "Stervensbegeleiding en begrafenisriten in de islam", 24, one finds it argued that the burial must take place on a graveyard destined for Muslims, except when this is not possible.

[66] Turkish Muslims in the Netherlands are not the only ones to put forward this argument. The same holds true for their fellow citizens in Turkey who expressed the wish to be buried in the village where their parents are buried, even though during the whole of their life they may have lived elsewhere in Turkey. This argument may sound familiar to the Dutch too.

For the Surinamese Muslims in the Netherlands, this factor does not seem to play such an important role, perhaps because of the fact that they mostly came to the Netherlands in family groups.

Several religious considerations may also account for the preference for burial in the country of origin. Some people argue that this gives them the assurance that family members will visit their graves on certain occasions.[67] They will pray for the salvation of their souls, recite the Koran, and donate money or food to the poor in the name of their dead.[68] A number of respondents emphasized that a Muslim should not be buried among non-Muslims, even though the implications drawn from this viewpoint varied among individuals.[69] Some respondents concluded that a Muslim must be buried in an Islamic country. Others stressed that the transport to the country of origin would not have been necessary if there had been Islamic graveyards in the Netherlands.[70] Some Moroccan and Turkish respondents stressed that special sections for Muslims within public cemeteries do not fully meet their wishes, since there a Muslim is still buried among non-Muslims. Surinamese Hindustani and Surinamese Javanese Muslims in the Netherlands do not object to this. On the contrary, burying their dead in the Netherlands has become common practice in those groups.

Moreover, people may feel more confident that in their country of origin the graves will not be emptied after a certain time. According to some respondents, an additional benefit is the fact that in the country of origin, unlike in the Netherlands, there is no charge for a grave. However, this is not necessarily so in the countries of origin, as a Turkish respondent learned from experience:

> My mother is buried in Istanbul, but I cannot find her grave any more. In all probability it has been emptied. If you do not pay for a grave, then it will be emptied after a period of time. That's the way it goes in Istanbul

[67] Cf. Karakaşoğlu, "Die Bestattung von Muslimen in der Bundesrepublik aus der Sicht türkisch-islamischer Organisationen", 101–102. She presents four explanations for the existing preference among Turkish Muslims for a burial in Turkey: a burial in Turkey gives one the guarantee of an everlasting resting place, of the observation of the Islamic prescriptions pertaining to burial, of a burial among Muslims, and of the prayers of those passing the grave. Whether future generations will prefer to be buried in Germany depends to a high degree, according to Karakaşoğlu, on the extent to which these requirements are met.

[68] Shadid & Van Koningsveld, *Moslims in Nederland*, 106.

[69] A Moroccan respondent argued as follows: "You want to be buried with your family and preferably not in a non-Islamic country, among Christians and Jews", whereas her sister disagreed with her. In her opinion, it does not matter where one is buried.

[70] We have also seen that, in the case of the nine-year-old murder victim Loubna Benaïssa, the main argument put forward in the press for her burial in Morocco in 1997 was the absence of Islamic cemeteries in Belgium.

and other big cities. I presume that this will be different in smaller places. There a grave will always be looked after. But in big cities, like Istanbul, that is not the way it goes.

Surinamese Hindustani and Javanese Muslims emphasized that one should be buried in the place where one dies. Some argued that their whole family came to the Netherlands when Surinam gained independence, and therefore they do not feel inclined to go to the expense of transport to Surinam. However, if the majority of the family had remained in Surinam, then they would prefer to be buried in Surinam. Shadid and Van Koningsveld suggest several reasons for the fact that Muslims who settled in Europe as a result of decolonization—such as the Surinamese Muslims in the Netherlands—are more frequently buried in Europe: among others, naturalization, the distance from the countries of origin, and the availibility of Muslim cemeteries or sections of public cemeteries reserved for Muslims.[71]

The Institution of Funeral Funds

The institution of funeral funds in the Netherlands ensued from the wish of many Moroccans and Turks to be buried in their country of origin and from the considerable expenses involved in repatriation.[72] Several Moroccan banks, such as the Banque Populaire du Maroc and the Banque Commerciale du Maroc, offer their accountholders the guarantee of the transport of their corpse (*naql al-juththa*) to Morocco for a small annual fee. Amounts charged range from *f*22 to *f*150 per year for an adult. The transport of the corpse of children is also covered, if both parents register for the scheme.

The same wish among Turkish Muslims in the Netherlands led to the foundation of Turkish funeral funds. These are organized by religious denominations rather than by banks. The *Diyanet*, or Presidium for Religious Affairs in Turkey,[73] and the *Milli Görüş*, for instance, have established funeral funds. For an annual fee, the funds guarantee the transport

[71] Shadid & Van Koningsveld, *Religious Freedom and the Position of Islam in Western Europe*, 99.

[72] The percentage of Turkish Muslims in the Netherlands who prefer a burial in Turkey is frequently estimated at 99%. This agrees with the findings of Karakaşoğlu, "Die Bestattung von Muslimen in der Bundesrepublik aus der Sicht türkisch-islamischer Organisationen", 97 and also 103 n. 2, as regards the percentage of Turkish Muslims in Germany who prefer a burial in Turkey.

[73] The *Diyanet* has branches in several Western European countries (for instance the DITIB in Germany and the ISN in the Netherlands). In the Netherlands the *Diyanet* coordinates some 96 mosques and 7 youth centres. Some 75 imams are employed in their affiliated mosques. These imams mostly received their training in Turkey. See Shadid & Van Koningsveld, *Religious Freedom and the Position of Islam in Western Europe*, 44.

of the corpse to Turkey accompanied by two family members and an ambulance to convey the body from the airport to the burial place.[74] The fee varies each year according to the number of bodies transported in the preceding year. Amounts quoted ranged from *f*120 to *f*150 per year for a family. Judging from the number of mosques affiliated to it, the largest funeral fund is the one run by the *Diyanet*.

If, upon death, it appears that someone from the Turkish or Moroccan community is not insured, his or her family may offer financial help or raise money among mosque members for the transport of the body.

Because funeral funds among Turkish Muslims in the Netherlands are managed by religious denominations, the mosques have come to play an important role in the burial preparations. In the course of time, members of the mosque staff, to whom people turn in the case of death, have gained experience in the required administrative tasks, such as collecting the documents required for the repatriation of the corpse. In towns in Turkey, however, as we will see, these tasks have increasingly been taken over by professional undertakers. In the countryside, by contrast, mosque organizations still play an important role by, for instance, providing the facilities for the ritual washing (such as washboard and pans for heating water).

In the Surinamese Hindustani community in the Netherlands, which mostly buries its dead in the Netherlands, one finds the beginnings of an increasing professionalization of the burial ritual. Up to now, this has not led to the employment of professional washers, who charge for their services. A Surinamese Hindustani funeral leader told me that he does not exclude that this development will occur in the near future. Unlike Turkish Muslims in the Netherlands, who, as a matter of course, turn to their mosques for the performance of the required tasks, Surinamese Hindustani Muslims seem to be less dependent on any one organization for the performance of these tasks.

Grave Construction and Interment

According to Islamic law a burial must take place as soon as possible after death, and not later than the day after the death.[75] It is considered reprehensible (Hanafites and Malikites) or prohibited (Malikites, Shafiᶜites, and Hanbalites) to bury more than one corpse in a grave,

[74] For a detailed account of the DITIB (*Diyanet*) funeral fund regulation concerning accession and procedures, see Karakaşoğlu, "Die Bestattung von Muslimen in der Bundesrepublik aus der Sicht türkisch-islamischer Organisationen", 99–101.

[75] Shadid & Van Koningsveld, *Moslims in Nederland*, 106.

except when necessary.[76] The *sunna* manner of bearing the corpse to its last resting place varies according to law school.[77] However, according to them all it is recommendable to walk briskly. Furthermore, it is recommended to take part in the funeral procession on foot rather than on a mount or in a wheeled vehicle.[78]

In early Islam, a corpse was not coffined: it was placed in the grave wrapped only in a shroud.[79] Thanks to the hardness of the soil in Islamic regions it was possible to construct a kind of cavity (called a *bait musaqqaf* or roofed house) into which the shrouded corpse was placed. Two variants of the *bait musaqqaf* became generally accepted, the *shaqq* and *laḥd* graves. The former is a narrower trench (*shaqq* or *ḍarîḥ*) dug at the bottom of a pit, into which the corpse is placed.[80] The latter is a niche (*laḥd* or *luḥd*), dug on the *qibla* side of the pit. The *laḥd* became more popular in the course of time, for the Prophet was allegedly buried in such a niche.[81] To prevent earth from collapsing onto the body, the niche, and according to some authorities the trench too,[82] is closed off, preferably with sun-dried stones,[83] and the gaps between the stones are

[76] Al-Jazîrî, *Al-fiqh ᶜalâ al-madhâhib al-arbaᶜa*, vol. 2, 538.

[77] Ibid., 530–532.

[78] Ibid., 532. Only the Hanafites take a slighty different position. However, in their view it is also better to walk.

[79] The six well-known collections of *ḥadîth* do not contain any reference to the use of a coffin. On the basis of this, Kamerlingh Onnes, "Kist of geen kist?", 26, reaches the conclusion that until the ninth century it was unusual for a body to be coffined.

[80] Dâr al-Iftâ' al-Miṣriyya, *Al-Fatâwâ al-Islâmiyya*, vol. 20, 7395. The *muftî* of this *fatwâ* (1985) defines the *shaqq* grave as an oblong excavation in the middle of a grave, built with sun-dried stones (*libn*) or something similar at its sides. After having placed the deceased in this grave, a roof is made of *libn*, wood or another material. This roof rises a little so as not to touch the body.

[81] Dâr al-Iftâ' al-Miṣriyya, *Al-Fatâwâ al-Islâmiyya*, vol. 20, 7394–7395, and Grütter, "Arabische Bestattungsbräuche in frühislamischer Zeit", part 3, 169.

[82] Grütter, "Arabische Bestattungsbräuche in frühislamischer Zeit", part 3, 168, indicates that, according to some, a *shaqq* grave is filled without the body being protected against earth. In the brochure of the Muslim World League, in the translation of Shadid & Van Koningsveld, "Stervensbegeleiding en begrafenisriten in de islam", 24, one finds it argued that a shelter should prevent earth from falling directly on the body without explicit reference to a special kind of grave: "Nadat de dode in het graf is gelegd, plaatst men een afdakje van stenen boven hem, waarvan de gaten met leem worden dichtgesmeerd, opdat de aarde niet direct op hem terecht komt." On the basis of this translation, one may assume that this passage concerns a *shaqq* grave, for the stones are placed above the body. Accordingly, from the Dâr al-Iftâ' al-Miṣriyya, *Al-Fatâwâ al-Islâmiyya*, vol. 20, 7395, it becomes clear that in the case of a *shaqq* grave, as in the case of a *laḥd* grave, the body is also protected against the earth with which the grave is filled.

[83] Other materials, such as bricks and plaster, may also be used to this end. In early Islam, the use of wood must have been rather unusual, for wood was rare in Islamic lands at that time, according to Grütter, "Arabische Bestattungsbräuche in frühislamischer Zeit", part 3, 173.

loamed. The *shaqq* grave is preferred if the soil is soft and moist, because under such conditions a *laḥd* grave would cave in.[84]

The corpse is laid on its right side in the niche, facing the *qibla*, and the knots of the *kafan* are untied.[85] It is recommended that those attending the burial each throw three handfuls of earth into the grave.[86] This may be done before or after the niche is closed off.[87] Subsequently, the grave is filled up with earth so as to form a heap approximately the size of a camel's hump.

The Hague is the only city in the Netherlands that has a separate Islamic graveyard. This dates from 1932, and was intended for Indonesian Muslims.[88] Surinamese Muslims in the Netherlands, who generally bury their dead in the Netherlands, make use of special sections of public cemeteries that are reserved for Muslims. These sections, which are marked, generally consist for the greater part of graves with an exclusive right. However, they may also contain a few public graves. The right to dispose of a grave rests with its owner in the case of graves with an exclusive right, and with the keeper of the graveyard in the case of public graves; in the latter case the keeper is required to observe certain legal prescriptions.[89] Among graves of both kinds, there are variants regarding the number of corpses that may be buried, the granting period, and the mode of construction.[90]

[84] Dâr al-Iftâ' al-Miṣriyya, *Al-Fatâwâ al-Islâmiyya*, vol. 20, 7394–7395.

[85] Shadid & Van Koningsveld, "Stervensbegeleiding en begrafenisriten in de islam", 24.

[86] Ibid., 24.

[87] Grütter, "Arabische Bestattungsbräuche in frühislamischer Zeit", part 3, 180, gives the following explanation: "Das Zuschütten des Grabes erfolgte zumindest zum Anfang durch die umstehenden Verwandten und Freunde, indem sie Hände voll Erde hineinwarfen. . . . Wie weit die Totengräber and dieser Arbeit Anteil hatten, erfahren wir nicht, aber wir dürfen wohl annehmen, daß sie den Rest des Zuschüttens mit ihren Spaten besorgten, mit denen sie auch das Grab gegraben hatten." In an addition, Grütter, ibid., 190, accounts for the fact that, in the Hadramaut, all those standing around the grave throw a handful of earth into the grave, and recite the *Fâtiḥa*. Then, the grave is filled up by those deputed to this task. Ibid., 180: "Die übrigen Nachrichten über das Werfen von Erde gehen auf einen alten heidnischen Brauch zurück, den auch Wellhausen, Reste S. 180 Anm. 1, erwähnt. Man pflegte auf den Toten, schon ehe er ins Grab gelegt wurde, Erde zu werfen. . . ."

[88] Landman, *Van mat tot minaret*, 20–21, and Bot, *Een laatste groet*, 148.

[89] Van der Putten, *Handboek Wet op de Lijkbezorging*, 104.

[90] Ibid., 102. Unfamiliarity with this distinction can lead to some confusion in practice. At first, people may choose a public grave because its cost is lower than that of a grave with an exclusive right. However, they may not be acquainted with the consequences regarding the granting period and the right of disposal. It may therefore occur that a corpse buried in a public grave is exhumed to be reburied in a grave with an exclusive right (Marrie Bot, oral communication). The reasons for this may be twofold. The family involved may have discovered after the burial that the public grave will be emptied after a certain time without their being given the possibility of extension. People may

Graves with an exclusive right in Islamic sections of cemeteries are designed to contain one corpse only, in accord with Islamic prescriptions.[91] However, in public graves, even in sections set aside for Muslims, the graveyard keeper will mostly inter three corpses on top of one another in the order in which they come in. For this reason Surinamese Hindustani and Javanese mosque organizations advise their members to opt for a grave with an exclusive right, for in this case the owner has the right to dispose of a grave and ensure that no more than one corpse is buried there. Moreover the possibility of extending the granting period applies only to graves with an exclusive right and not to public graves, a fact that makes people prefer the former.

In the Netherlands the construction of a *laḥd* grave is difficult because of the moistness of the soil. Also, Surinamese Muslims in the Netherlands did not introduce the *shaqq* construction, probably because this construction is not common usage even in Surinam. In time a special grave construction became generally accepted among Surinamese Muslims in the Netherlands.[92] The sides of the grave are supported by a wooden formwork, approximately 60 centimetres in height, installed before the interment. The construction of this formwork costs a few hundred guilders above normal burial costs. After having lowered the coffin without its lid into the grave, the upper edges of the formwork are covered from one side to the other with wooden slats (known as *taḥta*). The coffin lid is placed on these slats. Because the wooden formwork protrudes a little above the edge of the coffin, a kind of roofed house (*bait musaqqaf*) is created, which enables the deceased to sit up when the angels of death Munkar and Nakîr come to interrogate him or her.[93]

Burial in the Netherlands and in the countries of origin generally exhibit no further differences. The corpse is laid into the grave lying on its right side facing the *qibla*, or lying on its back with the face turned towards Mecca. The knots of the *kafan* are untied. Before the grave is filled up, those present throw three handfuls of earth into the grave either

discover also that they cannot dispose freely of the public grave. It may happen, in consequence, that the graveyard keeper decides to inter more than one corpse in a grave. This may bring people to rebury the corpse in a grave with an exclusive right, of which they can dispose themselves.

[91] There are also graves with an exclusive right into which two or three corpses can be buried. However, Muslims have a preference for graves into which only one corpse can be buried.

[92] This construction was introduced only recently. Until the end of the 1980s Muslims in the Netherlands commonly used a double-height coffin for a burial. See Bot, *Een laatste groet*, 149.

[93] For a photograph of this grave construction, see Bot, *Een laatste groet*, 152.

directly upon the body or upon the slats, which prevent the body being covered with earth. The recitation of a particular Koranic verse (20:55) on this occasion is considered recommendable (*mustaḥabb*): "From it [i.e. earth] we have created you, to it we will restore you and from it we will bring you to life again." Thereupon, a number of men present will fill up the grave. This task, like the bearing of the coffin in the funeral procession, is performed not by undertakers or other professional operators but by members of the Muslim community itself.

In the countries of origin, the dead are buried in either a *shaqq* or a *laḥd* grave. The former is the prevailing variant in Morocco and the latter in Turkey. The trench is closed off with a few stones to prevent earth from falling upon the body. In Turkey the grave of a woman is somewhat deeper than of a man, the former being dug breast-high and the latter waist-high.

Because the pre-1991 Dutch legislation on the disposal of corpses applied in Surinam, the use of a coffin was prescribed by law. However, according to Suparlan's findings,[94] in Surinam the dead are buried in a kind of *laḥd* grave, constructed by placing planks over the dead body at an angle, without a niche being dug on the *qibla* side of the pit. According to De Waal Malefijt, the coffin is placed upside down over the corpse.[95] According to a Surinamese Javanese respondent, the practice in Surinam is either to bury the dead with a coffin or to break up the coffin and lay the fragments at the bottom of the grave pit. Because the soil in Surinam is as moist as in the Netherlands, the corpse is laid on these planks to prevent it from getting wet.

Use of a Coffin

A subject that has been a matter of discussion in the course of Islamic history and that grew in importance in the Dutch migration context is the use of a coffin. The Malikite scholar Khalîl b. Isḥâq (d. 767/1365) held the opinion that, if sun-dried stones or other materials commonly used to close off the niche are unavailable, it is preferable to use earth for this purpose rather than to enclose the body in a coffin.[96] Commentaries on

[94] Suparlan, "The Javanese in Surinam", 270.

[95] De Waal Malefijt, *The Javanese of Surinam*, 169: "First the *ka'um* descends in the grave alone, and prays. Next, he makes three clots of earth, places one on the spot where the head will rest, one at waist level, and one at the feet. The body is lifted out of the coffin and placed directly on the earth, again in such a way that the face is turned towards Mecca. The coffin is placed over it, upside down. According to Shafi'ite law, a person should be buried directly in the earth, and use of a coffin is objectionable. But Surinam Government law makes burial in a coffin compulsory and a compromise is found by placing it over the body."

[96] Khalîl ben Ish'âq, *Abrégé de la loi musulmane selon le rite de l'Imâm Mâlek*, trans. Bousquet, vol. 1, 100: "Après l'enterrement, on recommande . . . de fermer le la'hd et la

the *Mukhtaṣar* of Khalîl b. Isḥâq further elucidated this point of view by stating that the use of a coffin is common practice among Christians and should therefore be rejected by Muslims.[97]

In two commentaries on the *Kitâb al-taqrîb fi'l-fiqh* of the Shafiᶜite scholar Abû Shujâᶜ (died after 500/1106)[98] it is argued additionally that a coffin is an unnecessary luxury and that its use is consequently to be rejected. Nonetheless, where the softness and moistness of the soil compel the use of a coffin for burial, this practice is not reprehensible.[99]

One finds the same line of reasoning, put forward even more explicitly, among Hanafite scholars, such as Al-Sarakhsî (d. 483/1090), Ibn Nujaim (d. 970/1562), and Ibn ᶜAbidîn.[100] Al-Sarakhsî points out that constructing a *laḥd* grave is not possible in his region, because of the softness of the soil. For this reason, a *shaqq* grave is generally preferred there. Its niche is closed off with sun-dried stones, canes or, if necessary, earth. The use of bricks for this purpose is, in the view of Al-Sarakhsî, reprehensible; a grave is a place of decomposition, whereas bricks are meant for structures of lasting value, being used for decoration or to fortify a building.[101] Al-Sarakhsî quotes an author named Muḥammad b. Al-Faḍl: "There is no objection against it in our region, in view of the softness of the soil. Thus, the use of wooden shelves and of a coffin for the deceased is permitted. It is also argued: I see no harm even in taking an iron coffin in our region."[102]

fosse, avec des briques cuites au soleil; à défaut avec des planches; à défaut avec des tuiles; à defaut avec des briques cuites au feu; à défaut avec des pierres; à défaut avec des roceaux; verser de l'eau sur la terre, si on n'a rien du tout ce qui précède, (pour en faire une pâte), est préférable à l'usage d'un cercueil, à l'instar des chrétiens."

[97] One finds this line of reasoning in the *Ḥâshiya* or glosses of Al-ᶜAdawî (d. 1189/1775) upon the commentary of Al-Kharâshî (d. 1101/1689) on the *Mukhtaṣar* and also in the commentary of Al-Dardîr (d. 1201/1786), says Kamerlingh Onnes, "Kist of geen kist?", 12–16. Ibid., 13–14: Al-ᶜAdawî refers more generally to this custom as pertaining to the *aᶜâjim* (non-Arabs or non-Muslims) and the *ahl al-kitâb* (the People of the Book).

[98] That is, in the glosses of Al-Bâjûrî (d. 1276/1860) upon the commentary of Al-Ghazzî (d. 928/1512) and in the commentary of Al-Shirbînî (d. 977/1569).

[99] Kamerlingh Onnes, "Kist of geen kist?", 10–12.

[100] Ibid., 16–19. Ibn ᶜAbidîn was born in Damascus in 1198/1784. He studied first Shafiᶜite and later Hanafite *fiqh*. He died in 1252/1836 or 1258/1842. I consulted his *Radd al-muḥtâr ᶜalâ l-Durr al-mukhtâr*, which is a refutation of the *Durr al-mukhtâr* of M. b. ᶜA. al-Ḥaṣkafî, a commentary on the *Tanwîr al-abṣâr wa-djâmiᶜ al-biḥâr* of Al-Timirtâshî. See Brockelmann, *Geschichte der Arabischen Litteratur*, SII, 427–428 and 773.

[101] Al-Sarakhsî, *Kitâb al-mabsûṭ*, vol. 2, 61–62. Ibn Nujaim rejects the use of wood for the same reason. Moreover, bricks have come in contact with fire, which is considered to bode ill.

[102] Al-Sarakhsî, *Kitâb al-mabsûṭ*, vol. 2, 62.

In a *fatwâ* delivered in 1936 by Shaykh ᶜAbd al-Majîd Salîm of the *Dâr al-Iftâ'*, a distinction is drawn according to sex.[103] If the dead person is male, a coffin is used only where the soil is soft. However, if the deceased is a female, the Hanafite scholars approve the use of a coffin regardless of the hardness of the soil, as it creates a kind of partition and protects the woman's body from being touched as it is placed in the grave.[104]

Karakaşoğlu refers to a Mecca judgement, which I could not identify, which approves the use of a coffin provided it is made of easily degradable wood: "Nach einem Gutachten der in islamischen Ländern als Autorität anerkannten Akademie für Islamisches Recht in Mekka vom März 1985 sind Beerdigungen von Muslimen in Särgen erlaubt, allerdings mit der Vorgabe, daß die Särge aus einfache, leicht vergänglichem Holz bestehen".[105]

With the introduction of the new Corpse Disposal Act (1991), it became possible for Muslims in the Netherlands to bury their dead within twenty-four hours and without a coffin on certain conditions. Before the introduction of the 1991 act, the mayor of the town of Ridderkerk, acting on behalf of the public prosecutor, had already occasionally given consent for the local Moluccan community to bury their dead within twenty-four hours and without a coffin.[106] With the introduction of the 1991 act, this local practice became further legalized.

Unlike the Moluccans, the Surinamese Hindustani and Surinamese Javanese communities in the Netherlands are not inclined to bury their

[103] Dâr al-Iftâ' al-Miṣriyya, *Al-Fatâwâ al-Islâmiyya*, vol. 4, 1264. The author refers to *Radd al-mukhtâr* and *Sharḥ al-munya* by Ibn ᶜAbidîn. I have been unable to identify the latter publication.

[104] A kind of partition is mentioned also in the brochure of the Muslim World League, translated by Shadid & Van Koningsveld, "Stervensbegeleiding en begrafenisriten in de islam", 24. According to this docuement it is recommendable to cover the grave of a woman with a cloth.

[105] Karakaşoğlu, "Die Bestattung von Muslimen in der Bundesrepublik aus der Sicht türkisch-islamischer Organisationen", 104.

[106] In Germany the policy concerning the use of a coffin varies locally. In Essen and Aachen, for instance, Muslims are allowed to bury their dead without a coffin, whereas in Frankfurt this is not allowed. See Karakaşoğlu, "Die Bestattung von Muslimen in der Bundesrepublik aus der Sicht türkisch-islamischer Organisationen", 87: "Der Verstorbene wird bis zum Grab im Sarg transportiert. Die Leiche kan auf Wunsch der Angehörigen im Leichentuch beerdigt werden, was im gesamten Bundesgebiet nur noch auf dem islamischen Gräberfeld in Aachen möglich ist. Es handelt sich hierbei nicht um eine feste Verordnung, sondern um eine Art 'Duldung'." However, the Muslims buried in Essen up to now have come mostly from from Afghanistan, Lebanon, and Bosnia, even though Karakaşoğlu predicts that the number of Turks buried there will increase in the long term.

dead without a coffin, notwithstanding the 1991 act.[107] They justified the use of a coffin in the Netherlands by reference to the softness of the Dutch soil. Additionally, some argued that there is no reason not to use a coffin, since insurance companies cover its cost. This preference may be explained also on the basis of the fact that in Surinam the use of a coffin was common practice and, moreover, prescribed by law.

If the corpse is to be transported from the Netherlands to the country of origin, the coffining of the deceased must comply with regulations concerning the material of the coffin, the way the coffin is sealed, and the accompanying documentation among other things.[108] Turkish respondents testified that in Turkey, corpses transported from Europe are in most cases committed to the earth uncoffined unless the corpse is badly damaged, for instance as a result of an accident or violence.[109] Moroccan respondents

[107] A Moroccan respondent reached the same conclusion. According to him, the choice in favour of or against the use of a coffin depends on the hardness of the soil. In the Netherlands a burial with a coffin is preferable due to the softness of its soil. In reponse to the burial practices of Moluccans in the town of Ridderkerk, he regarded a burial without a coffin as not necessary. He deemed it better to respect the Dutch law in this regard (here he assumed that Dutch law prohibits burials without a coffin). He further argued that, if a coffin is not necessary because of the hardness of the soil, then it is an unnecessary luxury. A Turkish respondent indicated that if a Turkish Muslim is buried in the Netherlands, it will not be done in the manner of Surinamese Hindustani Muslims. No slats will be used and the coffin will remain closed. He explained that, if the soil is soft, it is not possible to construct a niche, and it may even occur that the smell of the dead body will escape through the earth.

[108] Among the documents needed in the Netherlands for transport are the following: extract from death registration, laissez-passer for the corpse (requesting the authorities of all the countries across whose territory the shipment is to pass to allow it to pass freely and without hindrance), medical certificate, certificates concerning the sealing and material of the coffin, passport, residence permit, and work permit of the deceased. A Turkish respondent from the *Diyanet* indicated that in earlier times the undertaker often took responsibility for assembling the required documents. Nowadays, increasingly, the affiliated mosques of the *Diyanet*, being well informed of the requirements, will perform these tasks in order to lower the costs. The *Diyanet* thereby tries to keep the annual contributions towards the funeral fund to a minimum. As we have seen, the funeral funds of Moroccans in the Netherlands are managed by Moroccan banks. As a consequence, the performance of the aforementioned tasks has remained up to now in the hands of Dutch undertakers. This agrees with the findings concerning the Moroccans in Belgium of Renaerts, *La Mort, rites et valeurs dans l'islam maghrébin*, 108: "Les pompes funèbres s'occupent des formalités en collaboration avec les services consulaires."

[109] Bainbridge, *Life-Cycle Rituals of the Turks of Turkey*, 8, makes the following observation concerning the use of a coffin in Turkey: "However it is becoming common, especially in cities, for the coffin, properly used only for transporting the body to the grave, to be used for interment also; nevertheless, in order to bring the body into contact with the earth, as is proper, a hole is made in the coffin." From this one may conclude that customs vary locally and that process of urbanization is similar in many respects to the process of migration. On this similarity, see Schiffauer, "Migration and Religiousness", 156.

reported that in Morocco corpses from Europe are buried in a coffin. This applies not only to corpses from Europe but also to corpses transported over a long distance within Morocco. Moroccan respondents indicated that whether or not a dead person is coffined depends also on the financial position and the status of the family concerned.[110]

Leaving aside the need of a coffin arising from the transport of the corpse over long distance, both Turkish and Moroccan respondents explained a preference for a coffin by reference to the softness of the soil in which the corpse is to be buried. My respondents did not appeal to the argument put forward by a number of Hanafite scholars, who approved the use of a coffin especially in the case of a woman, to protect a woman from being touched when she is placed into the grave.[111] On the contrary, a Turkish respondent said that he disliked coffins for what he called their coolness. He had preferred to bury his parents without a coffin, so as to be able to touch them for a last time when putting them into their grave. In his view, the argument put forward by the Hanafite scholars did not apply here, for a woman is put into her grave by her closest relatives and therefore there is no reason to protect her from being touched.[112]

Attendance of Women at the Interment

We saw earlier that a dead man's body is washed generally by men and that of woman by women. However, placing the corpse into the grave is considered a men's task regardless of the sex of the deceased. According to the Shafiᶜites and the Hanbalites it is reprehensible for women to escort the dead in a funeral procession. In their view the participation of women is even forbidden if their participation leads to *fitna*. The Hanafites take the view that the participation of women is reprehensible and absolutely forbidden. The Malikites, by contrast, take the

[110] In this respect a Moroccan respondent asked me if I really thought that the king of Morocco would be buried without a coffin.

[111] One Moroccan respondent asserted that in Morocco it is more common for women than for men to be buried in a coffin. She was unable to offer any explanation of this. The findings concerning Tangier and the Bni ᶜAroṣ of Westermarck, *Ritual and Belief in Morocco*, vol. 2, 458, further substantiate this observation: "The body of a woman is placed in the grave under the shelter of a *ḥâyẹk*, and if she has been carried to the grave in a coffin she is also buried in it, though the blanket covering it is removed."

[112] These close relatives are the woman's *maḥrams*. A *maḥram* of a woman is one who, during her lifetime, is permitted to look at her and travel with her. The woman's husband falls within this category. See Shadid & Van Koningsveld, "Stervensbegeleiding en begrafenisriten in de islam", 24.

position that it is permitted for old women to escort the dead, if they join the end of the funeral procession. A young woman may also do so, if the deceased is a loved one, such as her father, child, husband or brother and if no-one is afraid of *fitna*, otherwise it is absolutely not permitted.[113]

According to a majority of the Muslims that I interviewed—particularly Moroccan, Surinamese Hindustani, and Turkish Muslims—women do not participate in the funeral procession, and their presence is not desirable at the burial itself. They justified this view on the grounds that women are more emotional and tender-hearted than men and therefore do better to remain at home. Surinamese Hindustani respondents further said that only Ahmadis, unlike Sunnites, raise no objection to the presence of women on such occasions.

However, there are indications that this pattern of behaviour is changing in the Netherlands as well as in the countries of origin.[114] Some people indicate that, if a woman is able to keep her emotions under control, she may be allowed to participate. In this case, her presence serves the same goal as that of the men, that is of bringing her to realize that one day she too will die. Whether women are present on this occasion in the countries of origin also depends on the locality. Some Turkish respondents, for instance, report that women take part in funerals in Istanbul but not in smaller towns.

Surinamese Javanese Muslims in the Netherlands, like Moluccan and Indonesian Muslims, did not object to the presence of women at the graveyard. Women are allowed to follow a short distance behind, but undertake none of the activities performed by men, such as filling up the grave. I did not come across indications that the presence of women at a burial had yet become common practice among Javanese Muslims in Surinam, although this may have happened recently.[115]

[113] Al-Jazîrî, *Al-fiqh ᶜalâ al-madhâhib al-arbaᶜa*, vol. 2, 532. What *fitna* consists of is not further elucidated. Grütter, "Arabische Bestattungsbräuche in frühislamischer Zeit", part 2, 95, explains that the Prophet no longer permitted women to take part in funeral processions, probably in support of his campaign against excessive lamentations. He expected women to be less able than men to take part without excessive and loud wailing. This prohibition notwithstanding, there are several accounts of women taking part in funeral processions, for instance on the occasion of the funeral of Aisha.

[114] At the funeral of Loubna Benaïssa in Morocco in 1997, her sister stood at the graveside at the moment of burial. She placed flowers on the coffin just before the grave was filled up.

[115] De Waal Malefijt, *The Javanese of Surinam*, 168, gives the following account of the procession and the burial: "Now the procession is formed. The *ka'um* goes in front with the bowl containing the money, then one of his helpers with the yellow rice, followed by a person carrying the grave-marker. Behind them the coffin, carried by six men on their shoulders, while a seventh holds an umbrella over the coffin thus shading the

Waiting at the Graveside and the Talqîn

According to Grütter, in early Islam the practice for mourners to wait at the grave after burial was not common, but there are a few documented cases of it.[116] According to a tradition recorded by Abû Dâwûd, for example, the Prophet used to seek forgiveness for the deceased and to beg for steadfastness before leaving a grave after a burial, because the deceased is believed to be interrogated at that moment.[117]

As we saw earlier, it is commonly believed that the devil (*shaiṭân*) appears to the dying person in an attempt to induce him or her to relinquish his or her faith, and that the angel ᶜIzrâ'îl appears at the moment of death (section 5.1). Many eschatological manuals[118] mention the appearance at the grave of two angels, named Munkar and Nakîr (Denied and Denying),[119] who pose the deceased some questions about his or her faith. There are various descriptions of the questions posed on this occasion: they concern God, the Prophet Muhammad, and the religion of the deceased.[120]

Islamic scholars are divided as to whether, in view of this questioning by Munkar and Nakîr, the *talqîn*, the teaching of the most important tenets of the Islamic faith at the graveside, should take place immediately after the interment. According to the Shafiᶜites and the Hanbalites the performance of the *talqîn* is recommendable (*mustaḥabb*), whereas the Malikites are of the opinion that this practice is reprehensible (*makrûh*).[121]

According to a Moroccan imam, reciting sura *YaSin* (36) and seeking forgiveness for the deceased on this occasion help prepare the deceased for the interrogation by the angels and render the *talqîn* unnecessary.[122]

head of the dead person. All other men walk behind. Women may not enter the graveyard but walk along a short way and then go home because their duties for the day are over." Suparlan, "The Javanese in Surinam", 270, does not distinguish between the sexes, using only the words "everyone who has accompanied the dead to the grave".

116 Grütter, "Arabische Bestattungsbräuche in frühislamischer Zeit", part 3, 182.

117 Ibid., 182.

118 Smith and Haddad, *The Islamic Understanding of Death and Resurrection*, 33–34, draw their material for their chapter on *barzakh*, the period between death and resurrection, according to classical Islam from five sources: Abû Ḥâmid al-Ghazâlî's *Al-Durra al-fâkhira*; Ibn Qayyim al-Jawzîya's *Kitâb al-rûḥ*; Jalâl al-Dîn Suyûṭî's *Bushrá al-ka'îb bi-liqâ'i al-ḥabîb*; Abû Layth al-Samarqandî's *Kitâb al-ḥaqâ'iq wa'l-daqâ'iq*; and the anonymous *Kitâb aḥwâl al-qiyâma*.

119 In the canonical traditions, one finds these names only in the collection of Al-Tirmidhî, according to Eklund, *Life between Death and Resurrection According to Islam*, 5–6 and 36–37.

120 Smith & Haddad, *The Islamic Understanding of Death and Resurrection*, 41–42.

121 Dâr al-Iftâ' al-Miṣriyya, *Al-Fatâwâ al-Islâmiyya*, vol. 4, 1266–1267.

122 According to Renaerts, *La Mort, rites et valeurs dans l'islam maghrébin*, 63, at most funerals sura *YaSin* is recited, which may be followed by the recitation of sura

According to a Turkish respondent, the *hoca* recites only the *Fâtiḥa*; later, once those present have left the grave, he returns to perform the *talqîn*. A Turkish imam emphasized that, while it is hoped that the *talqîn* will help the deceased, it should rather be considered a lesson to those staying behind. Before filling up the grave, Surinamese Hindustani respondents had the *Fâtiḥa* and the suras starting with *Qul* (112–114) recited.

Surinamese Javanese Muslims in the Netherlands may remain at the grave once it has been filled up for the *khutba al-qubûr* or *talqîn*, which takes approximately half an hour. This sermon serves as teaching for those attending the burial and provides guidance about the afterlife. After an opening *du*ᶜ*â'*, the programme is introduced briefly in Arabic. The imam then switches to Javanese and proceeds through the programme, which consists among other things of informing the deceased, and thereby also those present, of the angels Munkar and Nakîr and of the questions that they will pose.

5.3. Condolences and Mourning

According to Islam, one should offer one's condolences to the bereaved (*ta*ᶜ*ziya*) only once, that is at the funeral or, if one is not able to attend the funeral, at the earliest encounter to take place. Mourning (*iḥdâd*) consists of refraining from conspicuous dress, kohl, perfume, jewellery, and similar adornments for four months and ten days in the case of the widow of the deceased and for three days in the case of other relatives.[123] The mourning period for a widow is as long as the ᶜ*idda*, the legally prescribed waiting period during which a woman may not remarry after being widowed or divorced.

Al-Mulk or *Tabâraka* (67), sura *Taha* (20), and sura *Al-Ikhlâs* (112), the latter performed three times. It may be concluded with the recitation of the *Fâtiḥa*. Likewise, according to the earlier findings of Westermarck, *Ritual and Belief in Morocco*, vol. 2, 461, *YaSin* is most frequently recited, which may be followed by the Koranic verse *Al-Kursî* (2:255) and the last verse of sura *Al-Baqara* (2). According to him, alternatively, sura *Al-Mulk* (67), sura *Taha* (20), and sura *Al-Ikhlâs* (112) may also be recited. The recitation of the *Fâtiḥa* forms its conclusion. The point of view of the Moroccan imam as regards the importance of the *talqîn* may not be commonly accepted, since, according to Westermarck, *Ritual and Belief in Morocco*, vol. 2, 464–465, a *fqî* remains at the grave when everybody has left the graveyard, to instruct the deceased how to answer the questions of the interrogating angels.

[123] Dâr al-Iftâ' al-Miṣriyya, *Al-Fatâwâ al-Islâmiyya*, vol. 20, 7398–7399. A *ḥadîth* frequently cited in this respect runs as follows: "It is not allowed for a woman, who believes in God and the Last Day, to mourn longer than three days. However, when it concerns her husband, she mourns for four months and ten days." See also Koran 2:234.

The majority of Islamic scholars also rejects the memorial gatherings which are held on, among others, the third and fortieth days following the death and after a year. They argue that these gatherings revive pain at the loss, which should be avoided. Moreover, if these meetings were held, one would have to express one's sympathy once more, whereas according to *ḥadîth*, as we have seen in dealing with the *ta^c^ziya*, this should be done only once. Another argument put forward against the memorial gatherings is that the communal meals that are held on these occasions put the bereaved to unnecessary expense. This money would otherwise have gone to the family of the deceased, who may be in need of it. Besides, the deceased person receives no reward or grace from these meetings.[124] On this basis, it is argued that Muslims should refrain from holding memorial gatherings, but they are encouraged to ask for forgiveness on behalf of the deceased, to give alms or to perform the *hajj* in his or her name. In support of this the following *ḥadîth* is cited: "When a human being dies, his works come to an end except for three: a permanent charitable donation, profitable knowledge or a virtuous child that prays for him."[125]

In the Netherlands, the local Muslim community gathers at the home of the deceased immediately after hearing of a death to offer their condolences to the bereaved. It is not common for these visitors to view the body, even if the death occurred at home and the body has not yet been taken away yet for the ritual ablution and the shrouding. Only the closest relatives may be allowed to see the body.

A Turkish respondent indicated that in Turkey people normally offer their condolences after a burial and not beforehand. In Turkey the burial occurs within about two hours of a death. In the Netherlands, by contrast, especially if the body is transported to the country of origin, preparations for burial take at least one day. The bereaved family therefore receives condolences on several occasions: in the Netherlands immediately after having announced the death, in Turkey on the arrival of the corpse at the home village of the deceased, and again in the Netherlands after their return from Turkey.

The period of mourning and how the bereaved deal with the death in practice varies from person to person. Some people choose to remain at home for a few days; others avoid festivities for a year. In his description of mourning in Turkey, Tan distinguishes between the period of condolences ("Kondolenzzeit") and the period of mourning

[124] Dâr al-Iftâ' al-Miṣriyya, *Al-Fatâwâ al-Islâmiyya*, vol. 20, 7396–7397.
[125] Ibid., 7397.

("Trauerzeit"). During the period of condolences, which lasts—depending on the locality—either three or seven days from the day of burial, the bereaved remain at home and may not bathe, comb their hair, change their clothes, or eat. The period of mourning consists of several stages. The first of these is the period of condolences; further periods last forty days and one year from the day of the burial. For forty days following the burial, the bereaved may wear mourning clothes (clothes in colours that are not vivid, but certainly not black) and avoid festivities, and they neither play nor listen to music. During this period, neighbours may join the family for an evening meal, if only briefly.[126] A Turkish respondent buried her father in his native village. The family then left for their home in a nearby town. Upon their arrival they discovered that no-one from the neighbourhood had prepared a meal for them, a circumstance that they regarded as strange.

The ambivalence described above regarding the memorial gatherings can also be found in practice. According to my respondents, the bereaved family receives many visitors for three days after a death, and on the initiative of the family memorial gatherings are held at home or on the premises of a mosque on, for example, the third, seventh, and fortieth day following a death. These consist of praying for the deceased and a communal meal. At the same time, my respondents may also argue that it is better to refrain from these gatherings, for one could equally pray for the deceased at home at any time, without necessarily inviting the community. Their underlying reason may be that they regard these gatherings as a waste of money or are reluctant to bother the bereaved family. Nonetheless, in most cases, these considerations will not dissuade people from organizing a memorial gathering on particular days.

The days on which these gatherings are generally held vary. Moroccans may invite *ṭalba* and organize a *ṣadaqa* on the fortieth day following the death and again a year after the death. Renaerts for example reports the following observation concerning the *ṣadaqa* in Morocco, which is organized on the fortieth day, and also on the third and seventh day:

> Quoique la famille n'est tenu par aucune obligation, il y va de son honneur d'offrir une sadaqa. A l'origine la sadaqa est en fait une distribution de nourriture faite aux pauvres mais pratiquement il s'agit d'un repas communiel auquel participe la communauté entière. Il n'est pas rare qu'une famille s'endette afin que les funérailles soient dignes et conformes au prestige du groupe qu'elle représente.[127]

[126] Tan, "Wandlungen des Sterbens und der Trauerrituale in der Migration", 115–116.
[127] Renaerts, *La Mort, rites et valeurs dans l'islam maghrébin*, 68.

Turks may gather on the seventh, fortieth, and fifty-second day following the death. The bones are believed to have disintegrated fully on the fifty-second day. Javanese people from Surinam may organize a *ṣadaqa* or *slametan* after seven, forty, one hundred, and one thousand days and also annually. In the Netherlands, there is a tendency among this group to reduce the number of such gatherings. In earlier times, the gravestone would be put in place only after one thousand days. Nowadays, increasingly, this is done after a year, leading to a reduction in the number of gatherings. Surinamese Hindustani Muslims may organize a *kitaab* every day for forty days, and more elaborate gatherings may be held on the third (*tidja*) and the fortieth day (*jaliswa*).

According to a Turkish imam in the Netherlands, it is reprehensible (*makrûh*) to organize a memorial gathering on a particular day. In his view, one should prevent people from feeling obliged to organize such gatherings. Nevertheless, a *ṣadaqa*—consisting of a meal, a *mevlüt* or a donation of money—or undertaking a pilgrimage to Mecca in the name of the deceased proves that you are a good relative and raises the chance that the deceased will be forgiven. Another Turkish respondent stressed the importance of leaving behind virtuous children, capable of reciting the Koran. A Moluccan respondent stressed that only *ᶜilm*, *ṣadaqa*, and a child that prays for you are able to help you after your death. These points of view fit in particularly well with the *ḥadîth* cited earlier.

A group of bereaved Turkish Muslims in the Netherlands organized a *mevlüt* on the forty-second day following the death, during a weekend. This religious gathering, attended by men as well as women, took place in their mosque. In the prayer room allotted to women, about seventy women sat on the ground. At the moment in the story of the *mevlüt* at which the Prophet is born, the women stood and patted each other on the back, symbolically reliving the birth of a child, as they explained. As the *mevlüt* continued, sweets (*mevlüt şekeri*) were passed round and scented water was offered to those present.[128] After the *mevlüt*, a meal was served on the premises of the mosque.

[128] In describing the main differences between women's and men's performances of the *mevlüt*, Tapper & Tapper, "The Birth of the Prophet", 80, focus also on the section of the recital dealing with the birth of the Prophet. Their comment may throw some light on the events described above: "As the time of birth approaches, Emine [i.e. the mother of the Prophet] cries out with thirst and is offered sweet ice-cold water which fills her with light and joy; at recitals commemorating a very recent death, tall glasses of sugar water or very sweet lemonade (*cennet şerbeti*, lit. heavenly cordial) are then given to the congregation (though on other occasions, for both men and women, packages of sweet may be distributed, 'for respect (*hürmet*)', in their place). Then, at the moment of birth, when the white bird comes and strokes Emine's back, all the women stand facing Mecca, while

Likewise, the other groups may organize gatherings either at home or in the mosque, mostly consisting of a religious and a social part. In the religious part, apart from the *mevlüt*, participants may recite Koranic suras. The *Fâtiḥa*, sura *YaSin*, but also the Koran as a whole are frequently mentioned by respondents in this connection. Surinamese Javanese Muslims may also recite the *Tahlîl*, which consists among other things of the recitation of the opening sura *Al-Fâtiḥa*, suras starting with *Qul* (112 and 114), the *shahâda*, and the Koranic verse *Al-Kursî* (2:255), each repeated a number of times.

Thereafter, a more or less sumptuous meal may be served to those present, depending on the financial means of the family concerned among other things. In Morocco, the dishes served on this occasion vary locally.[129] One finds the same variety in the Netherlands: some Moroccan respondents served couscous whereas others offered bread and honey.

Turkish Muslims may present sweets on the fortieth day, indicating that life then resumes its normal course. Tan explains the Turkish practice of presenting sweets on the fortieth day on the assumption that sweets symbolize the positive order in human society. Eating these sweets together re-establishes the order. During the mourning period until the fortieth day, says Tan, sugar is taboo.[130] According to a Turkish respondent, however, *helva* may also be presented on the seventh day. In such cases the *mevlüt* may still be organized on the fortieth day.

Like the Turkish Muslims, Surinamese Hindustani Muslims may also pass around sweets (*siernie*, *halwa*). This may be done at the end of the religious part of the ceremony. Moroccan Muslims may bring sugar to the bereaved on the day of the burial and also upon their return to the Netherlands. A Moroccan family, for example, who had lost their son

the cantor sprinkles rosewater over them. The women then imitate both Emine and the white bird: they are in any case covered with waist-length diaphanous white prayer scarves and they now move through the room stroking each other on the back. When the flurry of movement and contact is over, women return to their places and the cantor recites the standing prayer (*ayak duası*), a prayer for the intercession of the Prophet in the lives of the congregation, which links images of birth with Muhammad's night journey to heaven [the latter explanation is severely criticized by Abu-Zahra, "The Comparative Study of Muslim Societies and Islamic Rituals", 15]. For women, the birth section of the *mevlûd* may be one of several high points. For men, this moment is the climax of the *mevlûd* but is marked simply by the congregation standing at the moment of birth and the sprinkling of rosewater and distribution of sweets by assistants; there is no physical contact or other movement among men."

129 See also Renaerts, *La Mort, rites et valeurs dans l'islam maghrébin*, 69–71.

130 Tan, "Wandlungen des Sterbens und der Trauerrituale in der Migration", 129 n. 13 and 17.

during a vacation in Morocco, received many visitors who came to offer their condolences upon the return of the family to the Netherlands. They brought about twenty sugar rods and fifty packs of sugar.

Surinamese Javanese Muslims may organize a *slametan* or a *ṣadaqa* on several occasions. The westward-prayers[131] among them may also make *sadjèn* offerings for the dead on each Thursday evening. These offerings may consist of special dishes and drinks that the deceased enjoyed during his life.[132] It is believed that these offerings prevent the spirits from turning against the surviving relatives. However, the Surinamese Javanese eastward-prayers reject this pattern of behaviour and keep to the *ṣadaqa* only.

5.4. Conclusions

The ritual of death has changed in several respects as a consequence of migration to the Netherlands. Clearly, the practice of repatriating the corpse to the country of origin, customary among Moroccan and Turkish Muslims, has greatly influenced the burial ritual. However, changes in this ritual have occurred also among Surinamese Muslims, who mostly opt for a burial in the Netherlands.

Generally, Surinamese Muslims in the Netherlands bury their dead in special Islamic sections of public graveyards. These sections consist mainly of graves with an exclusive right, each holding one corpse only. Until the end of the 1980s, a double-height coffin was in common use

[131] For a description of the eastward- and westward-prayers among the Surinamese Javanese Muslims, see section 2.1.

[132] Suparlan, "The Javanese in Surinam", 271, describes the *slametan* and the *sadjèn* in Surinam: "The kinds of food offered in the *sadjen* offerings and in the *slametan* of the first day after the burial (*njurtanah*) are the same as the kinds of food offered at the other six *sadjen* offerings and *slametan* for the funeral ceremonies. The *sadjen* offerings consist of burning incense, a glass of water filled with some *melati* blossoms, several kinds of food which the dead liked very much when he was still alive, a pair of *apem* (rice pancakes) and *kolak ketan* (a desert made of chunks of banana, sweet potatoes and others and cooked in sweetened coconut juice). These last two kinds of food are considered as being offered to the ancestors. The kinds of food offered in the *slametan* are almost the same as those for any other kinds of *slametan*. These consist of rice, chicken in several styles of cooking, seasoned vegetables, fried rice chips, *djadjan pasar*, boiled eggs, and several kinds of porridge. Some of them offer more varieties and greater quantities of food in the *slametan*, while others do it with simpler food and in smaller quantity. This depends upon their economic capacities." A Surinam Javanese respondent in the Netherlands described in detail the *sadjèn* offering that she made because of her anniversary (*waton*). It consisted of four plates of rice porridge, various kinds of fruit, various prepared dishes with rice, eggs and vegetables as ingredients, glasses containing water with and without blossom, coffee, tea, milk. Some of the dishes, covered with aluminium foil, were meant for wandering spirits, for whom no *sadjèn* is made.

with this group. Nowadays this type of coffin has disappeared, being replaced by a coffin of normal height. It is lowered without its lid into a special wooden formwork which supports the sides of the burial pit. The upper edges of this formwork are then covered with slats. The result is a kind of *bait musaqqaf* (roofed house), comparable in certain respects to a *laḥd* or a *shaqq* grave. This construction is unknown in Surinam, where either the dead are buried coffined, or the coffin is placed upside down over the body, or the coffin is broken up and the fragments are scattered under the corpse at the bottom of the burial pit, to prevent the corpse from getting wet.

The 1991 Dutch Corpse Disposal Act offers the option, specifically designed for Muslims, of burying the dead within twenty-four hours after death and without a coffin on certain conditions. Only the Moluccan Muslims make use of this option. Up to now Surinamese Muslims have not made use of this option: they still prefer to commit their dead to earth coffined. They explain this preference by reference to the moistness of the Dutch soil and prevailing custom in Surinam. They may also argue that there is no need to bury the dead without a coffin when insurance companies will cover its the costs.

Because of the practice of repatriating the dead to the countries of origin, prevalent among Turkish and Moroccan Muslims, the preparations for burial, the burial itself, and the subsequent mourning period have become split up both spatially and in time. For this reason, it may occur that the *ṣalât al-janâza* is held twice, once in the Netherlands and once in the home country. The condolence visits may also take place on several occasions: in the Netherlands immediately upon the announcement of the death, in Turkey or Morocco upon arrival of the corpse, and again in the Netherlands by those who have not yet had the opportunity to express their sympathy. Turkish Muslims further indicated that in the Netherlands the local Muslim community gathers at the home of the bereaved immediately upon hearing of a death to offer their condolences. If the death occurs in Turkey, however, these visits take place only after the burial and not beforehand, because of the short time that elapses between death and burial.

The wish to repatriate the corpse to the country of origin has led to the establishment of funeral funds among Moroccan and Turkish Muslims, to meet the considerable expenses involved. This shows that these Muslims attach greater importance to a burial in the country of origin than to a burial as soon as possible after death, as the preparations and the transport to the country of origin cost at least two days, while a burial in the Netherlands could have taken place one day earlier. In Morocco and

Turkey the burial mostly takes place on the day of the death, and often within a few hours of it.

Repatriation of the dead body requires the use a coffin for transport. Upon arrival in Turkey in most cases the body is removed from the coffin; in Morocco this occurs more rarely. Corpses transported within Morocco may also be buried coffined. Usually, however, those who die in Morocco or Turkey are buried without a coffin. In these countries the coffin is used only for carrying the corpse to its last resting place.

In the migrational context the role of the mosques in performing the preparatory *farḍ kifâya* tasks, that is the ritual ablution of the dead, the shrouding (*takfîn*), and the performance of the *ṣalât al-janâza*, seems to have increased. In both Turkey and Morocco, mosques may play a background role. They may provide the items needed for the washing, and they may have available a number of coffins of differing sizes, in which the dead are carried to the grave. In the Netherlands however mosques no longer provide such items. Rather they support the bereaved family in organizational matters of all kinds. This holds for Turkish Muslims in particular: as we have seen, their mosque organizations are responsible for the management of the funeral funds, whereas financial institutions have taken over this responsibility among Moroccans.

In the Netherlands the ritual purification of the dead is performed either at the funeral parlour or in the hospital where the death took place. Mosques in the Netherlands may also provide for washing facilities. In the countries of origin, however, this ritual usually takes place at home. A Surinamese Javanese respondent indicated that in Surinam, even if a person died in a hospital, his or her corpse is brought home for the preparatory tasks and is carried to his or her last resting place from there.

We have seen how gradually an organizational infrastructure for the performance of circumcisions has developed in the Netherlands. This development has only just begun with respect to the ritual of death. In the near future an increasing number of Muslims in the Netherlands will probably opt for a burial in the Netherlands. This may occur not only for future generations of Moroccans and Turks, whose ties with the countries of origin may grow weaker, but also for other groups of Muslims in the Netherlands, such as Pakistanis.

In 1998, the Pakistan Welfare Social Society obtained a section of the Zuiderbegraafplaats in Rotterdam, a public graveyard, for the exclusive use of its members. The negotiations of this mosque organization in Rotterdam with the graveyard keeper may offer an example of the organizational developments to be expected in the field of burial practices in the near future. The cost of a grave with an exclusive right is relatively high compared to that of transporting a corpse to Pakistan for burial. The two parties therefore agreed that the members of the Pakistan Welfare Social Society could opt for a public grave at first, which costs less than a grave with an exclusive right. After fifteen years the family of the deceased can decide to convert the public grave into a grave with an exclusive right, which will not be emptied at the end of the term. Relatives thus have fifteen years to raise money for a grave with an exclusive right. Muslims constitute an important customer group for graveyard keepers: Islamic law prescribes burial wherever possible, whereas native Dutch citizens increasingly prefer cremation to burial. Muslim organization therefore enjoy a strong negotiating position with graveyard keepers.

The growing number of Muslims opting for a burial in the Netherlands may lead to the establishment of separate Islamic graveyards and to a renewed discussion about burial on the day of death, the use of a coffin, the use of graves with an exclusive right, and the most suitable grave construction. We have seen that Surinamese Muslims have reservations against burials without a coffin, while Moluccan Muslims in the Netherlands do not use a coffin. Moroccans, Turks, and Pakistanis are likely to opt for yet another solution. The subsequent discussions may eventually bring about compromises similar to the one struck at the Zuiderbegraafplaats in Rotterdam.

6
CONTINUITY AND CHANGE

> Just as the experience of cognitive dissonance is disturbing, so the experience of consonance in layer after layer of experience and context after context is satisfying.
>
> —Mary Douglas, *Natural Symbols,* 74

> Das Leben in der Fremde, einem weitgehend entsymbolisierten Raum, ist . . . ein gestaltbares Leben. Es bietet dem einzelnen bislang ungeahnte Chancen, es kann und wird, jedenfalls eine Zeitlang, als Befreiung von traditionalen Zwängen erlebt. Das Leben in einem entsymbolisierten Raum hat jedoch auch eine Kehrseite, nämlich die einer prinzipiellen Leere.
>
> —Werner Schiffauer, *Migranten aus Subay,* 177

The development of lifecycle rituals of Muslims in the Netherlands is a delicate balance between continuity and change. It is shaped both by the wish to retain the significance of the rituals in a new social, cultural, and juridical context, and by the necessity to adapt them under the influence and in consequence of the new surroundings. In the foregoing chapters I presented many examples of continuity and change in lifecycle rituals. I shall not summarize them here, but rather shift to an analytic level.

I shall explore two theses. First, I suggest that the lifecycle rituals of migrant groups in a new setting, such as Muslims in the Netherlands, exhibit phenomena of attrition or erosion. Due to the transplantation of rituals from one social and cultural context to another that does not support them to the same degree, the ritual repertoire becomes smaller and displays less variety. The erosion of rituals arises from, and in turn results in, a loss of competence of the ritual actors and a reduction of ritual redundancy. The phenomena of ritual attrition are in many respects analogous to phenomena of language attrition, studied by historical linguists. Second, I will argue that the historical path and outcome of the transplantation process at a certain time is contingent. I conclude by indicating possible future trends in the development of Muslim lifecycle rituals in the Netherlands.

6.1. Competence and Consonance

How does the ritual repertoire of Moroccan, Surinamese, and Turkish migrants in the Netherlands differ from that in the countries of origin? By ritual repertoire I mean the entire stock of ceremonies and rites consisting of combinations of a particular type of circumstances (time and space), instruments, agents, movements, utterances, and gestures from which ritual actors draw in their performance of a ritual.[1] My fieldwork findings suggest that the ritual repertoire of Muslim migrants in the Netherlands has changed in two ways: it has become smaller than in the countries of origin and it has come to show a smaller degree of diversity.

First, some customs that are widespread in the countries of origin have partly or completely disappeared in the Netherlands. The practice that a Turkish boy appears in festive clothes for two or three days before his circumcision, for example, which is customary in certain parts of Turkey, is no longer extant in the Netherlands. The bride's ceremonial visit to the bathhouse and visits of friends and relatives to view her trousseau are less common in the Netherlands than in Morocco and Turkey. Likewise, the *mitoni* ceremony in the seventh month of a Surinamese Javanese woman's pregnancy has lost much of its performative character in the Netherlands. In Surinam the ceremony takes place in the open air, enabling many guests to attend. In the Netherlands, by contrast, the ceremony may be held in the bathroom of the bride's house or apartment. This prosaic location transforms the "feel" of the ceremony and ensures that only a few guests can attend.

Second, the lifecycle rituals of Muslims in the Netherlands display a smaller degree of diversity than in the countries of origin. The development apparent among certain strata of the population of Surinam and Turkey, that couples conclude a civil marriage but no religious marriage, is for example not found in the Netherlands. Similarly, whereas separate wedding parties for the families of the bride and groom are still held in Morocco and Turkey, this phenomenon seems to have disappeared in the Netherlands: the wedding parties are increasingly often held in a venue where the male and female guests of both families gather together. Furthermore, local differences that existed in the countries of origin have vanished in the Netherlands.

The limitations of a poorer ritual repertoire make themselves more strongly felt in a situation of diminished competence of the ritual actors and in a migrational setting of reduced consonance. Ritual actors are said to have "competence" if they know how to perform certain rituals. In a migrational context, where Muslims form a minority, the ritual actors lose the reinforcing stimuli of the native country. In this situation, the ritual actors are compelled to rely on their own competence in the performance of the relevant rites and ceremonies. However, most people

[1] I owe this combination of aspects, with the exception of "utterances", to Bourdieu, *Outline of a Theory of Practice*, 118.

have little or no knowledge of the details of the rituals. Parents may for instance be unversed in the words that should be whispered in a child's ear shortly after the birth, even though they may be familiar with the ceremony in general terms. If first-generation migrants are unable to provide adequate models for the performance of the rituals in the new situation where the strong influence of the native models is no longer present, the second and third generations may in turn experience difficulties in acquiring sufficient ritual competence to sustain the ritual repertoire. Bridal couples may not know what to expect at the religious wedding ceremony, or the bereaved may not know exactly how to perform the ritual ablution and shrouding of the dead. By contrast, in the countries of origin, someone is always available who knows what should be done or where to find the expertise.

The loss of competence of the ritual actors and the lack of models for the performance of rituals in a migrational setting is accompanied by a decreased degree of consonance. Consonance or redundancy is a feature that ritual practice may exhibit—particularly in well-integrated societies—if dense complexes of symbols replicate the social order and each other in multiple ways. In plural and pluralistic societies, where many systems of symbols exist side by side, consonance is often less profuse and comprehensive since it is accomplished only within those parts of the society that hold to a particular set of symbols. The smaller degree of consonance is a major factor responsible for the feeling of emptiness that migrants may experience in the Netherlands.[2]

The changes in the practice of dressing a boy in festive clothes on the occasion of his circumcision clearly convey the reduction in consonance and the sense of disappointment that follows from it. In Turkey, if a boy shows himself in festive clothes on the days preceding his circumcision, relatives and neighbours will offer him encouragement and give him a treat. Everyone knows that he will be circumcised on the third day or so. This combination of ingredients is lacking in the Netherlands. Most people in Dutch society have no knowledge of or experience with this pattern of behaviour. For fear of lack of understanding, parents may therefore prefer to postpone dressing their son in festive clothes until the circumcision celebrations, which take place within their own ethnic group. In this smaller group, the festive clothes retain their significance.

Another example of the reduction of consonance may be found in my respondents' experience that the support network that was normally available in the countries of origin is lacking in the Netherlands. In the

[2] On consonance, see Platvoet, "Ritual in Plural and Pluralist Societies", 32.

Netherlands, Moroccans in particular miss the conviviality experienced in Morocco on certain social occasions thanks to the involvement of everyone in the surroundings. Moreover, certain services, customarily available in the countries of origin, are less easy to obtain in the Netherlands. Dressers in Morocco, who accompany the bride during a wedding party, have for example a much wider assortment of bridal clothes and accessories than dressers in the Netherlands, and Morocco, unlike the Netherlands, offers a wide selection of professional Moroccan bands.

The impact of these processes of erosion has been counteracted to some extent by new initiatives, mostly in the field of the organization of the lifecycle rituals. The most notable initiatives have been taken on a local level in the performance of circumcisions. The establishment of funeral funds among Turks and Moroccans in the Netherlands is another example.

In summary, my findings show that the ritual repertoire is smaller and shows less variety in the migrational context than in the countries of origin. This both arises from and results in a reduction of competence and consonance.

6.2. Ritual Attrition

An analogous phenomenon is well known in historical linguistics, where it goes under the name of language attrition. The phenomenon of language attrition has been the object of research particularly since the 1980s.[3] It forms an important theme in studies of language maintenance, shift, and death, as well as in studies of language contact and bilingualism.[4]

Language attrition can be defined as erosion in the competence in and performance of a first or primary language, L1, in contact situations with a second language, L2.[5] The first-language vocabulary of bilingual Turkish children living in the Netherlands, for example, is less extensive than the vocabulary of monolingual Turkish children living in Turkey.[6] Even the language of first-generation migrants, who are native speakers, is

[3] Waas, *Language Attrition Downunder*, 16 and 33–35.

[4] On language attrition, see Lambert & Freed, *The Loss of Language Skills*, Seliger & Vago, *First Language Attrition*, Fase, Jaspaert & Kroon, *Maintenance and Loss of Minority Languages*, and Waas, *Language Attrition Downunder*.

[5] Sharwood Smith & Van Buren, "First Language Attrition and the Parameter Setting Model", 18–19; Seliger & Vago, "The Study of First Language Attrition", 4. For alternative definitions, see Waas, *Language Attrition Downunder*, 17–26, and Yağmur, *First Language Attrition among Turkish Speakers in Sydney*, 11–15.

[6] Schaufeli, "A Domain Approach to the Turkish Vocabulary of Bilingual Turkish Children in the Netherlands", 130.

often affected by attrition after their migration when the strong influence of the native language norms is no longer present.[7]

The standard case of language attrition is a bilingual or multilingual setting in which an attritted L1 is replaced by L2 in the course of two or three generations. The unlearning process consisting of a decline of first-language skills is initiated by a reduction of access to and use of L1 and an increasing exposure to L2. The changes can be divided into two classes. Some changes in L1 occur under the influence of L2: an element in L1 may for example be incorrectly patterned on analogy to L2. We call these external changes.[8] Other attrition phenomena, including generalization, simplification, and regularization, are changes internal to L1.[9]

There are considerable differences between various ethnic groups with respect to the degree of language loss. In Australia, for example, second-generation Dutch-born migrants show an almost complete shift to English, whereas the language shift among Greek migrants is far smaller.[10] Cultural similarity with the dominant group promotes a shift to L2, whereas cultural distance from the dominant group discourages this process.[11] Other variables that may promote language maintenance include a large concentration of L1 speakers in a particular area, the existence of supporting institutions such as ethnic schools, churches, newspapers, radio, and television, and a high cultural value of a minority language for the continued existence of a minority group as a group.[12] Furthermore, the degree of first-language loss among less-educated migrants is usually larger than among well-educated migrants.[13]

[7] Ibid., 118, with reference to Gonzo & Saltarelli, "Pidginization and Linguistic Change in Emigrant Languages", which I did not consult. For similar findings concerning Turkish migrants in Australia, see Yağmur, De Bot & Korzilius, "Language Attrition, Language Shift and Ethnolinguistic Vitality of Turkish in Australia". See also Hock & Joseph, *Language History, Language Change, and Language Relationship*, 449. According to De Bot & Clyne, "A 16-year Longitudinal Study of Language Attrition in Dutch Immigrants in Australia", 17, first-language attrition does not necessarily take place in the first generation of migrants.

[8] Seliger & Vago, "The Study of First Language Attrition", 7.

[9] Ibid., 10.

[10] Yağmur, De Bot & Korzilius, "Language Attrition, Language Shift and Ethnolinguistic Vitality of Turkish in Australia", 54, Clyne, *Community Languages*, 65, and De Bot & Clyne, "A 16-year Longitudinal Study of Language Attrition in Dutch Immigrants in Australia", 18.

[11] Clyne, "Linguistic and Sociolinguistic Aspects of Language Contact, Maintenance and Loss", 32–33; Clyne & Pauwels, "Use, Maintenance, Structures, and Future of Dutch in Australia", 42.

[12] Clyne, *Community Languages*, 61–111. For Smolicz's theory on language as a cultural core value, see Smolicz, "Minority Languages as Core Values of Ethnic Cultures".

[13] Yağmur, De Bot & Korzilius, "Language Attrition, Language Shift and Ethnolinguistic Vitality of Turkish in Australia", 55 and 64. For a critical discussion of the factors

I propose an analytic structure for rituals and ritual attrition in the migrational context analogous to that developed in historical linguistics for language attrition. I shall denote the repertoire of lifecycle rituals of Moroccans, Turks, and Surinamese in their countries of origin by R1; the quite different repertoire of lifecycle rituals that is commonplace in the Netherlands is denoted by R2.

Ritual attrition, by analogy with language attrition, is the process by which the ritual repertoire reduces in size and variety. This is accompanied by a decrease in competence and consonance. Attrition phenomena are likely to occur particularly among the first three generations of migrants. The degree of attrition will be determined among other things by the number of migrants in a particular area, the time elapsed since their migration, their educational level, and the institutional resources.[14]

In language attrition, as we have seen, the language actually spoken by the migrant group comes to differ from L1 as a result of internal and external factors. Internally induced changes consist of the intrinsic evolutionary drift of L1 that takes place in the circumstances of linguistic isolation, whereas externally induced changes result from the influence of L2. By analogy, the ritual repertoire of Muslims in the Netherlands comes to differ from the original R1 as a result of two sets of factors. Internally induced changes consist of the intrinsic evolutionary drift of lifecycle rituals of Moroccans, Turks, and Surinamese in the Netherlands. These are mainly processes intrinsic to the transplantation of rituals, such as the reduction of diversity, morphological reduction, and stylistic shrinkage.[15] Externally induced changes, by contrast, result from the influence of the migratory environment, including both what might be termed the local repertoire of lifecycle rituals R2, and the Dutch social and juridical context.

The decrease in ritual repertoire and the reduction of consonance and competence in a migrational setting seems to have exacted a greater psychological toll on Moroccan and Turkish than on Surinamese Muslims. My Moroccan and Turkish respondents report a greater degree of estrangement and feeling of emptiness when performing lifecycle rituals than my Surinamese respondents. I interpret this feeling as arising from the greater cultural distance of Morocco and Turkey than Surinam from

leading to language maintenance or shift, see Clyne & Pauwels, "Use, Maintenance, Structures, and Future of Dutch in Australia", 33–47.

[14] According to Fishman, "Mother-Tongue Claiming in the United States Since 1960", 158–159, the number of language claimants and the institutional resources for language maintenance determine the relative survival rates of languages.

[15] I owe these terms to Campbell, "Language Death", 1963.

the Netherlands. The disparity in cultural distance can be retraced to two factors.

First, Surinamese, unlike Moroccans and Turks, are familiar with the Dutch language and institutions, since Surinam was a Dutch colony until 1975. Moreover, Surinamese Muslims in the Netherlands have a family history of migration. The Muslims now living in Surinam are descendants of migrants from Java and Hindustan (India) who moved to Surinam in the late nineteenth century. The Muslim community in Surinam has built up its Muslim identity particularly since the 1920s. The generations that moved to the Netherlands thus have recent experience in transplanting lifecycle rituals to a new context.

Second, Surinamese Muslims, in contrast to Moroccans and Turks, were used to living in a pluralistic situation in Surinam and are therefore socially and psychologically better equipped to deal with the effects of the reduction of competence and consonance. For example, unlike their Turkish and Moroccan counterparts, Surinamese Hindustani and Javanese mosque organizations make up for the lack of competence in the washing and shrouding of the dead by periodically organizing courses on how to perform these tasks. Moreover, whereas Moroccans and Turks miss the conviviality experienced in their countries of origin, Surinamese do not expect the involvement of the broader social context in the performance of the lifecycle rituals.

Language and ritual attrition show different features in some respects. Language attrition generally increases with the time elapsed since migration, leading to the gradual replacement of L1 by L2 in the course of three generations. By contrast, if the cultural and religious distance between R1 and R2 is large, ritual attrition is likely to decrease with the time elapsed since the migration.[16] In a first phase of reconstruction of the ritual repertoire in the new context consisting of at least two generations of migrants, R1 is adapted under the influence of the new surroundings and exhibits attrition phenomena but nevertheless maintains its distinctness from R2 on the basis of its religious and cultural features. The transplantation of lifecycle rituals thus does not result in the gradual replacement of R1 by R2.

The influence of the Dutch physical, social, and juridical context on the lifecycle rituals of Moroccans, Turks, and Surinamese living in the Netherlands constitutes another disanalogy between language and ritual attrition. Lifecycle rituals are determined by the setting in which they are

[16] For the role of cultural similarity to the dominant group in language maintenance, see Clyne, "Linguistic and Sociolinguistic Aspects of Language Contact, Maintenance and Loss", 32–33.

performed to a greater extent than language. Ritual actors must take account of the physical conditions of the local setting, such as climate and other environmental factors, in the performance of a ritual. Furthermore, ritual actors are subject to rules regulating the local resources that they need in the performance of rituals. There is space for negotiation in some cases. However, the outcome of this process is historically contingent, as we will see in the next section.

I conclude this section with two hypotheses about the effect of ritual attrition on Muslim lifecycle rituals in the Dutch migrational setting and about the features of rituals that are more and less likely to survive attrition. My first hypothesis is that rites and ceremonies in which many people participate simultaneously are more easily transplanted to a migrational setting than those attended by a few people. In particular, rites and ceremonies of a private or individual character are the hardest to maintain. For example, the rites and ceremonies of whispering the call to prayer in the child's ear shortly after birth and of washing and shrouding the dead are more difficult to maintain than the bride's changing of her clothes that is characteristic of Moroccan weddings. This is because the wider the circle of people participating, the greater is the stock of knowledge that is brought to bear on the ritual.

My second hypothesis concerns what I call self-reliant rites and ceremonies. These are rites and ceremonies that are not dependent on local resources and institutions. I hypothesize that self-reliant rites and ceremonies are reconstructed first in the migrational setting. Examples are the offering of sweets wrapped in tulle to the guests when they leave a Moroccan party held on the occasion of the birth of a child, a Turkish bride's wearing of a red sash around her waist, and the shrouding of the deceased in white cotton cloths instead of items of clothing.

6.3. Historical Contingency

Like most historical processes, the development of lifecycle rituals of Moroccan, Surinamese, and Turkish Muslims in the Netherlands is historically contingent: the outcome that is instantiated is one of a large number of possible outcomes. The outcome is influenced by a complex network of causal factors, including local conditions, the influence of personalities, and sheer chance. Often it is difficult, despite the relatively short history of the Muslim presence in the Netherlands, to establish why a certain outcome or historical path at a particular moment was what it was, and not otherwise.[17] It is for instance unknown to me why a

[17] Ringer, *Max Weber's Methodology*, 3.

double-height coffin, previously in common use among Surinamese Muslims, came to be replaced by a coffin of normal height in Rotterdam and The Hague at the end of the 1980s.

The contingent nature of the processes described here is well illustrated by the differing fates of efforts to provide a new organizational infrastructure on a local level for the performance of circumcisions. As we saw in chapter 3, initiatives were launched in Rotterdam in 1994, in The Hague in 1996, and in Utrecht in 1997. The interested parties were in each case the same: Muslim organizations, the medical sector, and health insurance companies. But similar starting-points led to very different outcomes.

In Rotterdam, SPIOR, a platform of Muslim organizations in the city and its environs, proved a decisive factor in the establishment of Al-Gitaan, a foundation that performs circumcisions outside the hospital setting. In Utrecht, by contrast, the medical sector, and particularly a paediatrician of the Wilhelmina Children's Hospital, played an important role in the foundation of an organization comparable to Al-Gitaan. The Hague, unlike Rotterdam and Utrecht, was unable to develop an alternative to hospital circumcisions. The leader of SHIP, an organization similar to SPIOR, was unable to define a plan for The Hague that united all Muslim groups in the city. STIOM, a support organization of general practitioners, was unwilling to support an approach that failed to advance its main aim of improving relations with patients of Islamic background by performing circumcisions in the family setting. Moreover, hospitals in The Hague were willing to perform the operation, whereas in Rotterdam and Utrecht hospitals were no longer prepared to perform circumcisions except for medical reasons.

A second example of historical contingency can be found in the evolution of Muslim burial practices in Rotterdam. Thanks to strong lobbying, as we saw in chapter 5, the Pakistan Welfare Social Society in 1998 obtained a section of the Zuiderbegraafplaats for the exclusive use of its members. If requests for such a section had come from several Muslim groups, they would probably have been rejected. The graveyard keeper would have been obliged to choose to establish one section for all Muslims or several sections for the various ethnic groups and mosque organizations in Rotterdam. The fact that these groups were not reconciled to the same extent to the practice of burying their dead in the Netherlands contributed to the development of the present solution in Rotterdam.

These two examples suggest that the success of the initiatives in the field of the organization of circumcision and burial depends to a great extent on the strength of the leadership of the initiating parties, including local Muslim organizations and local authorities. The creativity that they were able to display on a local level has not yet been manifested on a national level where the disunity of Muslim organizations is prevalent.

6.4. Future Trends

What can be said about future trends in the evolution of lifecycle rituals of Muslims in the Netherlands? We have seen that, over two or three generations, migrants have developed radically new styles of lifecycle rituals based on models prevailing in the countries of origin. The relations with the countries of origin, particularly among Moroccans and Turks, have remained strong. The first generation cherishes the memory of their country of birth. The second and third generations regularly visit these countries during summer vacations, and like first-generation migrants mostly retain their original nationality. The continuous influx of migrants among other things through marriage, as well as the far-reaching influence of the mass media, further contribute to the maintenance of the knowledge of and contacts with the countries of origin.

This situation importantly defines the form and content of the lifecycle rituals. Most Moroccans and Turks conclude a marriage at the Moroccan or Turkish consulate in the Netherlands, or in the countries of origin, and prefer a burial in their country of origin. This practice will alter if the ties with the countries of origin grow weaker with generations to come. An increasing number of Moroccans and Turks will take Dutch nationality. As a result Moroccans, like Turks and Surinamese, may tend increasingly to conclude a marriage twice, once before a Dutch registrar and once in an Islamic manner. This will lead to renewed discussions about the marriage proceedings. Will they conclude a religious marriage on the premises of the mosque or at home like the Turks, or in the presence of the wedding guests like the Surinamese Muslims, or will they omit the ceremony and apply only for an *Acte de Reconnaissance de Mariage* at the Moroccan consulate? Furthermore, an increasing number of Moroccans and Turks will opt for a burial in the Netherlands. I expect that this will lead to renewed discussions between the several ethnic groups on how to proceed in the performance of the ritual.

If we pursue the comparison between language and ritual attrition further, we may forecast two alternative trends in the future development of lifecycle rituals of Muslims in the Netherlands. The first trend is one in which the distinct features of the ethnic groups are constantly revitalized and reactivated by continuing contact with the countries of origin through visits and new arrivals. This may show similarities to the phenomenon in language by which the population of L1 speakers in a migrational setting remains constant in size, with the number of new L1 speakers joining the population each year compensating for the number of second- and third-generation migrants shifting to L2.[18] The chance that a person belonging to a migrant group is a speaker of L2 rises with the time elapsed since migration. Likewise, in the case of rituals, one category consists of migrants—mainly first- to third-generation—whose ethnic background determines the form and content of the rituals. Another category consists of migrants with an early time of migration whose Muslim identity increasingly determines the form and content of the rituals. This trend is the most plausible scenario for the near future.

The second trend is a gradual development of Muslim lifecycle rituals in which the distinct traits of Moroccan, Surinamese, and Turkish rituals gradually disappear. This is similar to the process of reduction of variety in language after migration. This trend would be more likely to occur if Moroccan, Surinamese, and Turkish imams were to receive a common training in the Netherlands, including a general introduction on how to perform the lifecycle rituals according to Islamic law. This trend is more likely to obtain in the long run when the number of new arrivals and contacts with the countries of origin have decreased. It may be marked by a growing number of intermarriages across the various national Muslim communities.

In this study, I concentrated on the initial phase of the transplantation of lifecycle rituals to the Dutch context. Further research into the subsequent phases of this continuous process of adaptation of lifecycle rituals to the Dutch social circumstances is necessary. I hope that researchers entering this field will benefit from the approach developed in language attrition research. It will enable us to monitor the process of ritual attrition, to determine in more detail which factors promote and discourage it, and to ascertain the patterns and amount of loss.

[18] Personal communication, Pieter Muysken, Department of Languages and Cultures of Latin America, Leiden University.

BIBLIOGRAPHY

ᶜAbd al-Harî, Abû Sarîᶜ Muhammad. *Aḥkâm al-ṭahâra fî l-fiqh al-islâmî ᶜalâ al-madhâhib al-arbaᶜa maᶜa bayân al-ra'y al-râjiḥ*. N.p.: Dâr al-Iᶜtiṣâm, n.d.

ᶜAbd al-Muᶜnim Ibrâhîm, Abû ᶜA'ish. *Al-furqân fî ḥukm khitân al-banât wa l-ṣibyân*. [Cairo]: Dâr al-Fatḥ, 1995.

Abdurrahman Bewley, Aisha, trans. *Al-Muwatta of Imam Malik ibn Anas: The First Formulation of Islamic Law*. London: Kegan Paul International, 1989.

Abu-Zahra, Nadia. "The Comparative Study of Muslim Societies and Islamic Rituals." In *Arab Historical Review for Ottoman Studies* 3–4 (1991): 7–38.

Adhin, J. H. "Ontstaan en ontwikkeling van de z.g. Aziatische huwelijkswetgeving." In *Een eeuw Surinaamse codificatie: Gedenkboek (1869 – 1 mei – 1969)*, 93–142. Paramaribo: Surinaamse Juristen-Vereniging, 1969.

——. "Surinamisering van het huwelijksrecht." In *De Nieuwe West-Indische Gids* 50, 2–3 (1975): 77–88.

Alami, Dawoud Sudqi El, and Doreen Hinchcliffe. *Islamic Marriage and Divorce Laws of the Arab World*. London: Kluwer Law International, 1996.

Albânî, Muḥammad Nâṣir al-Dîn al-. *Aḥkâm al-janâ'iz wa-bidaᶜuhâ*. Beirut: Manshûrât al-Maktab al-Islâmî, 1969.

Aldeeb Abu-Sahlieh, Sami A. "To Mutilate in the Name of Jehovah or Allah: Legitimization of Male and Female Circumcision." In *Medicine and Law* 13 (1994): 575–622.

Alladien, Goelam Rasoel. *De baby en zijn naam in de islam*. Paramaribo: de Imaam v/d Surinaamse Moslim Associatie, 1975; Amsterdam: Mohammadi Stichting Nederland, 1992.

——. *Mohammed: De genade der werelden, de roem der werelden. Een Milaadboek met verhalen en gezangen over Allah's boodschapper*. Amsterdam: Mohammadi Stichting Nederland, 1992.

Ansay, Tuğrul. "Die Eheschliessung der Türken in der Bundesrepublik Deutschland." In *Die Welt des Islams* 15, 1–4 (1974): 26–38.

Ansay, Tuğrul, and Hilmar Krüger. "Gesetz Nr. 3716 vom 8. 5. 1991 über die Registrierung von außerehelichen Verbindungen als Ehen und von nichtehelich geborenen Kindern als eheliche Kinder." In *Das Standesamt* 45, 3 (1992): 87–88.

Antoun, Richard T. "Anthropology." In *The Study of the Middle East*, ed. Leonard Binder, 137–199. New York: John Wiley & Sons, 1976.

Ashqar, ᶜUmar Sulayman al-. *Thalâth shaᶜâ'ir: Al-ᶜaqîqa, al-uḍḥîya, al-liḥyaᶜ*. Ammân: Dâr al-Nafâ'is, Maktabat al-Falâh, 1991⁴.

Azharî, Shaihk Ṣâliḥ ᶜAbd al-Samiᶜ al-Abî al-. *Al-thamaru al-dânî: Sharḥ Risâla Ibn Abî Zaid al-Qairawânî*.

Bainbridge, Margaret. "Life-Cycle Rituals of Turks in Turkey: An Outline." In *Research Papers: Muslims in Europe* 16 (1982), 1–11.

Bartels, K., and I. Haaijer. *'s Lands wijs 's lands eer? Vrouwenbesnijdenis en Somalische vrouwen in Nederland.* Rijswijk: Centrum Gezondheidszorg Vluchtelingen, 1992.

Beatty, Andrew. *Varieties of Javanese Religion: An Anthropological Account.* Cambridge: Cambridge University Press, 1999.

Berg, Dora van den, Wilma van den Haak, Karin de Kiewit, Marijke Koggel, and Humphrey E. Lamur. "Javaans-Surinaamse rituelen: Zwangerschap en geboorte bij Javaanse contractarbeiders." In *OSO* 12, 1: 28–42.

Bergmann, A., and M. Ferid. *Internationales Ehe- und Kindschaftsrecht.* Frankfurt a. M.: Verlag für Standesamtswesen, 1983–.

Bilmen, Ömer Nasuhî. *Büyük islâm ilmihali.*

Biyar, Mohammed El. "Een goede besnijdenis is geen verminking." In *NRC Handelsblad*, 1 May 1997.

Boele-Woelki, K. "Bipatridie in het Nederlandse Internationaal Huwelijks- en Echtscheidingsrecht en de gevolgen daarop van een eventueel bilateraal verdrag met Marokko." In *De wenselijkheid van een bilateraal verdrag tussen Marokko en Nederland over conflicten aangaande het Internationaal Familierecht: Bijdragen aan de studiedag van 21 februari 1992 en de reactie van het NCB*, 14–22. Utrecht: Nederlands Centrum Buitenlanders, 1992.

Bommel, Abdulwahid van. "Rouwgebruiken bij moslims." In *Afscheid nemen van onze doden: Rouwen en rouwgebruiken in Nederland*, ed. Johanna Fortuin and Jan van Kilsdonk, 96–118. Kampen: Kok, 1988.

——."Wat zegt de islam over besnijdenis?" In *Al-Mizan: Marokkaans-Nederlands Maandblad* 4, 8 (1989): 8 and 11.

——. *Kom tot het gebed: Een korte inleiding tot de praktijk van de islam.* 's-Gravenhage: Uitgeverij Het Laatste Kwartier, [1989?].

Bot, Kees de, and Michael Clyne. "A 16-year Longitudinal Study of Language Attrition in Dutch Immigrants in Australia." In *Journal of Multilingual and Multicultural Development* 15, 1 (1994): 16–28.

Bot, Marrie. *Een laatste groet: Uitvaart- en rouwrituelen in multicultureel Nederland.* Rotterdam: Marrie Bot, 1998.

Bouhdiba, A. *La sexualité en islam.* Paris: PUF, 1975.

Bourdieu, Pierre. *Outline of a Theory of Practice.* Translated by Richard Nice. 1977. Reprint, Cambridge: Cambridge University Press, 1992.

Brockelmann, C. *Geschichte der Arabischen Litteratur.* 5 vols. Leiden: E. J. Brill, 1937–1949.

De buren vieren feest: Geboorte, overgang en huwelijk bij Antwerpse bevolkingsgroepen. (Exhibition catalogue, 13 September–15 December 1996, Koningin Fabiolazaal, Antwerp). Antwerpen: Provinciebestuur van Antwerpen, 1996.

Burkart, Dagmar. "Der rote Schleier: Zur traditionellen Brautausstattung bei den Türken und Bulgaren." In *Die Braut: Geliebt–erkauft–getauscht–geraubt: Zur Rolle der Frau im Kulturvergleich*, ed. Gisela Völger und Karin v. Welck, vol. 2, 450–455. Köln: Stadt Köln, 1985.

Buschkens, W. F. L., and J. A. Zevenbergen. "Surinaams huwelijksrecht: streven naar eenheid in verscheidenheid." In *Intermediair* 12 (1976): 36.

Buskens, Léon. "De recente hervorming van het Marokkaanse familierecht." In *Recht van de Islam* 12 (1995): 59–96.

——. *Islamitisch recht en familiebetrekkingen in Marokko*. Amsterdam: Bulaaq, 1999.

Cammaert, Marie-France. *Migranten en thuisblijvers: een confrontatie. De leefwereld van Marokkaanse Berbervrouwen*. Leuven: Universitaire Pers Leuven; Assen: Van Gorcum, 1985.

Campbell, Lyle. "Language Death." In *The Encyclopedia of Language and Linguistics*, ed. R. E. Asher and J. M. Y. Simpson, 4 (1994): 1960–1968.

Centraal Bureau voor de Statistiek. *Kerkelijke gezindte en kerkbezoek aan het einde van de 20e eeuw: Opvattingen en activiteiten*. Voorburg: Centraal Bureau voor de Statistiek, 2000.

——. "Allochtonen in Nederland (eerste en tweede generatie) naar geboorteland", updated on 4 May 2000. http://www.cbs.nl/nl/cijfers/kerncijfers/sbv0610d.htm, consulted on 20 December 2000.

——. "Niet-Nederlanders naar nationaliteit", updated on 4 May 2000. http://www.cbs.nl/nl/cijfers/kerncijfers/sbv0610b.htm, consulted on 20 December 2000

Cesari, Jocelyne. *Être musulman en France aujourd'hui*. Paris: Hachette, 1997.

Chaïb, Yassine. "L'Islam et la mort en France." Thèse Nouveau Régime, Université d'Aix-Marseille, Institut d'Etudes Politiques, 1992.

Chebel, Malek. *Histoire de la circoncision: Des origines à nos jours*. Paris: Éditions Balland, 1992.

Clyne, Michael. *Community Languages: The Australian Experience*. Cambridge: Cambridge University Press, 1991.

——. "Linguistic and Sociolinguistic Aspects of Language Contact, Maintenance and Loss: Towards a Multifacet Theory." In *Maintenance and Loss of Minority Languages*, ed. Willem Fase, Koen Jaspaert, and Sjaak Kroon, 17–36. Amsterdam: John Benjamins Publishing Company, 1992.

Clyne, Michael, and Anne Pauwels. "Use, Maintenance, Structures, and Future of Dutch in Australia." In *Dutch Overseas: Studies in Maintenance and Loss of Dutch as an Immigrant Language*, ed. Jetske Klatter-Folmer and Sjaak Kroon, 33–49. Tilburg: Tilburg University Press, 1997.

Crijnen, Ton. *Veertien portretten van nieuwe Nederlandse en Vlaamse moslims*. Amsterdam: Bulaaq, 1999.

Dâr al-Iftâ' al-Miṣriyya. *Al-Fatâwâ al-Islâmiyya min Dâr al-Iftâ' al-Miṣriyya*. Vol. 20. Al-Qâhira: Wizâra al-Awqâf, Al-Majlîs al-A[c]lâ li l-Shu'ûn al-Islâmiyya, 1993.

Dassetto, Felice. *La Construction de l'islam européen: Approche socio-anthropologique*. Paris: L'Harmattan, 1996.

Dassetto, Felice, and Albert Bastenier. "Organisations musulmanes de Belgique." In *La Belgique et le monde arabe*, ed. B. Khader and C. Roosens. Louvain-la-Neuve: Academia, 1990.

Dassetto, Felice, and Yves Conrad. *Musulmans en Europe occidentale: Bibliographie commentée / Muslims in Western Europe: An Annotated Bibliography*. Paris: L'Harmattan, 1996.

Dessing, Nathal M. "The Circumcision of Muslim Boys in the Netherlands: How Change Occurs in a Diaspora". In *Strangers and Sojourners: Religious Communities in the Diaspora*, ed. Gerrie ter Haar, 133–151. Leuven: Peeters, 1998.

——. "Continuïteit en verandering in de huwelijkssluiting bij Marokkaanse, Turkse en Surinaamse moslims in Nederland". In *Recht van de Islam* 16 (1999), 59–81.

——. "Uitvaart- en rouwrituelen bij moslims in Nederland". In *Handboek Sterven, Uitvaart en Rouw*, III 1.3, 1–16. Maarssen: Elsevier, 1999.

Diop, Amadou Moustapha. "France." In *Musulmans en Europe occidentale*, ed. Felice Dassetto and Yves Conrad, 21–51. Paris: L'Harmattan, 1996.

Dirks, Sabine. *La Famille musulmane turque: Son évolution au 20e siècle.* Paris: Mouton, 1969.

Douglas, Mary. *Natural Symbols: Explorations in Cosmology*. 3d ed. London: Routledge, 1996.

Dungen, Niek van den. "Masallah: Een exploratief onderzoek naar de ontwikkeling van moslimbesnijdenissen onder Turkse migranten in Nederland." Master's thesis, Etnische Studies en Minderheidsvraagstukken, Vrije Universiteit Amsterdam, 1993.

Eickelman, Dale F. "Rites of Passage: Muslim Rites." In *The Encyclopedia of Religion*, ed. Mircea Eliade, 12 (1987): 398–403.

Eklund, Ragnar. *Life between Death and Resurrection According to Islam*. Uppsala: Almqvist & Wiksells, 1941.

Elaroussi, Khalid. "Pratiques du mariage au Maroc: Le cas d'El Jadida." In *Le Mois en Afrique* 251–252 (1986–1987): 121–136.

Errazki-van Beek, Mariëtte. "Een vrouwenmuziekgroep uit Marrakech: De ᶜanṭriyat." In *Sharqiyyât* 7, 1 (1995): 28–56.

Étienne, B. *La France et l'islam*. Paris: Hachette, 1989.

Evers-Rosander, Eva. "Some Wedding Customs in Qbila Anjra Now (1976–87) and Then (1900–1910): Comparisons and Reflections Based on Westermarck's 'Marriage Ceremonies in Morocco'." In *Westermarck et la société marocaine*, ed. Rahma Bourqia and Mokhtar Al Harras, 111–124. Rabat: Publications de la Faculté des Lettres et des Sciences Humaines, 1993.

Fase, Willem, Koen Jaspaert, and Sjaak Kroon, ed. *Maintenance and Loss of Minority Languages*. Amsterdam: John Benjamins Publishing Company, 1992.

Fishman, Joshua A. "Mother-Tongue Claiming in the United States Since 1960: Trends and Correlates." In *The Rise and Fall of the Ethnic Revival*, ed. Joshua A. Fishman, 107–194. Berlin: Mouton, 1985.

Gailly, A. *Een dorp in Turkije*. Brussel: Cultuur en Migratie, 1983.

Geertz, Clifford. *The Religion of Java*. Chicago: University of Chicago Press, 1960.

Gellner, Ernest. *Muslim Society*. Cambridge: Cambridge University Press, 1981.

Gennep, Arnold van. *The Rites of Passage*. Chicago: University of Chicago Press, 1960.

Gerholm, Tomas, and Yngve Georg Lithman, ed. *The New Islamic Presence in Western Europe*. London: Mansell, 1988.

Gluckman, Max. "Rituals of Rebellion in South East Africa." In *Order and Rebellion in Tribal Africa*. London: Cohen & West, 1963.

Gonzo, S., and M. Saltarelli. "Pidginization and Linguistic Change in Emigrant Languages." In *Pidginization and Creolization as Language Acquisition*, ed. R. W. Anders. Rowley, Mass.: Newbury House, 1983.
Gooswit, Sylvia M. "Jaran képang, beheerste bezieling." In *Kalá: Tijdschrift van de Academie voor Hoger Kunst- en Cultuuronderwijs* 5, 1 (1991): 8–14.
Grütter, Irene. "Arabische Bestattungsbräuche in frühislamischer Zeit (nach Ibn Sa^c^d und Buhârî)." Parts 1–3. In *Der Islam* 31, 2–3 (1954): 147–173; 32, 3 (1957): 79–104, 168–194.

Haar, Gerrie ter. *Halfway to Paradise: African Christians in Europe*. Cardiff: Cardiff Academic Press, 1998.
Hart, David Montgomery. *The Aith Waryaghar of the Moroccan Rif: An Ethnography and History*. Tucson: University of Arizona Press, 1976.
Heine, Peter. "Die Bestattung von Muslimen außerhalb der islamischen Welt als Problem des islamischen Rechts." In *In fremder Erde: Zur Geschichte und Gegenwart der islamischen Bestattung in Deutschland*, ed. Gerhard Höpp and Gerdien Jonker, 11–18. Berlin: Das Arabische Buch, 1996.
Hock, Hans Henrich, and Brian D. Joseph. *Language History, Language Change, and Language Relationship: An Introduction to Historical and Comparative Linguistics*. Berlin: Mouton de Gruyter, 1996.
Hoefnagels, G. P. "Huwelijks- en concubinaatsvormen in Suriname." In *Familie- en Jeugdrecht* 3, 3 (1981): 98–103.
Hoefte, Rosemarijn. *De betovering verbroken: De migratie van Javanen naar Suriname en het rapport-Van Vleuten (1909)*. Dordrecht: Foris Publications, 1990.
Hoffer, C. B. M. *Moslimbesnijdenissen in Nederland: Een inventariserend onderzoek naar besnijdenissen bij islamitische groeperingen*. Leiden: LIDESCO, 1990.

Ibn Qayyim al-Jawziyya, Shams al-Dîn Abû Bakr Muḥammad b. Abî Bar al-Zar^c^i. "Fî khitân al-mawlûd wa aḥkâmihi." In *Al-khitân: Ra'y al-dîn wa l-^c^ilm fî khitân al-awlâd wa l-banât*, ed. Abu Bakr ^c^Abd al-Râziq, 99–151. Cairo: Dâr al-I^c^tiṣâm, 1989.
Ibn Rushd, Abû al-Walîd Muḥammad b. Aḥmad. *The Distinguished Jurist's Primer: A Translation of Bidâyat Al-Mujtahid*. Translated by Imran Asan Khan Nyazee. Reviewed by Muhammad Abdul Rauf. Vol. 1. Reading: Garnet, 1994.
Ibn Rushd al-Qurṭubî, Abû al-Walîd Muḥammad b. Aḥmad. *Al-muqaddamât al-mumahhadât li biyân mâ iqtaḍathu rusûm al-mudawwana min al-aḥkâm al-shar^c^iyyât wa al-taḥṣîlât al-muḥkamât li ummahât masa'ilaha al-mushkilât*. Vol. 1. Bayrut: Dâr al-Gharb al-Islâmiyya, 1988.
Ibn Ṭûlûn al-Dimashqî al-Ṣâliḥî, Shams al-Dîn Muḥammad b. ^c^Alî. *Faṣṣ al-khawâtim fîmâ qîla fî al-walâ'im*. Damascus: Dâr al-Fikr, 1983.
INSEE, Institut national de la statistique et des études économiques. *Tableaux références et analyses: Exploitation principale. Recensement de la population de 1999*. Paris: INSEE, 2000.

Jäschke, Gotthard. "Die 'Imam-Ehe' in der Türkei." In *Die Welt des Islams* 4 (1956): 164–201.

Jazîrî, ᶜAbd al-Raḥman al-. *Al-fiqh ᶜalâ al-madhâhib al-arbaᶜa*. Vol. 2–3. Istanbul: Maktaba al-Haqîqa, 1990–1991.

Jordens-Cotran, L. "Enkele wijzigingen van de Marokkaanse familiewetgeving." In *Migrantenrecht* 8, 10 (1993): 211–217.

——. "Het Marokkaanse huwelijks- en het Nederlandse internationaal huwelijksrecht (I): De verloving of khitba." In *Migrantenrecht* 8, 10 (1993): 218–223.

——. "Het Marokkaanse huwelijks- en het Nederlandse internationaal huwelijksrecht (II): De verloving in het Nederlandse internationaal familierecht." In *Migrantenrecht* 9, 1 (1994): 3–5.

Juynboll, Th. W. *Handleiding tot de kennis van de Mohammedaansche wet volgens de leer der Sjâfiᶜitische school*. Leiden: E. J. Brill, 1930.

Juynboll, Th. W., and J. Pedersen. "ᶜAḳîḳa." In *The Encyclopaedia of Islam*, 2d ed., 1 (1960): 337.

Kamerlingh Onnes, J. C. M. A. "Kist of geen kist? Voorschriften over het gebruik van een lijkkist bij moslims." Master's thesis, Vakgroep Talen en Culturen van het Islamitische Midden-Oosten, Universiteit Leiden, 1988.

Kapchan, Deborah A. "Moroccan Female Performers Defining the Social Body." In *Journal of American Folklore* 107, 423 (1994): 82–105.

Kaptein, Nico. "Circumcision in Indonesia: Muslim or Not?" In *Pluralism and Identity: Studies in Ritual Behaviour*, ed. Jan Platvoet and Karel van der Toorn, 285–302. Leiden: E. J. Brill, 1995.

Karakaşoğlu, Yasemin. "Die Bestattung von Muslimen in der Bundesrepublik aus der Sicht türkisch-islamischer Organisationen." In *In fremder Erde: Zur Geschichte und Gegenwart der islamischen Bestattung in Deutschland*, ed. Gerhard Höpp and Gerdien Jonker, 83–105. Berlin: Das Arabische Buch, 1996.

Kater, L., and R. Evers. "Besnijden is zonder risico's." In *NRC Handelsblad*, 1 May 1997.

——. "Besnijdenis is in belang van kind." In *NRC Handelsblad*, 10 June 1997.

Kaysî, Marwân Ibrâhim al-. *Morals and Manners in Islam: A Guide to Islamic Adâb*. London: The Islamic Foundation, 1986.

Khalîl ben Ish'âq. *Abrégé de la loi musulmane selon le rite de l'Imâm Mâlek*. Translated by G.-H. Bousquet. Vol. 1. Alger: Editions Algériennes en-Nahdha, 1956.

Kister, M. J. "... And he was born circumcised ...: Some Notes on Circumcision in Ḥadîth." In *Oriens* 34 (1994): 10–30.

Klerk, C. J. M. de. *Cultus en ritueel van het orthodoxe hindoeïsme in Suriname*. Amsterdam: Urbi et Orbi, 1951.

Koningsveld, Sjoerd van. "Between Communalism and Secularism: Modern Sunnite Discussion on Male Head-Gear and Coiffure." In *Pluralism and Identity: Studies in Ritual Behaviour*, ed. Jan Platvoet and Karel van der Toorn, 327–345. Leiden: E. J. Brill, 1995.

Kool, Martijn. "Vrouwenbesnijdenis in Nederland als moreel probleem." In *Amsterdams Sociologisch Tijdschrift* 21, 2 (1994): 71–85.

Kraan, C. A. *Hoofdlijnen van het Surinaamse huwelijksvermogensrecht*. Deventer: Kluwer, 1994.

Krüger, Hilmar. "Fragen des Familienrechts: Osmanisch-islamische Tradition versus Zivilgesetzbuch." In *Zeitschrift für Schweizerisches Recht* 95 (1976): 287–301.

——. "Grundzüge des türkischen Verlöbnisrechts." In *Das Standesamt* 43, 11 (1990): 313–325.

——. "Änderungen im türkischen Familienrecht." In *Das Standesamt* 44, 7 (1991): 181–183.

Kulu Glasgow, Işik. "Het huwelijk in Turkije: Zowel moderne als traditionele aspecten." In *Demos* 9, 9 (1993): 65–68.

Lahrichi, F. S. *Vivre musulmane au Maroc: Guide des droits et obligations.* Paris: Librairie Générale de Droit et de Jurisprudence, 1985.

Lambert, Richard D., and Barbara F. Freed, ed. *The Loss of Language Skills.* Rowley, Mass.: Newbury House Publishers, 1982.

Landman, Nico. *Van mat tot minaret: De institutionalisering van de islam in Nederland.* Amsterdam: VU Uitgeverij, 1992.

Lane, Edward William. *An Arabic-English Lexicon.* 8 vols. New York: Frederick Ungar Publishing, 1955–1956.

Lans, J. M. van der, and M. Rooijackers. "Types of Religious Belief and Unbelief among Second Generation Turkish Migrants." In *Islam in Dutch Society: Current Developments and Future Prospects*, ed. W. A. R. Shadid and P. S. van Koningsveld, 56–65. Kampen: Kok Pharos, 1992.

Le Coeur, Ch. "Les Rites de passage d'Azemmour." In *Hespéris: Archives Berbères et Bulletin de l'Institut des Hautes-Études Marocaines* 17, 1 (1933): 129–148.

Leveau, Rémy. "The Political Culture of the '*Beurs*'." In *Islam in Europe: The Politics of Religion and Community*, ed. Steven Vertovec and Ceri Peach, 147–155. New York: St. Martin's Press, 1997.

Leveau, R., and G. Kepel, ed. *Les musulmans dans la société française.* Paris: Éditions du CNRS, 1988.

Lewis, Philip. *Islamic Britain: Religion, Politics and Identity among British Muslims.* London: I. B. Tauris, 1994.

Linant de Bellefonds, Y. *Traité de droit musulman comparé.* Vol. 2, *Le mariage, la dissolution du mariage.* Paris: Mouton, 1965.

Magnarella, Paul J., and Orhan Türkdoğan. "Descent, Affinity, and Ritual Relations in Eastern Turkey." In *American Anthropologist* 75 (1973): 1626–1633.

Mantel, A. F. "Verbied het besnijden van jongens." In *NRC Handelsblad*, 28 April 1997.

——. "Besnijdenis is inbreuk op integriteit." In *NRC Handelsblad*, 13 May 1997.

M'Erad, Benali. "La Ziadah ou naissance à Safi (Maroc)." In *Revue Africaine* 57 (1913): 48–62.

Mir-Hosseini. Ziba. *Marriage on Trial: A Study of Islamic Family Law.* London: I. B. Tauris, 1993

Morris, Brian. *Anthropological Studies of Religion: An Introductory Text.* Cambridge: Cambridge University Press, 1987.

De Mudawwanah: Marokkaans wetboek inzake personen-, familie- en erfrecht. 2d ed. Translated by M. S. Berger and J. H. Kaldenhoven. Nijmegen: Ars Aequi Libri, 1997.

Mungra, G. *Hindoestaanse gezinnen in Nederland.* Leiden: COMT, 1990.

Muslim Council of Britain. "Population Statistics." http://www.mcb.org.uk/popstats.html, consulted on 10 January 2001.

Naamane-Guessous, Soumaya. *Au-delà de toute pudeur: La sexualité féminine au Maroc.* 8th ed. Casablanca: Eddif Maroc, 1992.

Nederlands Centrum Buitenlanders. "Regulering besnijdenissen bij jongetjes in Nederland: Projectverslag." Utrecht: Nederlands Centrum Buitenlanders, 1997.

Nicolas, Michèle. *Croyances et pratiques populaires turques concernant les naissances (Région de Bergama).* Paris: Publications Orientalistes de France, 1972.

Nicolasen, S. M. "Gewijzigd Turks familierecht." In *Het Personeel Statuut* 44 (1992): 6–7.

Nielsen, J. S. *Muslims in Western Europe.* Edinburgh: Edinburgh University Press, 1992.

Nielsen, J. S., and S. Vertovec. "Great Britain." In *Musulmans en Europe occidentale*, ed. Felice Dassetto and Yves Conrad, 67–94. Paris: L'Harmattan, 1996.

NRC Handelsblad. "Imam voor gemengd bidden." In *NRC Handelsblad*, 9 January 1998.

Oedayrajsingh Varma, E. G., and H. A. Ahmad Ali. *Surinaams familierecht.* Utrecht: Nederlands Centrum Buitenlanders, 1989.

Office for National Statistics. *Britain 2001: The Official Yearbook of the United Kingdom.* London: The Stationary Office, 2000. Also available at http://www.statistics.gov.uk, consulted on 12 January 2001.

Örücü, Esin. "Turkish Family Law: A New Phase." In *Journal of Family Law* 30 (1991–1992): 431–438.

Öztan, Bilge. "Das türkische Familienrecht unter besonderer Berücksichtigung der Familienrechtsnovelle." In *Zeitschrift für Rechtsvergleichung internationales Privatrecht und Europarecht* 33, 1 (1992): 20–42.

Platvoet, Jan. "Ritual in Plural and Pluralist Societies: Instruments for Analysis." In *Pluralism and Identity: Studies in Ritual Behaviour*, ed. Jan Platvoet and Karel van der Toorn, 25–51. Leiden: E. J. Brill, 1995.

Prins, J. "Een Surinaams rechtsgeding over een moslimse verstoting." In *De West-Indische Gids* 42 (1962–63): 201–207.

——. "Twintig jaar praktijk van de Aziatische huwelijkswetgeving in Suriname." In *De Nieuwe West-Indische Gids* 44, 1–2 (1965): 78–108.

Putten, W. G. H. M. van der. *Handboek Wet op de Lijkbezorging.* Lelystad: Koninklijke Vermande, 1993.

Rath, Jan, Rinus Penninx, Kees Groenendijk, Astrid Meijer. *Nederland en zijn islam: Een ontzuilende samenleving reageert op het ontstaan van een geloofsgemeenschap.* Amsterdam: Het Spinhuis, 1996.

REMID, Religionswissenschaftlicher Medien- und Informationsdienst e.V. "Religionsgemeinschaften in Deutschland: Mitgliederzahlen (Stand Dezember 2000)." http://www.uni-leipzig.de/~religion/remid_info.zahlen.htm, consulted on 8 January 2001.

Renaerts, Monique. *La Mort, rites et valeurs dans l'islam maghrébin*. Bruxelles: Université Libre de Bruxelles, 1986.

Reysoo, Fenneke. "Een collectieve besnijdenis in Noord-West Marokko." In *Lokale islam: Geloof en ritueel in Noord-Afrika en Iran*, ed. Willy Jansen, 42–52. Muiderberg: Coutinho, 1985.

Ringer, Fritz. *Max Weber's Methodology: The Unification of the Cultural and Social Sciences*. Cambridge, Mass.: Harvard University Press, 1997.

Rooijackers, M. "Religious Identity, Integration and Subjective Well-Being among Young Turkish Muslims." In *Islam in Dutch Society: Current Developments and Future Prospects*, ed. W. A. R. Shadid and P. S. van Koningsveld, 66–73. Kampen: Kok Pharos, 1992.

Rude-Antoine, Edwige. *Le Mariage maghrébin en France*. Paris: Éditions Karthala, 1990.

Rutten, Susan. *Moslims in de Nederlandse rechtspraak: Een inventarisatie van gepubliceerde rechterlijke beslissingen in zaken waar islamitische rechtsnormen en waarden een rol spelen 1973–1986*. Kampen: Kok, 1988.

Saint-Blancat, Chantal. *L'Islam de la diaspora*. Paris: Bayard Éditions, 1997.

Sander, Åke. "To What Extent is the Swedish Muslim Religious?" In *Islam in Europe: The Politics of Religion and Community*, ed. Steven Vertovec and Ceri Peach, 179–210. New York: St. Martin's Press, 1997.

Santing, Froukje. *Die vrouw, dat ben ik: Over het leven van Turkse vrouwen*. Rotterdam: Stichting Samen Wonen Samen Leven, 1987.

Sarakhsî, Shams al-Dîn al-. *Kitâb al-mabsûṭ*. 20 vols. [Cairo], 1906–1913.

Sawwaf, Muhammad Mahmud al-. *Waakt over uw gebeden!* Translated by Muhammad Tahir de Jong. Tilburg: Stichting Islam Informatie Centrum Zuid-Nederland, n.d.

Schaufeli, Anneli. "A Domain Approach to the Turkish Vocabulary of Bilingual Turkish Children in the Netherlands." In *Maintenance and Loss of Minority Languages*, ed. Willem Fase, Koen Jaspaert, Sjaak Kroon, 117–135. Amsterdam: John Benjamins Publishing Company, 1992.

Schiffauer, Werner. "Migration and Religiousness." In *The New Islamic Presence in Western Europe*, ed. Tomas Gerholm and Yngve Georg Lithman, 146–158. London: Mansell Publishing, 1988.

——. *Die Migranten aus Subay. Türken in Deutschland: Eine Ethnographie*. Stuttgart: Klett-Cotta, 1991.

Schmitz, Roderick. "Rituele besnijdenis van jongens in Nederland." Ph.D. diss., Utrecht University, 2001.

Seliger, Herbert W., and Robert M. Vago. "The Study of First Language Attrition: An Overview." In *First Language Attrition*, ed. Herbert W. Seliger and Robert M. Vago, 3–15. Cambridge: Cambridge University Press, 1991.

Seliger, Herbert W., and Robert M. Vago, ed. *First Language Attrition*. Cambridge: Cambridge University Press, 1991.

Shadid, W. A. R., and P. S. van Koningsveld. *Minderheden, hulpverlening en gezondheidszorg: Achtergrondinformatie ten behoeve van de zorg voor moslimse migranten*. Assen: Van Gorcum, 1983.

——. "Stervensbegeleiding en begrafenisriten in de islam." In *Qiblah: Islamitisch kwartaalblad* 7, 2 (1983): 18–26, 36.

——. *Religious Freedom and the Position of Islam in Western Europe: Opportunities and Obstacles in the Acquisition of Equal Rights (with an Extensive Bibliography).* Kampen: Kok Pharos, 1995.

——. "Loyalty to a Non-Muslim Government: An Analysis of Islamic Normative Discussions and of the Views of Some Contemporary Islamicists." In *Political Participation and Identities of Muslims in Non-Muslim States*, ed. W. A. R. Shadid and P. S. van Koningsveld, 84–114. Kampen: Kok Pharos, 1996.

——. *Moslims in Nederland: Minderheden en religie in een multiculturele samenleving*. 2d ed. Houten: Bohn Stafleu Van Loghum, 1997.

Sharwood Smith, Michael, and Paul van Buren. "First Language Attrition and the Parameter Setting Model." In *First Language Attrition*, ed. Herbert W. Seliger and Robert M. Vago, 17–30. Cambridge: Cambridge University Press, 1991.

Singels, Loes. "Op het raakvlak van twee geboortesystemen: Een analyse van de problemen die zich voordoen bij de verloskundige begeleiding van Marokkaanse vrouwen door de Nederlandse vroedvrouw in Amsterdam." Master's thesis, Cultural Anthropology, Vrije Universiteit Amsterdam, 1987.

Smith, Jane Idleman, and Yvonne Yazbeck Haddad. *The Islamic Understanding of Death and Resurrection.* Albany: State University of New York Press, 1981.

Smolicz, Jerzy J. "Minority Languages as Core Values of Ethnic Cultures: A Study of Maintenance and Erosion of Polish, Welsh, and Chinese Languages in Australia." In *Maintenance and Loss of Minority Languages*, ed. Willem Fase, Koen Jaspaert, Sjaak Kroon, 277–305. Amsterdam: John Benjamins Publishing Company, 1992.

Snoek, J. A. M. "Initiations: A Methodological Approach to the Application of Classification and Definition Theory in the Study of Rituals." Ph.D. diss., Leiden University, 1987.

Speckmann, J. D. *Marriage and Kinship among the Indians in Surinam.* Assen: Van Gorcum, 1965.

Spuler-Stegemann, Ursula. *Muslime in Deutschland: Nebeneinander oder Miteinander.* Freiburg: Herder, 1998.

Statistisches Bundesamt. *Statistisches Jahrbuch 2000 für das Ausland.* Stuttgart: Metzler-Poeschel, 2000.

Stichting Lalla Rookh. *Huwelijk, geboorte en overlijden bij moslims.* Utrecht: Stichting Lalla Rookh Nederland, 1986.

Sukkarî, ᶜAbd al-Salâm ᶜAbd al-Raḥîm al-. *Khitân al-dhakar wa khifâḍ al-unthâ min manẓûr islâmî.* Haliyûbûlus: Dâr al-Manâr li l-Nashr wa l-Tawzîᶜ, 1988.

Sunier, Thijl. *Islam in beweging: Turkse jongeren en islamitische organisaties.* Amsterdam: Het Spinhuis, 1996.

Sunier, Thijl, and Nico Landman. "Nederland." In *Musulmans en Europe occidentale*, ed. Felice Dassetto and Yves Conrad, 125–150. Paris: L'Harmattan, 1996.

Suparlan, Parsudi. "The Javanese in Surinam: Ethnicity in an Ethnically Plural Society." Ph.D. diss., University of Illinois at Urbana-Champaign, 1976.

Surinaamse Moeslim Associatie Ahle Sunnat-Wal-Jamaat (Hanafi). *Tartiebus-Swalaat (Moeslim gebeds-boekje)*. 2d ed. N.p.: Surinaamse Moeslim Associatie Ahle Sunnat-Wal-Jamaat (Hanafi), n.d.

Talbi, M. "ᶜIyâḍ b. Mûsâ." In *The Encyclopaedia of Islam*, 2d ed., 4 (1978): 289–290.

Tan, Dursun. "Wandlungen des Sterbens und der Trauerrituale in der Migration." In *In fremder Erde: Zur Geschichte und Gegenwart der islamischen Bestattung in Deutschland*, ed. Gerhard Höpp and Gerdien Jonker, 107–130. Berlin: Das Arabische Buch, 1996.

Tapper, Nancy. "'Traditional' and 'Modern' Wedding Rituals in a Turkish Town." In *International Journal of Turkish Studies* 5, 1–2 (1990–1991): 137–154.

Tapper, Nancy, and Richard Tapper. "The Birth of the Prophet: Ritual and Gender in Turkish Islam." In *Man: Journal of the Royal Anthropological Institute* 22, 1 (1987): 69–92.

Tekeli, Şirin. "Introduction: Women in Turkey in the 1980s." In *Women in Modern Turkish Society*, ed. Şirin Tekeli, 1–21. London: Zed Books, 1991.

Turner, Victor. *The Ritual Process: Structure and Anti-Structure*. New York: Aldine de Gruyter, 1969.

——. *Dramas, Field and Metaphors: Symbolic Action in Human Society*. Ithaca: Cornell University Press, 1974.

Tweede Kamer der Staten-Generaal. *Wijziging van de Wet van 25 maart 1981, houdende regeling van het conflictenrecht inzake ontbinding van het huwelijk en scheiding van tafel en bed en de erkenning daarvan, in verband met de bekrachtiging van de Verdragen van Luxemburg en 's-Gravenhage inzake erkenning van beslissingen betreffende de huwelijksband, onderscheidenlijk de erkenning van echtscheidingen en scheidingen van tafel en bed*. Vergaderjaar 1995–1996, 24709, no. 3.

Vertovec, Steven, and Ceri Peach, ed. *Islam in Europe: The Politics of Religion and Community*. New York: St. Martin's Press, 1997.

Vestdijk-van der Hoeven, A. C. M. *Religieus recht en minderheden*. Arnhem: Gouda Quint, 1991.

Vries, Marlene de. *Ogen in je rug: Turkse meisjes en jonge vrouwen in Nederland*. Alphen aan den Rijn: Samsom Uitgeverij, 1988.

Waal Malefijt, Annemarie de. *The Javanese of Surinam: Segment of Plural Society*. Assen: Van Gorcum, 1963.

Waas, Margit. *Language Attrition Downunder: German Speakers in Australia*. Frankfurt am Main: Peter Lang, 1996.

Waugh, Earle H. "Names and Naming." In *The Oxford Encyclopedia of the Modern Islamic World*, 3 (1995): 224–226.

De wenselijkheid van een bilateraal verdrag tussen Marokko en Nederland over conflicten aangaande het Internationaal Familierecht: Bijdragen aan de studiedag van 21 februari 1992 en de reactie van het NCB, 14–22. Utrecht: Nederlands Centrum Buitenlanders, 1992.

Westermarck, Edward. *Marriage Ceremonies in Morocco*. 1914. Reprint, London: Curzon Press, 1972.

——. *Ritual and Belief in Morocco.* 2 vols. 1926. Reprint, New Hyde Park, N.Y.: University Books, 1968.

Wiersma, Sytske. "De bruid in veranderende huwelijksrituelen in Ben Smim (Midden Atlas, Marokko)." Master's thesis, CA/SNWS, Vrije Universiteit Amsterdam, 1991.

Wing Önder, Sylvia. "Your Own Mother or Father State? Health Care Choices on the Black Sea Coast of Turkey." Paper presented at the 33rd annual meeting of the Middle East Studies Association (MESA), Washington, D.C., 19–22 November 1999.

Woodward, Mark R. "The Slametan: Textual Knowledge and Ritual Performance in Central Javanese Islam." In *History of Religions*, 28, 1 (1988): 54–89.

Yağmur, Kutlay. *First Language Attrition among Turkish Speakers in Sydney.* Tilburg: Tilburg University Press, 1997.

Yağmur, Kutlay, Kees de Bot, and Hubert Korzilius. "Language Attrition, Language Shift and Ethnolinguistic Vitality of Turkish in Australia." In *Journal of Multilingual and Multicultural Development* 20, 1 (1999): 51–69.

Yerden, Ibrahim. *Trouwen op z'n Turks: Huwelijksprocedures bij Turkse jongeren in Nederland en hun strijd om meer inspraak.* Utrecht: Uitgeverij Jan van Arkel, 1995.

Zabîdî, Muhammad b. Muhammad al-Ḥusainî al-. *Kitâb itḥafu l-sâdati al-muttaqîn bi-sharḥ asrar Iḥya' ᶜulûm al-dîn.* 10 vols. Cairo: Al-Matbaᶜa al-Maymuniyya, 1893.

Zevenbergen, J. A. *De Surinaamse huwelijkswetgeving in historisch en maatschappelijk perspectief.* Deventer: Kluwer, 1980.

Zevkliler, Aydin. "Die neuen Formvorschriften im türkischen Eheschließungsrecht." In *Das Standesamt* 40, 4 (1987): 99–103.

Zwemer, S. M. "The ᶜAkika Sacrifice". In *The Moslem World* 6, 3 (1916): 236–252.

INDEX

Abraham, 30, 43–47, 51, 70, 154
Abû Shujâ[c], 167
Abu-Zahra, Nadia, 8–9
[c]*adl* (professional witness), pl. [c]*udûl*, 85, 91–92, 94, 131, 138
afterbirth. *See* placenta
age
 of circumcision, 51–55, 75
 of marriage, 87, 92, 95–96, 99, 102
Alladien, Goelam Rasoel, 23–24, 35, 38–40
amulets, 23–24
angels
 [c]Izrâ'îl, 142, 172
 Munkar and Nakîr, 165, 172–173
aniconism, 123
Antoun, Richard, 8
[c]*aqîqa*, 26–38
 alms, 31–32
 Islamic law, 26–30, 35
 religious qualification, 27–29
 sacrifice, 26–33, 35–36
 shaving the child's hair, 36–38
 substitution, 28, 37
 timing, 28, 35–36
Ashqar, [c]Umar Sulayman al-, 24, 27–28, 37
attrition
 language, 186–190, 193
 ritual, 183, 186–190

Bergmann, A., 100
Bilmen, Ömer Nasuhî, 12
birth
 delivery, 19–20
 husband's presence, 20–21
 Islamic law, 15, 24
 naming of child, 25–26, 31, 38–40
 postnatal period, 21–22
 registration, 40
 services of district nurses, 23
 taḥnîk, 24–25, 39
 whispering in the child's ear, 24–25, 185, 190
 See also [c]*aqîqa*; *lohusalık*; *mitoni*; pregnancy
Bot, Marrie, 5, 148
bridal gift
 amount, 81, 86, 104–108
 Huwelijksbesluit Mohammedanen, 102
 Islamic law, 88–90
 Mudawwana, 93
 Turkish Civil Code, 96
Britain, Muslims in, 1–2
burial, 157–173
 country of, 7, 141, 158–161, 178, 192
 interment, 162, 164–166
 memorial gatherings, 174–178
 of placenta, 20–21
 preparations, 144–157, 180
 talqîn (teaching at graveside), 172–173
 See also coffin; funeral; grave
Buskens, Léon, 92, 130

Cammaert, Marie-France, 119
Çelebi, Süleyman, 111
celebrations, venue of
 hall, 65, 68–69, 72, 74, 113, 120–123, 125–127, 129, 131, 133, 139
 home, 65, 66–68, 113, 120–121, 125, 127, 130–131, 133, 139
 mosque premises, 65, 69–70, 120, 123, 125, 139
cemeteries, 159–160, 164–165, 171, 178, 180, 191
Centrum Santoso, 13, 59, 69
ceremony. *See* rites and ceremonies
Chaïb, Yassine, 5
chékai. *See* engagement
circumcisers, professional, 56–57, 63, 75
 dukun sunat, 55
 hajjam, 55, 77
 sünnetçi, 55, 64, 69, 77
 tjallak, 55
circumcision
 age, 51–55, 75
 costs, 60–61, 64, 76
 definition and terminology, 44
 female, 43–44
 festivities, 64–75
 hospital, 55–58, 64, 75–77
 Islamic law, 44–49
 Jews, 44, 51, 58
 medicalization, 77
 organization, 43, 55–64, 186, 191
 professional circumciser, 55–57, 63–64, 69, 75, 77
 religious qualification, 44–51
 techniques, 56, 61
clothing, festive
 circumcision, 66, 68, 70, 73, 76, 184–185

engagement, 84–85
henna party, 114, 116
marriage, 85, 97, 103, 123–129, 132, 138
mitoni, 18
women, 68, 125, 131
coffin
double-height, 178, 190–191
use of, 141, 158, 163, 166–170, 179–181
communitas, 6
competence, ritual, 184, 188–190
condolences, 144, 173–176, 178–179
consonance, 184–186, 188–189
conspicuity, 43, 73, 76
contingency, historical, 190–192
conviviality, 36, 41, 185, 188–189
corpse
shrouding, 144–145, 149–153, 180, 185, 189–190
transport, 144, 162, 169–170, 174, 178–181
washing, 144–149, 180, 185, 189–190
country of origin, 10–11
ᶜaqîqa, 31, 36, 42
burial, 7, 141, 144, 156, 159, 161–162, 178–179, 192
circumcision, 55, 65, 74–75
marriage, 110, 192
relations with, 110, 141, 159, 180, 188–189, 192–193
cremation, 157, 181

dancing. *See* music and dancing
death and dying, 141–144
See also burial; funeral; *ṣalât al-janâza*; corpse, shrouding; corpse, washing
devil, 24, 81–82, 98, 142, 172
Diyanet, 161–162
dresser. *See neggafa*
drink. *See* food and drink
Dungen, Niek van den, 55, 57
Durkheim, Emile, 6

eastward-prayers, 17, 19, 73, 178
Eickelman, Dale F., 37
Elaroussi, Khalid, 117, 119
emptiness, feeling of, 185, 188
engagement, 80–81, 83–84
Evers-Rosander, Eva, 127
evil influences, 18, 22–23, 37, 66, 99–100, 114

farḍ kifâya (collective duty), 79, 144, 147, 149, 153, 155, 157, 180
Ferid, M., 100
festivities. *See* celebrations, venue of; clothing, festive; meals, festive
fiṭra, 48, 50
food and drink, 16–19, 34, 68, 73, 124, 127, 132
See also meals, festive; wedding cake
France, Muslims in, 1
funeral
funds, 158, 161–162, 179, 186
prayer. *See ṣalât al-janâza*
procession, 158, 163, 166, 170–171
See also burial; corpse; grave

games, 34–35, 120, 122–123, 134
gatherings, religious
circumcision, 67–68, 70–72
marriage, 111–113
death, 175–178
gecekondu, 19–20
Gellner, Ernest, 8
Gennep, Arnold van, 5–6
Germany, Muslims in, 1
Ghannouchi, Al-, 158
gifts, 34, 67, 69–70, 84, 106, 115, 118, 120, 124–125, 134, 137
See also bridal gift; *takı*
Gitaan, Al-, 13, 58–60, 62–65, 69–70, 76, 191
Gluckman, Max, 6
grave
design, 158, 162–167, 179, 181
exclusive right, 164, 178, 180
granting period, 160–161, 164–165
number of corpses, 162–165
public, 164, 180
visit, 160
waiting at, 172–173
graveyard. *See* cemeteries, Grütter, Irene, 172
guardianship, 85, 87–88, 91–92, 98, 102

Haddad, Yvonne Yazbeck, 142
Hague, The, 9, 11–13, 20, 62–63, 75–76, 117, 164, 191
hajjam (professional circumciser), 55, 77
ḥammâm. *See* marriage, visit to bathhouse
ḥanîf, 46
Hanafites, 27, 29, 45, 64, 79, 81, 86–89, 99, 109, 145–146, 150–151, 153–156, 162, 167, 170
Hanbalites, 45, 79, 81, 86–89, 109, 146, 150–151, 153–155, 162, 170, 172
Hart, David, 53, 70
headscarves, 2, 4, 5, 125
health insurance, 19, 57–58, 76
ANOVA, 61
Zilveren Kruis, 59–60

henna, 65–66, 73–74, 128
significance of, 114–115, 117
See also marriage, henna party
hoca. *See* imam
Hoffer, Cor, 5
hospital
birth, 19–21, 41
circumcision, 55–58, 66, 75–77, 191
death, 143, 180
Juliana Children's (The Hague), 13, 63
Sophia Children's (Rotterdam), 59–60, 62–63
Wilhelmina Children's (Utrecht), 61–63, 75, 191
housing, 67, 77, 139
Huwelijksbesluit Mohammedanen, 101–103

Ibn ᶜAbidîn, 167
Ibn al-Siddîq, 158
Ibn Nujaim, 167
Ibn Qayyim al-Jawziyya, 45, 48, 54
Ibn Rushd al-Qurṭubî, 24, 27–29
Ibn Ṭûlûn, 16
Ibrâhîm. *See* Abraham
ᶜidda (waiting period), 80, 145, 173
iᶜdhâr, 33, 64, 109
imam, 12, 16, 26, 37, 39–40, 67, 71, 82, 84, 95, 98–99, 101, 104–105, 111, 128–129, 138, 143, 148, 172–173, 193
imam nikâhı. *See* marriage, religious
incense, 17–19, 116, 146, 149
Islam, identification with, 4, 39, 112, 120, 130, 138–139, 193

jaran képang (horse dances), 71, 73–75
Jäschke, Gotthard, 99
Javanese religion, 18–19
Jazîrî, ᶜAbd al-Raḥman al-, 16
Jordens-Cotran, Leila, 84

Karakaşoğlu, Yasemin, 5, 156, 168
ka'um. *See* imam
Kaysî, Marwân Ibrâhîm al-, 31, 40
Khalîl b. Isḥâq, 26, 36, 166–167
khiṭba. *See* engagement
kına gecesi. *See* marriage, henna party
kirve (co-parent), 69
Kister, M. J., 64
kitaab. *See* gatherings, religious
Koningsveld, P. S. van, 23, 161
Koran, 15, 23, 25, 32, 34, 38–39, 43, 46–47, 50, 54, 88, 128, 141, 176
recitation, 16, 64, 67–71, 76–77, 84, 97, 105, 111–112, 125, 129, 142–143, 160, 166, 172, 177
Krüger, Hilmar, 100

language attrition, 186–190, 193
law
Corpse Disposal Act, 141, 158, 168–169, 179
Dutch, 31, 40–42, 44, 56, 90, 103, 138, 141, 158, 166, 168–169, 179
Huwelijksbesluit Mohammedanen, 101–103
Islamic law. *See* Hanafites, Hanbalites, Malikites, Shafiᶜites
Mudawwana, 79, 83–84, 91–93, 138
Surinamese Civil Code, 101–103
Turkish Civil Code, 40, 94–97
liminality, 5–6
Linant de Bellefonds, Y., 85–90
lohusalık, 21–22

mahr. *See* bridal gift
Malikites, 24, 27–28, 30, 39, 40, 51–52, 64, 79, 81, 86–93, 109, 145–146, 150, 153–155, 162, 166, 170, 172
marriage
age, 87, 92, 95–96, 99, 102
bathhouse, visit to, 110, 117, 119, 184
bridal gift, 85–90, 93, 96–97, 102, 104–108, 118
civil, 95–101, 103, 107, 129, 134, 138, 184, 192
consulate, 90, 97, 110, 112, 137–138, 192
consummation, 87–89, 92–94, 109, 128–129, 134
contracting, 85–88, 109–110, 112
guardianship, 85, 87–88, 91–92, 98, 102
henna party, 110, 112–120, 130, 133
Islamic law, 85–90
legislation, 80, 90–106
polygamy, 91, 94, 100
proposal, 80–85
reception of bride, 110, 133–137
religious, 82, 95–101, 103–107, 110, 122, 19, 134, 138–139, 184–185, 192
religious qualification, 79
trousseau, 106, 108, 117, 128, 137, 184
wedding cake, 122–124
wedding party, 81, 110, 120–133, 184
witnesses, 85, 88, 91–92, 96, 102, 104
mawlana. *See* imam
meals, festive, 16, 70, 72, 112–113, 116, 120, 122–123, 127, 132, 135
religious qualification, 33, 64, 109
See also ᶜ*aqîqa*; food and drink; *iᶜdhâr*; *slâmetan*; *walîma*; wedding cake
Mecca, 4, 26, 141, 150, 165, 168, 176
medical services

birth, 19–20, 23, 41
Districts Huisartsen Vereniging, 61
female doctors, 20
GG & GD, 61–62, 76
Gitaan, Al-, 13, 58–60, 62–65, 191
health insurance, 19, 57–58, 76
hospital, 19–20, 55–58
Public Health Inspectorate, 56
STIOM, 62–63, 191
Stichting Informatiecentrum Gezondheidszorg, 55
Thuiszorg, 59
women's clinic, 20
Ziekenfondsraad (Medical Insurance Board), 57
mehndie. *See* henna
M'Erad, Benali, 26
mevlüt, 8, 34, 71–72, 111–112, 128–129, 176–177
migration, history of, 7, 189
mijadji. *See* imam
military service, 50
milla (religion), 46
Milli Görüş, 82, 98, 100, 123, 125, 134, 139, 161
mitoni, 16–19, 41, 184
moe dighauni. *See* marriage, reception of bride
Moluccans, 2, 168, 171, 176, 181
Moroccans
birth, 16, 19, 21–23, 25–27, 29, 31, 33–37, 40–41
circumcision, 43, 49, 53, 55, 65–68
marriage, 81, 83–85, 90, 94, 107, 110–117, 121, 125–127, 136, 138–139
death, 141, 143–144, 147–148, 152, 155–156, 159–162, 170–172, 175, 177–181
Morocco, 21, 31, 36, 38, 40–42, 57, 63–64, 67, 70–71, 73–75, 77, 79, 85, 94, 107, 130 112–113, 116–117, 119, 127, 131–133, 135–136, 138, 166, 169, 177–180, 184, 186, 188–189
mosques, 3, 162, 180, 189
mourning, 173–175, 179
Mudawwana, 79, 83–84, 91–93, 138
Muhammad, Prophet, 9, 28–30, 37, 64, 115, 128, 142, 150–152, 163, 172, 176
music and dancing, 68–70, 74, 112, 115–116, 120, 122–125, 127, 129, 132, 135
Muslims, numbers of, 1–2

nafaqa (obligation to provide for wife's living), 85, 87, 89, 91, 93
naming of child, 25–26, 31, 38–40
nationality, 79–80, 90, 93, 137–138, 192
neggafa (dresser), 110, 115–116, 119, 121, 126–127
Nicolas, Michèle, 21, 39
nişan. *See* engagement

Pakistanis, 2, 180–181, 191
placenta, 20–21
polygamy, 91, 94, 100
prayer, 16, 23–24, 34
pregnancy, 16–19
See also mitoni
professionalization, 139, 143, 149, 162

Qairawânî, Ibn Abî Zaid al-, 12

redundancy. *See* consonance
Renaerts, Monique, 152, 175
resmî nikâh. *See* marriage, civil
rings, exchange of, 81, 84, 122
rites and ceremonies, 8
private, 15, 190
self-reliant, 190
ritual
attrition, 183, 186–190
competence, 184, 188–190
consonance, 184–186, 188–189
evolution of, 8, 31–33, 188
knowledge, 15, 25, 41, 184, 188–190
repertoire, 183–184
self-evidence, 34, 43, 75–76, 185
theory of, 5–8
Rotterdam, 9, 11–13, 58–60, 75–76, 191
Rude-Antoine, Edwige, 5
Rushdie affair, 4

sabᶜa or *subûᶜ*. *See ᶜaqîqa*
sacrifice. *See ᶜaqîqa*
ṣadâq. *See* bridal gift
ṣadaqa (charitable gift), 36–37, 71, 73, 75, 111–113, 175–176, 178
sadjèn (offering to spirits), 17, 72, 149, 178
sağdıç, 133–134, 136
ṣalât, 47, 50, 52, 70, 134, 145
ṣalât al-janâza, 143–145, 153–157, 179–180
helal etmek (absolution of deceased), 143, 157
Islamic law, 153–155
women at, 156
Santing, Froukje, 19, 137
Sarakhsî, Shams al-Dîn al-, 153, 167
services, availability of
bands, 126, 139, 186
circumcisers, professional, 63
district nurses, 23
health services, 19–20, 41

Koran reciters, 76, 112–113
wedding accessories, 110, 126, 139, 186
sexes, segregation of, 33–34, 66–67, 77, 84, 98, 120–121, 124–125, 130–131, 139
Shadid, W. A. R., 23, 161
Shafi^c^ites, 24, 27, 30, 36, 39, 45, 51–52, 54, 64, 79, 81, 86–89, 109, 145–146, 150–151, 153–154, 162, 167, 170, 172
shahâda (profession of faith), 25, 39, 50, 54–55, 69, 71–73, 104, 142–143, 177
shi^c^âr (distinguishing marks), 47, 49, 75
SHIP, 13, 62–63, 191
shrouding of corpse. *See* corpse, shrouding
ṣibgha, 46, 49
slametan, 16–17, 70–73, 176, 178
Smith, Jane Idleman, 142
söz kesme (official acceptance of marriage proposal), 81–82
Speckmann, J. D., 104, 117, 119–120, 133, 135
SPIOR, 12, 58–60, 191
STIOM, 62–63, 191
Sukkarî, ^c^Abd al-Salâm ^c^Abd al-Raḥîm al-, 48, 51
sünnetçi (professional circumciser), 55, 64, 69, 77
Suparlan, Parsudi, 17, 26, 53, 72, 166
support network, 34, 36, 41, 43
Surinam, 16–19, 21, 41, 53–54, 64, 71–73, 79, 104, 107, 111, 117, 119–120, 133, 135, 138, 149, 165–166, 179–180, 184, 188–189
Surinamese, 43, 55, 137, 141, 159, 164, 178, 179, 181
Surinamese Hindustani
birth, 16, 22–23, 26–27, 29, 31–32, 36, 38–39
marriage, 103–106, 108–111, 113–115, 117, 120–123, 125, 133–136, 138–139
death, 147–148, 151–152, 155, 160–161, 162, 165, 168–169, 171, 173, 176–177
Surinamese Javanese
birth, 15–19, 38–39, 41
circumicision, 50, 53–54, 65–67, 69–71, 73, 75
marriage, 81
death, 147–149, 155–157, 160–161, 165, 168–169, 171, 173, 176–178
See also eastward-prayers; westward-prayers

takı (present-giving), 67, 124–125
talqîn. *See* burial
Tan, Dursun, 143, 174, 177
Tapper, Nancy, 8, 71, 97, 117, 121, 127–130, 136–137
Tapper, Richard, 8, 71
The Hague. *See* Hague, The
trousseau, 106, 108, 117–118, 128, 137, 184
Turkey, 19–22, 25–26, 31, 34, 41, 57, 63–64, 68, 70–71, 73–75, 77, 79, 97, 110, 117–118, 127, 129, 133, 136–139, 143, 149, 162, 166, 169, 171, 174–175, 179–180, 184–185, 188–189
Turks
birth, 16, 19, 22–23, 25, 27, 29, 31–34, 37, 39–41
circumcision, 43, 49–50, 55, 65–68, 69
marriage, 81, 83–85, 90, 97–101, 107, 109, 113–117, 120–121, 123–125, 133–134, 136–139
death, 141, 143–144, 147–149, 152, 155–157, 159–162, 170–171, 173, 176–181
Turner, Victor, 6

United Kingdom, Muslims in. *See* Britain, Muslims in
Utrecht, 11–12, 61–62, 75–76, 191

virginity, 87–88, 123, 136

Waal Malefijt, Annemarie de, 16–17, 53–54, 71, 73, 166
wajang (shadow play), 71, 73–74
walîma, 33, 109, 120
washing of corpse. *See* corpse, washing
Waugh, Earle, 40–41
wedding
accessories, 110, 125–126, 133, 135, 139
cake, 122–124
dress, 85, 97, 123–127, 129, 132
night, 136–137
See also marriage
Westermarck, Edward, 114, 119, 153
westward-prayers, 17, 19, 73, 178
widow, 80, 145, 173
wilâya. *See* guardianship
Wing Önder, Sylvia, 20
witnesses, marriage, 85, 88, 91–92, 96, 102, 104
See also *^c^adl* (professional witness), pl. *^c^udûl*
women at burial, 145, 148, 156, 158, 166, 168, 170–171
See also clothing, festive; *ṣalât al-janâza*; sexes, segregation of

Yerden, Ibrahim, 5, 84, 110

PRINTED ON PERMANENT PAPER • IMPRIME SUR PAPIER PERMANENT • GEDRUKT OP DUURZAAM PAPIER - ISO 9706

N.V. PEETERS S.A., KLEIN DALENSTRAAT 42, B-3020 HERENT